The Personal Camera
SUBJECTIVE CINEMA AND THE ESSAY FILM

Laura Rascaroli

WALLFLOWER PRESS
LONDON & NEW YORK

A Wallflower Press Book
Published by
Columbia University Press
Publishers Since 1893
New York • Chichester, West Sussex
cup.columbia.edu

A complete CIP record is available from the Library of Congress

ISBN 978-1-906660-13-0 (cloth : alk. paper)
ISBN 978-1-906660-12-3 (pbk. : alk. paper)
ISBN 978-0-231-50314-3 (e-book)

Book design by Elsa Mathern

Columbia University Press books are printed on permanent
and durable acid-free paper.
This book is printed on paper with recycled content.
Printed in the United States of America

The Personal Camera

contents

acknowledgements   vii

introduction Subjective cinema and the I/eye of the camera   1

part one | **the essay film**

1   The essay film: problems, definitions, textual commitments   21

2   The metacritical voice(over) of the essay film: Harun Farocki, found footage and the essayist as spectator   44

3   The musealisation of experience: Chris Marker's digital subject between archive, museum and database   64

4   Performance and negotiation: Jean-Luc Godard plays Jean-Luc Godard   84

part two | **personal cinema**

5   First-person filmmaking: history, theory, practices   106

6   The diary film: Aleksandr Sokurov's *Spiritual Voices* and the feeling of time   115

7   The notebook film: Pier Paolo Pasolini and the film that cannot be made   146

8   The self-portrait film: Michelangelo's last gaze   170

afterword   189
notes   192
bibliography   206
index   220

acknowledgements

I wish to express my gratitude to the friends, colleagues and students who have contributed in many generous and priceless ways to my work on this project. Their presence in this book may be invisible to the reader, but is conspicuous to me; in many cases, the roles they have played cannot be adequately acknowledged in these notes. Most of all, I am thankful for their friendship.

My students, Stefano Baschiera, Marian Hurley, Abigail Keating, Stefano Odorico and Aidan Power gladly lent a helping hand whenever needed; Gianluca Cinelli let me borrow his indispensable notes on literary autobiography; Sarah Cooper and Catherine Lupton provided me with unpublished material; Patrick Crowley looked over some of my translations, and had erudite answers to give on literary self-representation; Antje Ehmann at Harun Farocki Filmproduktion always responded promptly and kindly to my many requests and queries; Harun Farocki kindly agreed to provide access to stills from his films; Jacopo Benci, Sabine Kriebel, Federica Mazzocchi, Luca Mosso, Stefano Odorico and Anita Trivelli were instrumental in locating elusive primary and secondary sources; David Montero shared his bibliography and his thoughts on the essay film; Patrick O'Donovan, John David Rhodes, Anita Trivelli and Michael Witt agreed to read sections of the manuscript, on which they offered learned, insightful, invaluable feedback.

I am thankful to Francesco Casetti, Winfried Pauleit, John David Rhodes and Pauline Small for kindly inviting me to present my work in progress, thus giving me the opportunity to rehearse my ideas in public – as well as to enjoy their company. I am forever indebted to Francesco Casetti, who taught me what cinema is all about when I was twenty, and then reminded me again twenty years later; his influence on my way of thinking about film is deeper than I can ever acknowledge.

I am grateful to the staff at Wallflower Press and, especially, to Yoram Allon, for his competence, energy and enthusiasm, and for believing in this book from day one; to the Nonfictions Series Editor, Brian Winston, for being such a generous reader of my manuscript; and to Editorial Manager Jacqueline Downs for doing her work with much proficiency and good humour.

A version of chapter one, 'The essay film: problems, definitions, textual commitments', was published in *Framework* (49:2); the insightful observations I received from the late Paul Arthur and from Drake Stutesman prompted me to further refine and sharpen my argument. A section of chapter four appeared in *Studies in French Cinema* (9:1) with the title 'Performance in and of the essay film: Jean-Luc Godard plays Jean-Luc Godard in *Notre musique*'; I especially wish to thank Phil Powrie and Michael Witt for their encouragement. For this project, I have obtained the generous support of the Research Publication Fund of the College of Arts, Celtic Studies and Social Sciences, University College Cork.

A special and loving thank you goes to my family, and particularly to Tom and Alice, for always supporting me, and for putting up uncomplainingly with the hours I devoted to this book; to my parents, for insisting in seeing in me more than I can; and to Norah (1928–2008), who accepted me, respected me and, I think, loved me.

The best pages in this book are for Jean-Luc and, in memoriam, for Michelangelo: *merci beaucoup, grazie infinite,* thank you so much for your devastating visions – *fatale beauté.*

introduction
SUBJECTIVE CINEMA AND THE I/EYE OF THE CAMERA

The object of study of this book is sited at the intersection of documentary, art film and avant-garde practices, and is best defined as subjective, first-person, essayistic cinema. This ostensibly simple definition is, however, burdened with problems, for it implies a range of theoretical and terminological questions. 'Essay film' is no doubt an increasingly germane expression, frequently encountered in both film reviews and scholarly writings on nonfiction cinema. Despite its widespread use, however, there is much confusion as to the meaning of the term, which is applied to a puzzling variety of films and cinematic forms: it has been used for anything from, for instance, Chris Marker's *Le Mystère Koumiko* (1965) to Michael Moore's *Fahrenheit 9/11* (2004), from Dziga Vertov's *Chelovek s kino-apparatom* (*Man with a Movie Camera*, 1929) to Errol Morris's *The Thin Blue Line* (1988), from Luis Buñuel's *Las Hurdes* (*Land Without Bread*, 1933) to Agnès Varda's *Les Glaneurs et la glaneuse* (*The Gleaners and I*, 2000), from Orson Welles' *Vérités et mensonges* (*F For Fake*, 1974) to Morgan Spurlock's *Supersize Me* (2004). From such an expansive use one derives the impression that essay is almost becoming synonymous with documentary. This critical practice, which may be prompted by the difficulty of coming to terms with an increasingly complex nonfictional landscape, in which both documentary and fictional impulses come to merge in challenging ways, and in which the source of the communication is ever more visible, is perhaps not totally inaccurate, as it points to the fact that all documentaries, even those that are most successful at appearing unbiased and objective, are based on a specific point of view, and purport a given interpretation of the world; it suggests, in other words, that all nonfictions are films 'with a thesis'. On the other hand, the practice is not particularly productive if one seeks to define the experience of the essayistic in the cinema – an experience that is as incontrovertible as it is hazy and difficult to locate.

At the opposite of this critical practice, this monograph will adopt a much more restrictive use of the term, and ask why such a question is prompted when watching certain films, such as Alain Resnais' *Nuit et brouillard* (*Night and Fog*, 1955), Chris Marker's *Lettre de Sibérie* (*Letter from Siberia*, 1957), Groupe Dziga Vertov's *Ici et ailleurs* (*Here and Elsewhere*, 1976), Harun Farocki's *Arbeiter verlassen die Fabrik* (*Workers Leaving the Factory*, 1995), Aleksandr Sokurov's *Hubert Robert. Schastlivanya zhizn* (*Hubert Robert, A Fortunate Life*, 1996), Jean-Luc Godard's *Histoire(s) du cinéma* (1997–98), Thom Andersen's *Los Angeles Plays Itself* (2003), just to recall a few relevant titles from the mid-1950s to date, we the audience feel that we are viewing an essay, quite the cinematic version of a literary one, as opposed to a documentary, or a film-poem, or an autofiction, or an audiovisual letter or an experimental film.

Another way in which the expression 'essay film' is frequently used today is as a straightforward synonym of engaged, overtly political cinema, both with reference to a rather mainstream, critical documentary practice, as exemplified by the work of Michael Moore, and to forms of alternative filmmaking and videomaking that identify with the production of minority, diasporic or accented subjects. This is perhaps unsurprising, given that, traditionally, personal viewpoint films were just about limited to the category of political cinema – to speak 'I' is, after all, firstly a political act of self-awareness and self-affirmation. This tradition continues today, and is a fundamental component of the contemporary essay film. I believe, however, that a proper consideration of the essay documentary involves more than the strictly political; hence, with respect to this current critical practice, my use of the term will be broader. In this monograph, furthermore, I will not only engage with the essay film, but also with other cognate although distinct forms of subjective filmmaking: diary films, travelogues, notebooks and self-portraits.

Made in various countries at different times, roughly between the 1950s and the present time, either as ephemeral, occasional texts or else produced for theatrical release or TV broadcasting, the films grouped together here are, then, deeply idiosyncratic and form a diverse, paradoxical, heretical body of work. The very issue of categorising these films and videos – one thinks of such directors as Jean-Luc Godard, Chris Marker, Harun Farocki, Pier Paolo Pasolini, Aleksandr Sokurov, Michelangelo Antonioni, Derek Jarman, Federico Fellini, Wim Wenders, Jonas Mekas, Jean-Marie Straub and Danièle Huillet, Yvonne Rainer, Chantal Akerman, Ed Pincus, Patrick Keiller, Agnès Varda, Werner Herzog, Michelle Citron and Ross McElwee – is both challenging and problematic. It could be suggested that unorthodoxy (of technical formats, of subject matter, of aesthetic values, of narrative structures and of practices of production and distribution) is the only trademark common to all the films discussed in this book, and of other comparable works. However, if on the one hand I will argue that we should resist the urge to overtheorise essayistic cinema and to crystallise it into a genre, on the other hand the simple act of grouping these films together is a classificatory exercise, one that suggests the existence of a field, of a domain, if not of a coherent genre as such.

While these films, indeed, do not belong to a genre as we might normally think of it, they nevertheless share a number of distinguishing features. Metalinguistic, autobiographical and reflective, they all posit a well-defined, extra-textual authorial figure as their point of origin and of constant reference; they strongly articulate a subjective, personal point of view; and they set up a particular communicative structure, largely based, as I will argue, on the address to the spectator, or interpellation.[1] The ways in which they generate such address, and articulate questions of authorship, enunciation,[2] narration and communication, vary significantly; it is, however, my conviction that the identification of the general rhetorical structures by which essayistic films express a subjective viewpoint and construct their spectatorship is not only possible, but is in fact essential to attain an understanding of their internal dynamics and of the distinctive ways in which they engage the spectator.

Documentary and communicative subjectivity

> All great fictional films tend towards documentary, just as all great documentaries tend towards fiction. (Jean-Luc Godard 1985: 181–2; author's translation)

Although belonging to a liminal (but ever more relevant) zone of filmmaking, in which fictional and nonfictional, experimental and mainstream practices mix and merge, all these films are documentaries, or else tend towards documentary – at least in the broadest, less restrictive meaning of the term. Over the last decade, prompted by the evolution of our conception of issues of realism and representation, as well as by the emergence and successful establishment, in terms of distribution and audience response, of an increasingly more ambiguous and challenging nonfictional practice, scholars have begun to challenge the accepted understanding of documentary as the field of total objectivity.[3] As Bill Nichols has proposed, 'Traditionally, the word documentary has suggested fullness, and completion, knowledge and fact, explanations of the social world and its motivating mechanisms. More recently, though, documentary has come to suggest incompleteness and uncertainty, recollection and impression, images of personal worlds and their subjective construction' (1994: 1). Such a tendency to subjectivity and uncertainty, which is certainly valid at least in the case of personal, essayistic cinema (if not for all current nonfictional production, much of which is still rather traditional), can be framed historically and theoretically in at least two ways, which are not necessarily contradictory: on the one hand, as the outcome of the process of postmodernisation of both the social and the artistic fields and, on the other, as a continuation and evolution of filmic practices that first emerged within European modernism.

It is evident that the foregrounding of subjectivity and autobiography are today widespread tendencies: one need only consider the proliferation of personal accounts, memoirs and diaries both in literature and in other arts: 'publishers and critics agree that, for better and for worse, the production and popular consumption of life writing, and interest in the biographical details of contemporary authors, are experiencing a notable boom' (Douglas 2001: 806). Subjectivity and autobiography are, for instance, at the root of the worldwide popular acclaim and commercial success of such books as Frank McCourt's *Angela's Ashes*, James McBride's *The Color of Water* or Helen Fielding's *Bridget Jones' Diary* (all 1996).

Subjectivity and autobiography are also a prominent aspect of the contemporary mass media: I refer primarily to the Internet, with the booming practice of maintaining first-person blogs and online diaries, as well as of producing 'the confessional video, the electronic essay, and the personal Web page' (Renov 2004a: xi); but also to the increasing 'personalisation' of television, with reality programmes which, starting with the *Big Brother* format, offer the audience the impression of watching somebody's real life in real time. Indeed, Stella Bruzzi, who reminds us that reality programmes on British television are currently categorised not as entertainment but as 'factual', explains them within the evolution of the observational documentary: 'The emergence of these strands signals the growing unhappiness with classical observational transparency and passivity, the absenting of an authorial voice and the abstention from any overt means of demonstrating the filmmakers' presence' (2006: 121).

This phenomenon embraces film as well. The last four decades have witnessed a noteworthy increase in the production of subjective nonfiction in international cinema, a phenomenon that includes what Michael Renov referred to as 'the autobiographical outbreak of the 1980s and 1990s' (2004a: xxii). Such an outbreak may in part be explained by the spread of new technology, and in particular the wide availability of digital video and the Internet. Other more abstract causes have also contributed. At both a thematic and philosophical level, subjectivity in nonfiction forms of contemporary filmmaking is, I argue, a reflection and a consequence of the increased fragmentation of the human experience in the postmodern, globalised world, and of our need and desire to find ways to represent such fragmentation, and to cope with it. I refer of course to that body of theory claiming that insecurity and fluidity are prevalent experiences of the postmodern condition. According to many contemporary thinkers, in postmodernity it is impossible to find anything solid, and we are all condemned to decentredness, fragmentation and 'liquidity'.[4] Autobiographical accounts feed the hope of finding or of creating unity in a life that is increasingly experienced as disjointed, displaced and dispersed. It is not by accident that a profound critical interest for first-person narratives developed in literary theory, narratology and semiotics in the years associated with the first appearance of the postmodern condition. In the early 1970s, literary studies witnessed a flourishing of publications on autobiography and self-reflexive narrative structures; it suffices here to mention the works of theorists such as Maurice Blanchot, Gérard Genette, Seymour Chatman and Philippe Lejeune.

An important factor in the emergence of subjective nonfictional cinematic forms may be identified with the end of metanarratives heralded by Jean-François Lyotard in 1979 (see 1984), and with the consequent phenomenon of the diminishing of authority found in and promoted by postmodern discourse – as well as the 'waning of objectivity as a compelling social narrative' (Renov 2004a: xvii). The decline of the social persuasiveness of objectivity and authority has had visible consequences for the documentary film. In this sceptical era, in which grand narratives are mistrusted and the existence of an external and unchanging perspective from which to construct an objective vision of the world is problematised, the margins become more attractive than the centre, and contingency replaces necessity and immutability. Accordingly, the authority of the traditional documentary is also weakened; its aura of objectiveness is no longer tenable; its apparent impartiality and ability to produce a truthful discourse are exposed as linguistic, rhetorical forms, and are either parodied (as in the mockumentary) or replaced by an overt exhibition of the source of the act of communication. In the second phenomenon, which I intend to analyse in greater depth, the filmmaker comes to the fore, uses the pronoun 'I', admits to his or her partiality and purposefully weakens her or his authority by embracing a contingent, personal viewpoint. Obviously, this is only another rhetorical strategy, which aims to construct a discourse that is believed to be honest and truthful, at least to itself.

It is, however, also a form of tangible personal commitment on the part of the filmmaker. It is, indeed, important to clarify that I will not use expressions such as 'rhetorical strategy', or utilise poststructuralist analytical tools, with the aim of undermining the first-person documentary's claims to its nonfictional status; rather, the opposite. It is not in spite of embracing contingency, but precisely because of it, that the documentary continues today, in this post-grand narratives era, to gain access to the real, albeit on a radically different basis; and while being partial, as well as overtly personal, essayistic films both express biased opinions on reality, and are capable of significantly connecting with that reality, but in ways which are unpredictable and difficult to codify. Similarly to Carl Plantinga, I do not see a contradiction, although one seems to be implied by a poststructuralist approach to the documentary, between 'the recording function of nonfiction film and its rhetoric' (Plantinga 1996: 319). By engaging with these questions, this study aims to contribute both to our understanding of the general problem of realism and of the construction of the effect of reality in the cinema, and to our knowledge of the workings of the documentary in particular and its ability to access the real.

Although postmodernity is, for the reasons outlined above, a ripe time for the spread of subjective practices of nonfiction filmmaking, these forms in fact have their roots in an earlier era. The idea of the possibility of expressing subjectivity through film can be traced back to the very origins of film theory; in particular, some of the pioneers influenced by poetic impressionism, such as Ricciotto Canudo, Louis Delluc and Jean Epstein, urged directors to express their inner self and their personal dreams in their films. However, it is in the 1940s that the reflection on cinematic subjectivity emerges in European film theory, preparing the formulation of the *nouvelle vague*'s auteur theory in the second half of the 1950s, and the establishment of the personal cinema of the avant-gardes of the 1950s and 1960s. Some of the key moments of this line of reflection, which will be discussed in detail over the following chapters, are Hans Richter's 1940 article on the essay film (see Richter 1992); Alexandre Astruc's 1948 contribution on the *caméra-stylo* (see Astruc 1999); Cesare Zavattini's writings of the 1950s and 1960s on personal cinema (see Zavattini 1979); and Pier Paolo Pasolini's 1965 conference presentation on the 'cinema of poetry' (see Pasolini 1988).[5]

These contributions anticipated or paralleled the emergence of a modernist and, in some cases, truly avant-garde practice of first-person filmmaking, which included the *nouvelle vague*'s personal, almost private cinema; experiments in *cinéma vérité*, such as Jean Rouch and Edgar Morin's *Chronique d'un été* (*Chronicle of a Summer*, 1961), in which the authors simultaneously filmed themselves as the source of the act of communication, and set out to undermine their own authority; Zavattini's *Free Newsreels* of 1968, self-produced and made by ordinary people; Pasolini's documentaries; and the New American Cinema and Underground, with artists such as Jonas Mekas, Stan Brakhage and Andy Warhol.[6] Writing about Mekas's autobiographical and diaristic cinema, Maureen Turim rightly suggested: 'It is important to remember that the development of autobiographical cinema comes at a specific point in cinema history. It involves a process of rupture … The cinematic autobiographer says not only "I want to tell my life through the cinema", but also, "enough of cinema as a mass medium and as an industrial and collective activity"' (1992: 193). Subjectivity in contemporary nonfiction films can consequently be seen – perhaps in contradiction of their apparent claim to be modest and anti-authoritarian – as an inheritance of the decidedly auteurist and anti-mainstream, anti-establishment cinema of the new waves, and of European and North-American avant-gardes.

It is precisely because they belong to this tradition that the films in this book can be so decidedly personal and subjective, and point to their extra-textual authors as the true source of the act of communication. They are all, in fact, the work of strong auteurs, who happen to be granted a higher expressive and artistic freedom than the norm; or whose effective autonomy is otherwise guaranteed by the economic and artistic marginality of their films. And yet, the very possibility of expressing subjectivity and autobiographical perspectives in film is not a given; in fact, it has often been questioned, or even denied. So, the first problem that needs to be tackled here is whether subjectivity and autobiography are indeed possible in the cinema. I will address this issue by considering first the case of autobiography, because this question directly implies that of authorship, and hence also that of subjectivity.

The performance of the self: autobiography in the cinema

Although many films are labelled as autobiographical, and many directors are described by critics as eminently engaged in creating autobiographical cinema, whether fictional (for instance, Ingmar Bergman, Federico Fellini, Woody Allen) or nonfictional (Jonas Mekas, Ross McElwee, Ed Pincus), the actual possibility of realising a filmic autobiography is a moot point. In a short but influential study dedicated precisely to this question, literary theorist Elizabeth W. Bruss claimed that 'there is no real cinematic equivalent for autobiography' (1980: 296). Bruss maintained that 'Film lacks the capacity for self-observation and self-analysis that we associate with language and literature' (1980: 298); it is, in fact, unable to produce the unity, crucial to autobiography, of observer and observed. While Bruss acknowledged that films are signifying practices producing meanings, she postulated a clear difference between the subject who writes and the subject who films; whereas the first can achieve 'the capacity to know and simultaneously be that which one knows' (1980: 301), the second is deprived of this possibility because of the 'shortcomings' of cinematic language. Indeed, truth-telling for Bruss does not belong to the cinema; 'under what conditions would we call a film sincere or say that it expresses a belief in, a commitment to, the images it presents – the very wording sounds bizarre', she claims (1980: 303).

While correct in her analysis of the impossibility for the filmmaker to film herself directly,[7] hence reproducing the unity of the observer and the observed, it could be argued that Bruss cannot see how a film can be personal or sincere because she bases her theory on a conception of the cinematic language strongly indebted to Christian Metz's film semiotics (1974) – which holds that cinema is not a *langue* because there is no dictionary of images, as images do not hold fixed meanings. Indeed, Bruss claims, 'there is no way of marking a personal attachment to one image rather than another, no way of discriminating a shot of the director from a shot of any other, indifferent individual' (1980: 305). Thus, the expression of subjectivity in film seems impossible. The same goes for autobiography: for Bruss, not even films in which writer, director and protagonist are the same person (notoriously, Philippe Lejeune's prerequisite of the 'autobiographical pact') succeed in being autobiographical.[8]

It is certainly true that a single filmic image cannot easily carry the mark of individuality as can the use of the first-person pronoun in language (unless voice-over or captions introduce the 'I' verbally). Maureen Turim does indeed warn us that the equation of the 'I' with the 'eye', with visual perception, 'belies the gap between what the subject sees and what the subject is' (1992: 195); but she concedes that the image can bear traces of the subject who filmed or selected it, because the filmmaker can choose to signal his presence in the act of filming through his absence, a strategy that equates a subjective camera with the filmmaker's consciousness: 'This marking of presence through absence entails the following implicit enunciations: "I was there behind the camera. I chose this image. I chose this transformative process of registering the image to mark my presence as filmmaker. I inscribed myself through the ways I manipulated the camera"' (1992: 194). Of course, this is a figurative or metaphorical process of self-representation: 'The self is created in film through the mediation of the processes of narrative and symbolic representation, even if those processes rest on a phenomenology of vision' (1992: 196). However, even when these distinctions between film and literature are taken into account, one has to question the opinion that sincerity, subjectivity and autobiography are unachievable in film, in a different way from how they may be, or may not be, possible in literature. In fact, if we problematise Bruss's claims, we see that film and literature converge on a self at once empirical and performative.

Indeed, in literature also the use of the pronoun 'I' is, ultimately, problematic, because it raises the thorny question of identity: 'It is hard to remain on a level of strictly grammatical description: any sustained analysis of the interplay of pronouns and persons in enunciation is eventually faced with the vertiginous necessity of constructing a theory of the subject' (Lejeune 1977: 30). Within such perspective, one must note that not only the Romantic baggage of introspection of a unified self as evoked by the idea of autobiography has been problematised, but so has the view that autobiography *tout court* is possible. If autobiography is that practice that asks the question 'who am I?', various philosophers, for instance Gabriel Marcel and, more recently, Paul Ricoeur, have discarded the Cartesian's transparency of the self, hence challenging the viability of this activity. For Ricoeur, 'who am I?' corresponds to the notion of 'how the self can be at one and the same time a person of whom we speak and a subject who designates herself in the first person while addressing a second person' (1992: 34). 'Who am I?', for the philosopher, is not an objective fact, a truth to be discovered, but something that must be achieved or created, as well as attested. This achievement requires us to deal with a complex set of elements and ways of understanding, which involve material, temporal, linguistic and social discourses. Self-understanding is mediated by signs, symbols and texts, and is always an act of interpretation. In terms of language, the sign 'I' for Ricoeur is empty; it does not create the subject, but only shows it. The subject is presupposed by language, which indicates it without describing it.

In what way does literary autobiography create its subject? Not only the sign 'I' is empty; he who pronounces it has become a figure, a fiction. The poststructuralist 'death of the author' (to use Roland Barthes' notorious slogan; but references to other deconstructionists and poststructuralists such as Jacques Derrida and Michel Foucault remain *de rigueur*) impinges on any claim of the possibility of producing first-person expression in literature, or any other art. How can the author be a fiction, and at the same time offer a faithful autobiographical portrait or a compelling subjective account? Among the arguments that recur in writings on literary autobiography is, for instance, that of the impossibility of obtaining an absolute coincidence of identity between author and narrator. Not only does the 'I' tend to be a character for the author of autobiography, but the past 'I' for an author always becomes an other, as in the title of one of Philippe Lejeune's volumes on autobiography, which reproduces Rimbaud's formula: *Je est un autre*. Another frequent critical argument, concerning the unreliability of memory, is hinted at in the following quotation:

> The very fact of memory and its peculiar operation, bringing back some things, neglecting other things and other times entirely, seems to argue that selfhood is not continuous; for it brings up one self here and another self there, and they are not the same as one another, nor do they even seem to the same degree selves. (Olney 1972: 24)

Finally, a third recurrent observation is that only death is the ultimate limit that would allow the completeness and clarity that any autobiography requires. As Pier Paolo Pasolini wrote:

> It is therefore absolutely necessary to die, because so long as we live, we have no meaning, and the language of our lives ... is untranslatable, a chaos of possibilities, a search for relations and meanings without resolution. Death effects an instantaneous montage of our lives; that is, it chooses the truly meaningful moments (which are no longer modifiable by other possible

contrary or incoherent moments) [and] puts them in a sequence, transforming an infinite, unstable and uncertain – and therefore linguistically not describable – present into a clear, stable, certain, and therefore easily describable past. (1988: 236–7)

Nonetheless, it is obviously impossible for a writer to include her own death in her autobiography, which therefore remains the tentative description of an indescribable past.

The (im)possibility of autobiography extends well beyond the sphere of art. For many postmodernist thinkers, not only the self of the author, but the self in general is an utter fabrication. Cultural theorist Stuart Hall, for instance, drawing on Louis Althusser and Jacques Lacan, suggests:

Rather than speaking of identity as a finished thing, we should speak of *identification*, and see it as an ongoing process. Identity arises, not so much from the fullness of identity which is already inside us as individuals, but from a *lack* of wholeness which is 'filled' from *outside us*, by the ways we imagine ourselves to be seen by *others*. (1992: 287–8; emphasis in original)

In postmodern times, the (Western) self has become decentred, split, liquid, protean, displaced, multiple, schizophrenic, as well as socially constructed. As in Zygmunt Bauman's perceptive motto: 'If the *modern* "problem of identity" was how to construct an identity and keep it solid and stable, the *postmodern* "problem of identity" is primarily how to avoid fixation and keep the options open' (1996: 18; emphasis in original). Walter Truett Anderson thus summarises these arguments: 'In the postmodern world, you just don't get to be a single and consistent somebody' (1997: 26).

And yet, this book deals with subjective and, at times, autobiographical expression in film, hence, it would appear, accepting the precondition of the existence, somewhere, of an author who talks, and who talks of and for himself/ herself. How real are the authors of the films analysed in the chapters that follow? How trustworthy their enunciators? How sincere their narrators?

When describing the category of accented cinema,[9] which almost invariably foregrounds the directors and their personal and autobiographical experiences, Hamid Naficy confronted the same problems, and postulated that:

Exile discourse needs to counter the move by some postmodern critics to separate the author of the film from the enunciating subject in the film, for exile and authorship are fundamentally intertwined with historical movements of empirical subjects across boundaries of nations. (2001: 34)

The exiled author's historical/empirical existence, as Naficy suggests, does not, however, exclude the construction of fictional selves; nor does it avoid the problems connected to the activity of autobiography in general. The authors are still discursive figures who 'inhabit and are constructed not only by history but also by their own filmic texts ... How they inhabit their films, or, in [David] Bordwell's term ... how they are "personified" varies: they may inhabit them as real empirical persons, enunciating subjects, structured absences, fictive structures, or a combination of these' (2001: 35).

The same claim applies to first-person, essayistic cinema. In all cases, I will argue that these films' enunciators postulate the existence of authors who are empirical subjects, explicitly engaged in the production of an account of themselves and their point of view on the world.[10] This is possible because we are dealing here with filmmakers who – although never unproblematically or unreflexively – relate to the tradition of the Western Artist, and of the director-auteur, a figure who exerts a strong influence and control over the creative process and its final product. This is not to say that the object of study of this book is the truth of the self; for, as Turim suggested:

> If film artists found visual metaphors that expressed their subjective truths, we no longer find ourselves necessarily privileging that vision as the profound truth of the universe per se, or even as the truth of a singular and unique individual. We can now see subjectivities and truths as plural not only among subjects, but within a given subject, the self that is divided, and even in part unknown to itself. (1992: 202)

The object of this study, accordingly, is not the extra-textual author, seen as a coherent subject directly reflected in his or her textual product; my concern will be with the texts, their communicative strategies and, ultimately, with their enunciators as figures that offer themselves as a (sustainably truthful) representation and performance of their authors.

What vindicates this approach is the fact that all the films considered in this volume employ textual and extra-textual strategies to promote a certain form of reception, a certain viewing position. In other words, they encourage a *subjective* and sometimes an *autobiographical* reading – and this effect is crucial, given Paul de Man's (1984) claim that autobiography cannot be experienced as a genre or modus, but only as modality of reading. Similarly, for H. Porter Abbott, at the opposite of new criticism, whose approach 'aspires to a purity of fictive response, erasing the author altogether ... to read autobiographically is not to erase the author but to keep him or her in view' (1988: 608). The reader, in other words, asks the text to reveal its author. 'The difference ... between an autobiography and a novel lies not in the factuality of the one and fictiveness of the other but in the different orientations toward the text that they elicit in the reader' (1988: 603).

This shift impinges decisively on the problem of the essay film as object, to which I referred at the onset. Noël Carroll is not far from the above view when he persuasively claims that 'The distinction between nonfiction and fiction is a distinction between the commitments of the texts, not between the surface structures of the texts' (1996: 287). Precisely the same can be said of various types of nonfiction: the distinction is a matter of textual commitment or, to put it another way, of modality of viewing. So, to quote Dai Vaughan, 'What makes a "documentary" is the way we look at it' (1999: 84). This monograph will ask questions about the way in which we look at essayistic, first-person nonfictions, and about the modality of viewing they produce; and will argue that these films demand of their spectators that they always keep their authors in view.

Strong implicit authors, embodied enunciators

My attitude here, then, will be to conceive filmic autobiography as an effect, and as a modality of viewing. I have suggested that autobiography is not a matter of content (of factuality), or even of the strict adoption of a set of preconditions, such as those of Lejeune's autobiographical pact in literature, which relate to language (prose), subject (the life of an individual), the author's situation (coincidence between author and narrator), and narrator's positioning (coincidence between narrator and protagonist; see Lejeune 1996). Accordingly, I will look at subjectivity as the product of the text's adoption of certain strategies. Such strategies, which will be at the core of my analysis, usually imply strong enunciators, who produce an audiovisual discourse that asks to be experienced by the viewer as eminently personal. This does not exclude the possibility that these films' enunciators may also be, in many cases, empirical authors – quite the opposite. However, my interest will rest not so much on their biographies, or the factuality of their personal accounts, but on their performance of subjectivity in the text. I borrow Stella Bruzzi's definition of documentaries as 'performative acts, inherently fluid and unstable and informed by issues of performance and performativity' (2006: 1). In fact, most of the documentaries I will examine offer the performance of the filmmaker in the text, which is highly significant if we accept that 'the performance for the camera [is] the "ultimate document" ... the truth around which a documentary is built' (Bruzzi 2006: 154). Furthermore, they are also performative, because the essay film always and emphatically does what all nonfictions do in perhaps less evident ways – that is, in Bruzzi's words, 'enact the process of factual and intellectual discovery that goes into completing a documentary' (2006: 196).[11]

Film theorists have viewed subjectivity in the cinema in different ways, according to their adopted perspective, be it linguistic, semiotic, psychoanalytical, representational or political/ideological (for instance, Marxist, feminist, postcolonial). Traditionally, elements such as point-of-view shots and voice-over narration attracted particular attention for their ability to express the narrator's perceptions, or her psychological and emotional perspectives and responses. In his examination of classical fiction cinema, Edward Branigan has concisely defined subjectivity in relation to narration as 'a specific instance or level of narration where the telling is *attributed to* a character in the narrative and received by us *as if* we were in the situation of a character' (1984: 73; emphasis in original) – hence stressing that subjectivity in film is a form of narration, and highlighting the role of the spectator in its definition. I will unavoidably make reference to character point of view; however, the films included in this book not only present narrators, as all films do, but also strong enunciators.

Indeed, the presence of embodied enunciators is in contrast with many types of standard and mainstream cinema and, in particular, as is obvious, with various historical forms of realism, including classical Hollywood cinema; but they also contrast with what we could call the traditional documentary. In traditional forms of cinematic realism, in fact, the enunciator tends to hide; most of the time, it is disguised, and if it emerges forcefully it does so in a disembodied manner, through musical commentary, or camera angles and movements, or instances of voice-over. It is rare that his or her presence is seen more overtly than this in fiction films. Some examples do come to mind, for instance the signature appearances of Alfred Hitchcock in his movies; or images of, or relating to, the real author, such as the poster of *Andrey Rublyov* (*Andrei Rublev*, 1969) hanging on a wall of the protagonist's Moscow apartment in Andrei Tarkovsky's autobiographical *Zerkalo* (*Mirror*, 1975). In the documentary, it is of course far less unusual to see the filmmakers onscreen, or to be in the presence of a strong, outspoken enunciator. This happens, for instance, in what Bill Nichols (1991) calls the 'expository' mode of documentary, in which we find a 'voice-of-God' commentary directed towards the viewer; or in the 'interactive' mode, in which the filmmaker's presence in the film is apparent and synchronous to the filming, rather than superimposed in post-production. However, even in these modes, the enunciator is not necessarily to be taken as a strong expression of authorial subjectivity; indeed, in the expository mode, as Nichols himself recognises, he often represents a broad, institutional authority, while in the interactive mode he is sometimes structured as an absence.

It seems to me that the explicit enunciators of essayistic films are special, in the sense that they come forward to present their own, personal viewpoints. At times, they do so while talking of themselves or of topics that concern them directly; at other times, they offer a commentary on conceptual matters or public issues that affect not only them, but also culture and society at large. They can be pure voice-over or written linguistic presence (through captions and subtitles); on other occasions, they are embodied onscreen. In all cases, they create a stronger impression of authorial presence than that to be experienced in most classical and narrative films.

But it is crucial to recognise that, if much attention will be devoted to authors, one cannot forget that every 'I' implies a 'you'. Structuralism and enunciation theory have rightly been critiqued for presenting an abstract image of the reader/spectator, who used to be seen as a viewing position, as a standardised and passive figure produced and controlled by the text. The subjective enunciators of first-person films often address spectators directly, sometimes by looking into the camera lens, or else by speaking to them, or simply by presenting their discourse as a confession, as a shared reflection, or as a persuasive argument. My claim is that the (real) spectators of these films are called upon in an unremitting effect of interpellation. In the case of the essay film proper, they are asked to take the film as its author's subjective reflection and to connect with her, to share or reject her line of reasoning. In the case of essayistic forms such as diaries, notebooks and self-portraits, they are invited to engage with the truth that the author is telling about himself and his experiences. Hence, spectators of first-person films may feel closer to the text and to its author – and may themselves have a more personal, subjective spectatorial experience than with other types of cinema.

I am, however, far from suggesting that this structure is unique to essayistic cinema. But I do claim, more simply, that it is a characterising feature of this form. There is, indeed, a significant tradition of interpellation in fiction cinema: in terms of looks, a range of examples spring to mind, from the gaze into the lens of the robber who shoots the audience at the end (or at the beginning, as the scene could be equally used to either open or close the film) of Edwin S. Porter's *The Great Train Robbery* (1903),[12] to Jean-Paul Belmondo's asides in Godard's *À bout de souffle* (*Breathless*, 1960); from Alma and Elisabeth's monologues in Bergman's *Persona* (1966) to the several intense looks that different characters exchange with the spectator in Tarkovsky's *Mirror*; from the asides in the musical film to those in comedies. Direct address in fiction cinema may work as a Brechtian distancing device, based on its ability to interrupt the flow of the narration and highlight the permeability of the 'fourth wall' (Godard); as a manner to shock the audience and elicit emotional participation (*The Great Train Robbery*); or as a route to complicity and humour (musical and comedy). Examples of direct address through voice-over or captions are not infrequent either; in these cases, the interpellation is a form of narration that creates participation. In traditional documentaries, however, the direct address through gaze is rare.[13] Voice-over, by contrast, is pervasive in nonfiction; however, the voice does not always belong to the director, nor is it automatically connected by the spectator to the filmmaker, rather it often represents a generalised authority. In first-person cinema, instead, the address is unmistakably characterised as personal, as coming from an enunciator that overtly identifies with the empirical author.

These considerations suggest that essayistic films reveal and embody two fundamental and intertwined, although clearly paradoxical, aspirations of cinema, both fictional and documentary. The first is the filmmaker's desire to use the camera as a flexible, lucid, incisive means of personal, individual expression. The second is her wish to communicate with the spectator directly, to establish a contact with the embodied audience, based on an elective affinity. Such ambitions mark essayistic cinema as utopian; but also testify to the urgency of its project in the panorama of filmmaking.

First-person cinema: the basis of an investigation

The claim I made concerning the difference between fiction and nonfiction cinema can be reiterated with regard to different types of nonfiction: the distinction is a matter of textual commitments or, to put it another way, of modalities of viewing mobilised by these different types. Hence, I will draw a distinction between forms of subjective cinema. For this reason, *The Personal Camera* is divided into two sections: the first is devoted to the essay film proper; the second to other cognate but independent forms of first-person filmmaking, namely the diary film, the notebook film and the self-portrait film.[14]

All these forms share some fundamental traits, the most evident of which is that they derive from pre-existing artistic genres, mostly literary ones – with the exception of the self-portrait, which comes about first (and predominantly, despite the existence of literary examples) in the fine arts. This is an important factor, of course, which connects these films to a tradition of work that is reflective, introspective and authorial. Secondly, all these forms present, as I already claimed, strong and embodied enunciators.

However, there also are some key distinctions: the textual commitments of each type differ, and so does the spectatorial pact they set up. The commitment and the pact of the essay film can be summarised as follows: 'I, the author, am reflecting on a problem, and share my thoughts with you, the spectator.' In the diary, notebook and self-portrait, instead, the textual commitments can be expressed as follows: 'I am recording events that I have witnessed and impressions and emotions I have experienced' (the diary); 'I am taking notes of ideas, events, existents for future use' (the notebook); 'I am making a representation of myself' (the self-portrait). In each of these three cases, the spectator is not so much urged to share the director's experience or line of reasoning as an equal partner in the communication, but is admitted as a third party, who 'overhears' a private, self-addressed discourse. Furthermore, the essay is always subjective, but is not necessarily autobiographical; diaries, notebooks and self-portraits are always both personal and autobiographical. A compelling corpus of film texts exists which illustrates these trends and I shall bring to bear on these a range of theoretical discourses which are themselves the sites of important contemporary debates.

While a study of the workings of textual structures like these is indispensable to a comprehension of first-person, essayistic cinema, I do not believe that any simple formula can resolve all the interpretative and formal issues. These texts do not offer final answers but, quite the opposite, open up problems; they are original and diverse by nature. Through their idiosyncrasy, experimentalism and hybridism, they confound and challenge definitions. It is only by respecting their fluidity that we can comprehend the way they work. Hence, while proposing possible categorisations, I do not wish to offer an easy solution, a recipe that may be rigidly applied to such utterly volatile matter. Indeed, it seems to me that one of the characteristics shared by these films is a sort of fragility – perhaps due to their tentative nature and uniqueness, to their existing in a contextual void, as well as to their generic in-betweenness. This study, however, aims to do more than uncover the communicative structures of these forms; it aspires to investigate how these structures can themselves be said to be problematic.

The first section of the book, devoted to the essay film proper, opens with a chapter that explores the history of this form in the theory and practice of filmmaking, assesses existing definitions and offers a discussion of its particular rhetorical structures. The following three chapters address a number of areas that are, in my view, of topical importance today; they do so through an engagement with both scholarship and specific films. The case studies that occupy the first section of the book are, intentionally, the work of three directors who are widely associated with essayistic cinema, three of the main recognised representatives of this form.

The first area I will tackle is the question of voice-over as privileged site of the textual construction of the enunciator, and as an instrument of expression of the author's subjectivity and thought – topics that I will debate through an engagement with existing theorisations of voice-over in film, and in the documentary in particular; and through an analysis of two films by Harun Farocki. In this chapter, I will also discuss the issue of found footage and the use of archival images.

The second area of concern is the essay as musealisation of the experience and of the self. While the cinema in general can rightfully be described as a technology of memory, the essay film, which displays a constitutive preoccupation with the articulation of the author's subjective vision of herself and of the world, is a privileged site for memorialisation. In the context of the contemporary phenomenon of the spread of practices of audiovisual musealisation, I will also reflect on the evolution of the cinematic essay in the age of new, computerised and digital technologies of memory. I will engage with this topic through a discussion of Chris Marker's work.

The third chapter explores the related topics of performance and of negotiation. Both are of paramount importance to the essay film. I will claim, indeed, that the essay sets up a communication with an embodied spectator, and that each act of communication is a form of negotiation. Furthermore, the essay film displays its performativity in an especially emphatic way, because it tends to include in the textual fabric the process of its own coming into being. As a concept, as a field of study and as a practice, performance has not yet received much attention in writings on documentary. I propose to look at performance as one of the main sites of the negotiation between author and film, film and subject matter, spectator and film. My case study is work by Jean-Luc Godard, in which the filmmaker plays himself.

The second section of the book focuses on essayistic first-person cinema, and explicitly the diary film, the notebook film and the self-portrait film. An introductory chapter will offer an overview of these forms, of their connections to theoretical ideas about authorial cinema, and their relation to the personal cinema of the avant-gardes, to art cinema and to the first-person documentary. Then, the specific history and tenets of each category, their relationship with their models in other arts (and especially literature and painting), and the main theoretical issues they raise, will be investigated in three separate chapters. Each chapter will also discuss some of the best-known textual examples of diary films, notebook films and self-portrait films respectively, and then focus on three case studies – three nonfictions by Aleksandr Sokurov, Pier Paolo Pasolini and Michelangelo Antonioni. Ideas regarding self-representation, autobiography, voice-over, gaze, performance and address, which are equally relevant to the first part of the monograph, will also be explored in the second section. So the specific concern I have with the formal fluidity of these works carries over from the first part to the second; and the second extends the range of interpretative approaches that can be brought to bear on the materials considered in the book as a whole.

Overall, then, in *The Personal Camera* I aim to strike a fine balance between, on the one hand, describing the history of subjective cinema, tracing its theoretical roots, defining its workings, and exploring some of its principal issues and problems, and, on the other hand, respecting its heretical nature – an objective that will be achieved by avoiding an overtheorisation of the form, and by analysing real texts and their idiosyncratic articulation of the essayistic in film. Furthermore, I look at essayistic cinema as a transnational form, made by international filmmakers in dialogue with one another; but also one which has its own local histories and individual embodiments.[15] And finally, I see it as a practice that derives some of its current prestige from its affinity with contemporary discourses on the self, on identity, on the waning of the myth of objectivity; but that also springs from the auteurist and anti-establishment cinema of modernism and the avant-gardes.

Ultimately, I aim to offer an exploration and elucidation of a field that still lacks clarity, but that is of growing relevance not only for Film Studies, but also for the various and evolving forms of subjective and autobiographical expression which dominate the current mass media, literary, audiovisual, electronic and artistic landscapes.

part one | **the essay film**

chapter one
THE ESSAY FILM:
PROBLEMS, DEFINITIONS, TEXTUAL COMMITMENTS

The label 'essay film' is encountered with ever-increasing frequency in both film reviews and scholarly writings on the cinema, owing to the recent proliferation of unorthodox, personal, reflexive 'new' documentaries. In an article dedicated to the phenomenon that he defines as the 'recent onslaught of essay films', Paul Arthur proposes: 'Galvanized by the intersection of personal, subjective and social history, the essay has emerged as the leading nonfiction form for both intellectual and artistic innovation' (2003: 58). Although widely used, the category is under-theorised, more so than other forms of nonfiction. By tracing the birth of the essay in both film theory and film history, and by examining and evaluating existing definitions, a theory of the essay film can be shaped, some order in its intricate field made, and some light shed on this erratic but fascinating and ever more relevant cinematic form. Against such historical and theoretical backdrops, the following chapters will delve further into both the form's key features and its problematic areas.

Most of the existing scholarly contributions acknowledge that the definition of essay film is challenging, and suggest that it is a hybrid form, which crosses boundaries and rests somewhere in between fiction and nonfiction cinema. According to Louis D. Giannetti, for instance, 'an essay is neither fiction nor fact, but a personal investigation involving both the passion and intellect of the author' (1975: 26). Arthur's framing of such in-betweenness is particularly instructive: 'one way to think about the essay film is as a meeting ground for documentary, avant-garde, and art film impulses' (2003: 62). Nora M. Alter insists that the essay film is '*not* a genre, as it strives to be beyond formal, conceptual, and social constraint. Like "heresy" in the Adornean literary essay, the essay film disrespects traditional boundaries, is transgressive both structurally and conceptually, it is self-reflective and self-reflexive' (1996: 171; emphasis in original).

Transgression is a characteristic that the essay film shares with the literary essay, which is also frequently described as a protean form. The two foremost theorists of the essay are, as is well known, Theodor Adorno and György Lukács; both describe it as indeterminate, open and, ultimately, indefinable. According to Adorno, 'the essay's innermost formal law is heresy' (1991: 23); for Lukács, it must manufacture the conditions of its own existence: 'the essay has to create from within itself all the preconditions for the effectiveness and solidity of its vision' (1974: 11). Other theorists and essayists make similar claims: for Jean Starobinski, the essay 'does not obey any rules' quoted in Liandrat-Guigues 2004: 8; author's translation); for Aldous Huxley, it 'is a literary device for saying almost everything about almost anything' (1960: v); for John Snyder, it is a 'nongenre' (1991: 12). As these examples indicate, many existing definitions of both literary and filmic essays are simultaneously vague and sweeping. Indeed, elusiveness and inclusiveness seem to be the only characterising features of the essayistic; as Michael Renov observes: 'the essay form, notable for its tendency towards complication (digression, fragmentation, repetition, and dispersion) rather than composition, has, in its four-hundred-years history, continued to resist the efforts of literary taxonomists, confounding the laws of genre and classification, challenging the very notion of text and textual economy' (2004b: 70).

As José Moure (2004) has argued, the fact that we resort to a literary term such as 'essay' points to the difficulty that we experience when attempting to categorise some unclassifiable films. This observation flags the risk that we accept the current state of under-theorisation of the form, and use the term indiscriminately, in order to classify films that escape all other labelling, as the following remark appears to endorse: 'The essayistic quality becomes the only means of categorising cinema that offers resistance in the face of commercial production' (Liandrat-Guigues 2004: 10; author's translation). The temptation to assign the label of essay film to all that is non-commercial or experimental or unclassifiable must, however, be resisted, or else the term will cease being epistemologically useful, and we will end up equating very diverse films, as sometimes happens in critical literature – for instance, works such as Chris Marker's *Sans soleil* (*Sunless*, 1983) and Michael Moore's *Fahrenheit 9/11*, which have very little in common aside from their extensive voice-overs, and the fact that they both present problems of classification.

Of all the features that are most frequently identified in the essay form, both literary and filmic, two stand out as specific, essential and characteristic: reflectiveness and subjectivity. Jean-Luc Godard, for instance, who is widely considered to be an essayistic director, has suggested in his *Histoire(s) du cinéma* that cinema is a 'form that thinks' as well as 'thought that forms'; elsewhere, he defined himself as an essayist, and specified: 'As a critic, I thought of myself as a filmmaker. Today I still think of myself as a critic … Instead of writing criticism, I make a film, but the critical dimension is subsumed' (1972a: 171). In both quotes, Godard stresses the importance of the reflective component of the essay form.

If we follow Huxley, this component may engage with or, in the best cases, combine, three main spheres: 'Essays belong to a literary species whose extreme variability can be studied most effectively within a three-poled frame of reference. There is the pole of the personal and the autobiographical; there is the pole of the objective, the factual, the concrete-particular; and there is the pole of the abstract-universal' (1960: v). The critical stance, which for Huxley can address different spheres, is a key component of all essayistic forms. Indeed, the most important stamp that Montaigne left on the genre, and which derives from classical philosophical traditions, consists in the sceptical evaluation (from the Latin *exagium* – meaning weight, test, trial) of the subject matter, which self-reflexively includes the evaluation of the author's same conclusions. The essay contains and incorporates in the text the act of reasoning; as Graham Good writes, 'The essay aims, in other words, to preserve something of the *process* of thinking' (1988: 20; emphasis in original) – which is also why Adorno could claim that 'In the essay, concepts do not build a continuum of operation, thought does not advance in a single direction, rather the aspects of the argument interweave as in a carpet' (1991: 160). In what ways, however, does an artistic essay differ from other forms containing a similar critical engagement, such as an academic essay or journalistic reportage?

Most, if not all, accounts of the essayistic also place emphasis on its personal, almost autobiographical nature. Subjectivity is so important to the essay that Montaigne's motto was, famously, 'I am myself the matter of my book'; he wrote not in order to 'pretend to discover things, but to lay open my self' (1700: 254). As Lukács put it, 'the essayist must now become conscious of his own self, must find himself and build something of himself' (1974: 15). However, the essay film produces a particular articulation of subjectivity; the mere presence of a strong subject does not make an essay film. We can safely argue that Federico Fellini's films, for instance, were always highly subjective as well as deeply autobiographical; yet, this does not make them all essays – even though the author is at times listed among essayist filmmakers. Furthermore, it could be argued that many documentaries display the source of the act of communication, hence foregrounding their subjectivity; however, as Renov has reminded us, invoking Bill Nichols' words, 'standard tropes of subjective editing familiar from fiction films become, in the realm of documentary, the foundation for "a social subjectivity … dissociated from any single individual character". Here our identification is with the audience as a collectivity rather than with an individual behind the camera'

(2004a: xviii). In what ways does the subjectivity of the essay film differ from the subjectivity of other cinematic forms, be they fictional or documentary?

An examination of the textual commitments of the essay film, of its deep structures, as well as of the modality of viewing that it produces, will help to clarify matters. Firstly, it is opportune to understand when and where the concept of the filmic essay emerges in film theory, as well as in the practice of film-making. The idea of the possibility of expressing subjectivity through film can, in truth, be traced back to the very origins of film theory – in particular, some of the French pioneers influenced by poetic impressionism, such as Ricciotto Canudo, Louis Delluc and Jean Epstein, urged directors to express their inner self and their personal dreams in their films. As mentioned in the introduction, however, it is in the late 1940s that the reflection on cinematic subjectivity clearly emerges in European film theory, preparing the formulation of the *nouvelle vague*'s auteur theory in the second half of the 1950s. It is within this context that the theory of an essayistic use of the camera first emerges.

A certain tendency:
the emergence of the essay in film theory and film practice

Guy Fihman believes that the first reference to the term 'essay' in a cinematographic context occurs in Sergei Eisenstein's notes on his own work, and in particular in an entry of 13 October 1927 dedicated to his project of making a film based on *Das Kapital*: '*October* presents a new form of cinematographic work – a collection of "*Essays*" on the series of themes that form *Das Kapital*' (Eisenstein, quoted in Fihman 2004: 41; author's translation). In 1948, in the context of his seminal reflection on the cinema's ability to express ideas, Alexandre Astruc had indeed mentioned Eisenstein's project of illustrating Marx's *Das Kapital*, but did not regard it as an example of the new type of cinema he announced (see Astruc 1999: 160). Noël Burch, writing on the essay film in 1961, also mentioned another early, unrealised project, Jacques Feyder's adaptation of Montaigne's essays (see Burch 1981: 162).

The first contribution explicitly devoted to the essay film is probably Hans Richter's 'Der Filmessay, eine neue form de Dokumentarfilm', which was published on 24 April 1940 in *Nationalzeitung* (see 1992). In his article, Richter (himself often listed as an author of essay films) announces a new type of intellectual but also emotional cinema, able to provide 'images for mental notions' and to 'portray a concept'. Its relationship with documentary cinema is explored: 'In this effort to give body to the invisible world of imagination, thought and ideas, the essay film can employ an incomparably greater reservoir of expressive means than can the pure documentary film. Freed from recording external phenomena in simple sequence the film essay must collect its material from everywhere; its space and time must be conditioned only by the need to explain and show the idea' (in Leyda 1964: 31). Nora M. Alter comments:

> Unlike the documentary film, which presents facts and information, the essay film produces complex thought that at times is not grounded in reality but can be contradictory, irrational, and fantastic. This new type of film, according to Richter, no longer binds the filmmaker to the rules and parameters of traditional documentary practice, such as chronological sequencing or the depiction of external phenomena. Rather, it gives free reign to the imagination, with all its artistic potentiality. The term essay is used because it signifies a composition that is in between categories and as such is transgressive, digressive, playful, contradictory, and political. (2002: 7–8)

The transgressive quality that the essay film inherits from the literary essay, its derivation from but also betrayal of documentary, and its ability to be a meeting point between intellect and emotion are already identified in this first contribution.

By far the most important of the early contributions, for the impact it had on both the emergent critical category of the essay film and for author theory, is 'Naissance d'une nouvelle avant-garde: la caméra-stylo', the legendary article by Alexandre Astruc first published in *L'Ecran Français* on 30 March 1948, and translated into English with the title 'The Birth of a New Avant-Garde: La Caméra-Stylo' (see 1999). In his contribution, Astruc notices a new tendency, the first signs of a new type of cinema, equally distant from the conventionality of classical fiction film (which he compares to filmed theatre) and from the surrealist avant-garde (which he does not consider to be truly cinematic), from the visual experiments of Soviet montage and from silent cinema, with its static quality. For Astruc, who looks at Jean Renoir, Orson Welles and Robert Bresson as good approximations of what he has in mind, the new cinema will be able to express thought in a flexible, subtle and efficient manner, in the same way as literature does. This possibility, Astruc argues, has been brought about by technological developments, which will impinge on the distribution market: up to now films could only be shown in large auditoriums, hence production was limited to entertainment products. 'But with the development of 16mm and television, the day is not far off when everyone will possess a projector, will go to the local bookstore and hire films written on any subject, of any form, from literary criticism and novels to mathematics, history and general science' (Astruc 1999: 159). Astruc, hence, is not announcing the birth of the essay film, but of an authorial cinema able to produce a variety of linguistic and discursive registers, including the essayistic one, and that applies itself to a range of topics and disciplines, precisely as books do. This is possible because cinema is 'gradually becoming a language':

> By language I mean a form in which and by which an artist can express his thoughts, however abstract they may be, or translate his obsessions exactly as he does in the contemporary essay or novel. That is why I would like to call this new age of the cinema the age of *caméra-stylo* (camera-pen). This metaphor has a very precise sense. By it I mean that the cinema will gradually break free from the tyranny of what is visual, from the image for its own sake, from the immediate and concrete demands of the narrative, to become a means of writing just as flexible and subtle as written language. (1999: 159)

In order for this to fully happen, the role of the scriptwriter and that of the film-maker must merge: 'Direction is no longer a means of illustrating or presenting a scene, but a true act of writing. The filmmaker/author writes with his camera as a writer writes with his pen' (1999: 161).[1] There is, of course, some affinity between this article and François Truffaut's 'Une Certain Tendance du Cinéma Français', his 1954 manifesto of *la politique des auteurs* first published in *Cahiers du cinéma* (see Truffaut 1976), not only because of the directors taken as examples of the new 'tendency' (Truffaut includes Renoir, Bresson, Cocteau, Becker, Tati, Ophuls, Leenhardt and Gance), but also because both manifestos introduce a concept of cinematic auteurism borrowed from literature.

The first article that compared a film to an essay is, probably, Jacques Rivette's 'Lettre sur Roberto Rossellini', published in 1955 in *Cahiers du cinéma* (see Rivette 1977). For Rivette, *Viaggio in Italia* (*Voyage to Italy*, 1954) is the first film that offers the cinema the possibility of the essay, which was so far confined to literature, and, for its freedom, inquisitiveness and spontaneity, the true language of modern art. Rossellini's film is, simultaneously, a metaphysical essay, a confession, a logbook and an intimate journal – in other words, an essay *à la* Montaigne, because in it Rossellini filmed both his ideas and the most everyday details of his life (a life which, for Rivette, is thoroughly exemplary and instructive).

The most famous among the early articles that deliberately analysed a film by comparing it to an essay is, undoubtedly, André Bazin's review of Chris Marker's *Letter from Siberia*, first published in 1958 in *France-Observateur*. Remarking that *Letter from Siberia* resembles 'nothing that we have ever seen before in films with a documentary basis' (2003: 44), Bazin calls Marker's work 'an essay documented by film', hence highlighting the prominence of the written text over the images. He goes on to elucidate:

The important word is 'essay', understood in the same sense that it has in literature – an essay at once historical and political, written by a poet as well. Generally, even in politically engaged documentaries or those with a specific point to make, the image (which is to say, the uniquely cinematic element) effectively constitutes the primary material of the film. The orientation of the work is expressed through the choices made by the filmmaker in the montage, with the commentary completing the organisation of the sense thus conferred on the document. With Marker it works quite differently. I would say that the primary material is intelligence, that its immediate means of expression is language, and that the image only intervenes in the third position, in reference to this verbal intelligence. (Ibid.)

Although placing much importance on the written text, Bazin goes beyond literature and looks at the relationship between text and image, and between shots:

Marker brings to his films an absolutely new notion of montage that I will call 'horizontal', as opposed to traditional montage that plays with the sense of duration through the relationship of shot to shot. Here, a given image doesn't refer to the one that preceded it or the one that will follow, but rather it refers laterally, in some way, to what is said. (Ibid.)

This lateral or horizontal montage (which recalls Adorno's already mentioned idea of the carpet, in which 'thought does not advance in a single direction', and in which 'the aspects of the argument interweave'), allows the beauty and intelligence of words to transfer also to the visual component: 'The montage has been forged from ear to eye' (ibid.).

Bazin here analyses a specific film, and does not propose Marker as a case study of a more ample phenomenon; however, if his comments are to be referred to essayistic cinema in general, Bazin's conception is that of a cinema of the word, which cannot do without a poetic, intelligent, written text read by a voice-over. Similarly to Richter, Bazin places emphasis on the meeting between 'beauty and intelligence', and on the freedom of the essayist filmmaker, who may use 'all filmic material that might help the case – including still images (engravings and photos), of course, but also animated cartoons' (2003: 45).

It is not by accident that, after Richter's 1940 announcement, the two texts that signal the oncoming of the essay film, the first as a prediction, the second as an observation and an analysis, are both French and linked, although separated by a ten-year interval, to the *nouvelle vague* and the establishment of *la politique des auteurs*. It is indeed in this context that the essay film truly emerges as a cinematic form, although critics have labelled as essays a number of earlier films, even from different geographical areas (for instance, those of the already cited Hans Richter). However, most contributions on the cinematic essay rightly include among the early examples films by French directors Chris Marker, Alain Resnais and Agnès Varda (the Rive Gauche auteurs), and by one of the leading figures of the *nouvelle vague*'s other *rive*, Jean-Luc Godard. This may be explained by historical circumstances. Pierre Sorlin (2005) recalls how a 1940 law of the Vichy government had already boosted the production of nonfiction in France, with an increase from 400 documentaries made during the German occupation to 4000 made between 1945 and 1955. Catherine Lupton (2006) observes that France experienced a decade of flourishing of short filmmaking after the introduction in 1955 of a new system of grants which, together with the work of such sympathetic producers as Anatole Dauman (Argos Films) and Pierre Braunberger (Les Films de la Pléiade), favoured the debuts of many young directors in a situation of increased creative freedom. Bazin himself in his above-mentioned piece on Marker stressed how short filmmaking was at the time 'the liveliest fringe of French cinema' (2003: 44). French short filmmaking historically developed a close association with the personal documentary, either as a result of the influence of poetic impressionism and naturalism, as in the case of Alberto Cavalcanti's *Rien que les heures* (*Nothing but the Hours*, 1926) and Jean Vigo's *À propos de Nice* (*On Nice*, 1930), or of surrealism, as in Luis Buñuel's *Las Hurdes*, and Jean Painlevé's *L'Hippocampe* (*The Sea Horse*, 1932). As Lupton argues, the new postwar poetic documentaries, including works by Alain Resnais and Georges Franju, were made in a climate in which, thanks to the surrealist (and, I would add, impressionist) antecedents, the boundaries between documentary and fiction (and art film) were fluid, and the filmmaker's personal style in the approach to reality was valued, in contrast to other established documentary practices, and especially those linked to John Grierson's legacy: 'In France, documentary flourished within a continuum of short film production, and came to be regarded at its best as a mode of personal reflection on the world, more closely aligned to the authored literary essay than the social or legal document' (Lupton 2006: 48).[2]

Such first-person essayistic documentary production developed alongside, on the one hand, experiments in *cinéma vérité* such as *Chronicle of a Summer*, in which, as mentioned earlier, the authors filmed themselves as source of the act of communication, and inscribed a self-reflexive gesture into the text; and, on the other hand, the new first-person and autobiographical fiction cinema of the Parisian *nouvelle vague* of the late 1950s and 1960s, with its theorisation of the personal 'cinema of authors'. The essay provided filmmakers with a flexible form of cinewriting, able to tackle topics and experiences of various types. Often, it offered a channel to express a committed and political vision of the world, as in the tradition initiated, in particular, by Godard, Resnais and Marker in France, and by Pier Paolo Pasolini in Italy. It is not surprising, then, that in their famous manifesto Fernando Solanas and Octavio Getino mentioned the essay film as one of the privileged filmic languages for the development of a Third Cinema (see 1976: 55).

Solanas and Getino's manifesto was first published in 1969, a date by which the term 'essay film' had truly become accepted. The same year, in fact, saw the publication of Noël Burch's *Theory of Film Practice*. In a chapter on 'Nonfictional Subjects', Burch discusses the essay film as a type of documentary that he sees as particularly current and relevant. For Burch, the first examples of essay films are Georges Franju's *Le Sang des bêtes* (*Blood of the Beasts*, 1949) and *Hôtel des Invalides* (1952),[3] which differ from the 'old-style documentary' because they do not take a 'passive subject', but an 'active theme': '[Franju's] subject is, in and of itself, a development or rather, an interpretation, of this theme and it thereby becomes "active"' (1981: 159). Franju's films propose not an objective rendering of reality, but conflicts of ideas; they are meditations, reflections on non-fictional subjects that 'set forth thesis and antithesis through the very texture of the film' (ibid.). These films also represent for Burch 'the first use in the documentary film of a formal approach that previously had been exclusively employed in the fiction film' (ibid.). The essay film is, indeed, a 'dialectics of fiction and nonfiction' (1981: 164); it is 'a cinema of pure reflection, where the subject becomes the basis of an intellectual construct, which in turn is capable of engendering the overall form and even the texture of a film without being denatured or distorted' (1981: 162). The accent for Burch is, therefore, on reflexivity, form and aesthetic attitude.

In 1966, in a contribution to a symposium on 'Cinema and the Novel' published in *Cahiers du cinéma*, novelist Italo Calvino had stated his interest in 'everything that tends towards the essay-film' (1986: 79). Referring to Godard's *Masculin Féminin* (1966), and to Francesco Rosi's cinema, Calvino remarked that the essayistic 'sociological-inquiry film' and 'historical-research film' should not simply be 'filmed explanations of a truth that sociology and historiography have already established … For the true essay-film I envisage an attitude not of pedagogy but of interrogation, with none of that inferiority complex toward the written word that has bedevilled relations between literature and the cinema' (ibid.).

Definitions

While some critics and film reviewers today use the expressions 'film essay' and 'essay film' in an ostensibly unproblematic manner, to label an array of very diverse works either of nonfiction or in between fiction and nonfiction, there exist some scholarly contributions that have attempted to define the field. I will review below, in chronological order of publication, four such contributions which, although brief, are particularly relevant and coherent, and present and summarise arguments that also recur in other works.[4]

In an article entitled 'In Search of the Centaur', Phillip Lopate begins by claiming that we must distinguish between a 'reflective, self-conscious style' and a truly essayistic one. Lopate identifies the essay with the literary tradition that starts with Cicero and Seneca and crystallises with Montaigne and Bacon, and defines the essay film's principal characteristics as follows: 'An essay film must have words, in the form of a text, either spoken, subtitled, or intertitled'; 'The text must represent a single voice'; 'The text must represent and attempt to work out some reasoned line of discourse on a problem'; 'The text must impart more than information; it must have a strong, personal point of view'; 'The text's language should be as eloquent, well written and interesting as possible' (1998: 283–4). All these features derive from a comparison with the literary essay; the emphasis is firmly placed on the film's verbal component, as opposed to the visuals. Lopate, indeed, admits that he 'cannot accept an utterly pure, silent flow of images as constituting essayistic discourse' (1998: 283). For the critic, an early example of essay is Alain Resnais' *Night and Fog*, with its 'self-interrogatory voice, like a true essayist's, dubious, ironical, wheeling and searching for the heart of the subject matter' (1998: 286); Resnais' tracking shots form a 'visual analogue' of the voice's searching. Lopate also discusses a number of other filmmakers and films; his focus is always primarily on the authorial voice and the verbal text, but also on several other questions, including the use of interviews and collage, and the contrast between the voice-over's subjectivity and the predominant objectivity of the camera. While not listing it among the form's main characteristics, Lopate makes a passing, almost casual comment on a feature that, in my opinion, is crucial for a definition of the essay film. Similarly to the literary essay, in which 'Readers must feel included in a true conversation, allowed to follow through mental processes of contradiction and digression' (1998: 282), the spectators of the essay film must be 'forced to acknowledge a conversation' with the filmmaker (1998: 286).

In a very brief contribution to be found in a volume dedicated to the relationship between film and literature, Timothy Corrigan acknowledges that the essay film, while it can be traced in a documentary practice that extends as far back as the Lumière brothers, emerges more distinctly in postwar European cinema, and especially in France. Corrigan argues for three fundamental characteristics of the essay film:

> (1) a usually – but not necessarily – short documentary subject, (2) the lack of a dominant narrative organisation (although narrative may provide one of several patterns in the film), and (3) the interaction of a personal voice or vision, sometimes in the form of a voice-over. In the essay film, the interaction

of that subjective perspective and the reality before it becomes a testing or questioning of both, and the structure of the film, like the literary essay, follows the undetermined movement of that dialogue. (1999: 58)

Again, the emphasis is on a personal authorial vision, although the centrality of a text read by a voice-over is less prescriptive than in Lopate.[5]

In his volume on *The Subject of the Documentary*, which collects a number of essays published over the years, Michael Renov touches on the question of the essayistic a number of times. Drawing on that tradition of essay writing, and reflection on the essay, that includes names such as Montaigne, Lukàcs and Barthes, Renov focuses on the question of the borderline status of the essay film, and suggests that its subjectivity is not in contrast with its inquisitive attitude, but is, indeed, its marker: 'Descriptive and reflexive modalities are coupled; the representation of the historical real is consciously filtered through the flux of subjectivity' (2004b: 70). For Renov, the essay film (seen, in particular, through the example of Jonas Mekas's *Lost, Lost, Lost*, 1976) can encompass all the functions that documentaries have displayed since their origin (although at times over- or underfavouring one or more of them): to record, reveal and preserve; to persuade or promote; to express; and to analyse or interrogate (see 2004b: 74–85). In other words, Renov restores to the documentary, of which the essay film is an ever more vital component, all those abilities and inclinations that for a long time have not been seen as part of its dominion, in this agreeing with Stella Bruzzi, who also reminds us that 'it is the function of a documentary to provide structure and meaning' (2006: 27). Renov suggests that 'there is no contradiction between the elemental documentary impulse, the will to preservation, and the exploration of subjectivity; indeed, it is their obsessive convergence that marks the essayistic work' (2004b: 81). For Renov, in fact, subjectivity and reflexivity are the marks of the essay film:

> While all documentary films retain an interest in some portion of the world out there – recording, and less frequently interrogating, at times with the intent to persuade and with varying degrees of attention to formal issues – the essayist's gaze is drawn inward with equal intensity. That inward gaze accounts for the digressive and fragmentary character of the essayistic, as Andre Tournon's assessment of Montaigne's *Essays* suggests: 'Thought can abandon its theme at any time to examine its own workings, question its acquired knowledge or exploit its incidental potentialities.' (2004b: 85)

According to Paul Arthur, in his aforementioned article on the essay film, the elusiveness of the genre defeats attempts at categorisation, so much so that contributions such as those of Lopate and Renov 'are inconclusive and tend to diverge on issues such as the necessity of spoken narration or irony versus sincerity' (2003: 59). Arthur also attempts to define the form, and observes that film essays

> fracture epistemological unities of time and place associated with documentary practices from John Grierson and Thirties New Deal tracts through Sixties vérité. The binding aspect of personal commentary is typically constituted by voice-over narration enhanced by musical selections, editorial as well as factual intertitles, and is often reinforced by compositional devices. When spoken narration is either subdued or absent, other traces of authorial presence may replace direct speech. (Ibid.)

Arthur also attracts attention to the use of 'found footage and collage', which produce juxtapositions between the past tense of archival images and the present tense of the commentary, and in which, at the opposite of what happens in pastiche, the emphasis is on inquiry rather than on nostalgia. In terms of the question of authority, for Arthur, essay films 'confound the perception of untroubled authority or comprehensive knowledge that a singular mode of address projects onto a topic' (ibid.); however, he also recognises that 'Argument must proceed from one person's set of assumptions, a particular framework of consciousness, rather than from a transparent, collective "We"' (2003: 60). Because of its emphasis on the first person, the essay is, for Arthur, especially apt to express oppositional positions, and is indeed often employed by women directors and artists of colour.[6]

Theorising the essay: heresy, form, textual commitments

All these attempts at defining the essay film are productive, in that they identify a number of characteristics that are undoubtedly relevant; and, principally, the two primary markers of the form – reflectiveness and subjectivity. However, they also diverge in some substantial ways, perhaps due to that 'heretical' factor that we recognise in the literary essay first and, consequently, in its cinematic versions. While the heretical aspect of the essay should be respected, and an over-theorisation of the form avoided, it is important to understand why certain films produce in the spectator the impression of watching an essay, as opposed to a documentary, a fiction, a poem, a travelogue or an experimental film.

At the level of textual commitments (which can be summarised as follows: 'I am going to share with you my personal line of reasoning on this topic'), an essay is the expression of a personal, critical reflection on a problem or set of problems. Such reflection does not propose itself as anonymous or collective, but as originating from a single authorial voice; as Arthur writes, 'a quality shared by all film essays is the inscription of a blatant, self-searching authorial presence' (2003: 59). This authorial 'voice'[7] approaches the subject matter not in order to present an ostensibly factual report (the field of traditional documentary), but to offer an overtly personal, in-depth, thought-provoking reflection.

At the level of rhetorical structures, in order to convey such reflection, the filmic essay decidedly points to the enunciating subject, who literally inhabits the text. This enunciator is embodied in a narrator, who (although never unproblematically or unreflexively) is close to the real, extra-textual author. The distance between the two is slight, as the enunciator represents the author's views, and the narrator is her spokesperson (even when hiding behind a different name, or multiple personae, or when problematising the existence of the subject itself). The essay's enunciator may remain a voice-over or also physically appear in the text, and usually does not conceal that she is the film's director. As examples of these strong enunciators, and in order to further clarify my claims, in the course of the following three chapters I will examine a film by Chris Marker, in which the director briefly appears as himself in voice-over (and includes a shot of his hand), but also speaks extensively through a diegetic, fictional female narrator; two films by Harun Farocki, in which the filmmaker speaks in voice-over either directly, or through an extra-diegetic narrator, and – in one of the two films – shows parts of his body (his hand, the back of his head); finally, two films by Jean-Luc Godard, in which the director appears in person, but also uses an array of both real and fictional diegetic narrators. All these texts, although in idiosyncratic ways, point to the enunciating subjects in an extraordinarily strong (although never unproblematic and straightforward) manner; the authors inscribe themselves in the films, and play roles that position them as the source of the act of communication, and as essayists: they are filmmakers, researchers, film editors, intellectuals, lecturers. I have suggested, however, that the relationship between narrator(s), enunciator and author is never unproblematic or unreflexive; indeed, the essay is a field in which the author problematises and questions not only her subject matter, but also her authorship and her subjectivity. I will suggest, and try to demonstrate by analysing specific films over the following chapters, that authorship in the essay film is interstitial; it is played, indeed, in the liminal spaces between the empirical author and his or her textual figures.[8]

One could argue that fiction cinema and documentaries may also present strong or overt enunciators, who speak through a narrator (who can be either internal or external to the narration). In the essay film, however, this choice is structural rather than occasional (as is, instead, usually the case of fiction cinema); and is personal and individual, rather than social and collective (as often happens in traditional documentaries).[9] Furthermore, and this is a fundamental point, the enunciator addresses the spectator directly, and attempts to establish a dialogue. The 'I' of the essay film always clearly and strongly implicates a 'you' – and, for me, this is a key aspect of the deep structures of the form. 'You' is called upon to participate and share the enunciator's reflections. It is important to understand that this 'you' is not a generic audience, but an embodied spectator. The essay film constructs such a spectatorial position by adopting a certain rhetorical structure: rather than answering all the questions that it raises, and delivering a complete, 'closed' argument, the essay's rhetoric is such that it opens up problems, and interrogates the spectator; instead of guiding her through emotional and intellectual responses, the essay urges her to engage individually with the film, and reflect on the same subject matter the author is musing about. This structure accounts for the 'openness' of the essay film.

Writing about the CD-ROM *Immemory* (1997) by Chris Marker, Raymond Bellour touched on the question of the essay film, and rightly pointed to the importance of the presence of the spectator and of the dialogical structure that I just described:

> Still one thing is sure: the subjectivity expressed here with such force and such ease does not only stem from the power to say 'I,' of which Marker makes immoderate use. It springs from a more general capacity: the viewer is always taken as a third party to what he sees, through what he hears. Marker's formula is exchange, in the elective modes of conversation and correspondence. But since he does not believe in the communication under which our epoch agonises, he knows that the only real exchange resides in the address, the way the person who speaks to us situates himself in what he says, with respect to what he shows. (1997: 111)

Bellour's brief but persuasive reflection attracts our attention to two important aspects of the essay's textual structures: the person who speaks must situate herself in what she says, must display her own subjectivity, and take a risk; and must address the person who watches, who is hence invited to enter into a dialogue. Of course, this dialogue is achieved textually – in the negotiation of the embodied spectator with the text. The spectatorial position is not that of a generic audience; it is not in the plural but in the singular – it is the position of a real spectator, who is directly and personally addressed and summoned. For instance, as Bellour again notices, by varying the mode of address (as well as by giving the right to speak, the right to the image, to an extraordinary mass of people), Chris Marker is able to speak to the single spectator:

In this way the different persons of the verb can circulate even more fluidly through *Immemory* and through all his texts, as well as the commentaries and voices of his films: I, you, he, she, one, we, they, returning finally to 'I'. This fluidity implies knowing how to address oneself in order to move toward others, and knowing how to touch the other of each one who becomes involved. Beyond humanism, it is a gift of alterity, guaranteed perhaps by an ethos of reserve. (1997: 111)

Bellour's comments have been prompted by a CD-ROM – a text normally thought to instigate a different, more active type of viewing experience than that produced by a film; however, the author extends them to Marker's entire cinematic work. This move is, in my opinion, fully justified, not so much because the interactivity of a CD-ROM is, ultimately, always limited to the possibilities offered and prearranged by its author, but because Marker, in his films, attempts to approximate precisely the same type of direct and involved spectatorial experience achieved by the CD-ROM. My claim is that this same attempt characterises essayistic cinema as a form.

The structure of the essay film (as well as of the literary essay), in other words, is that of a constant interpellation; each spectator, as an individual and not as a member of an anonymous, collective audience, is called upon to engage in a dialogical relationship with the enunciator, hence to become active, intellectually and emotionally, and interact with the text. The spectatorial position is in the singular, because the genuine essay film raises problems and asks questions, and

Interpellation through the gaze: Chris Marker's *Sans soleil* (1983)

does not offer clear-cut answers; as suggested in an already quoted passage by Montaigne, the essayist writes not in order to 'pretend to discover things, but to lay open my self' (Montaigne 1700: 254).

The essayist does not pretend to discover truths to which he holds the key, but allows the answers to emerge somewhere else, precisely in the position occupied by the embodied spectator. The meaning of the film is created via this dialogue, in which the spectator has an important part to play; meanings are presented by the speaking subject as a personal, subjective meditation, rather than as objective truths. It is this subjective move, this speaking in the first person that mobilises the subjectivity of the spectator. As Christa Blümlinger has put it, the representation of social reality becomes an expression of the subjectivity through which it is mediated: self-reflexivity is the condition through which the essayist develops his considerations on the world (see 2004a: 56). The author's personal reflection asks to be either shared or rejected by the viewer. Indeed, implicit in the essay structure is the tentative assumption of a certain unity of the human experience, which allows two subjects to meet and communicate on the basis of such a shared experience. The two subject positions, the 'I' and the 'you', determine and shape one another.

This structure is likely to generate a more personal spectatorial experience than that of a fiction film, which – even when it is the autobiographical product of a strong auteur – rarely addresses the spectator directly, and as an individual; or of a traditional documentary, in which the public may not be addressed overtly, or else may be addressed as the anonymous audience constructed by the position of generalised authority taken up by the enunciator. Or, even, of the spectator of a diary, a notebook or a travelogue film, who might have the impression of being let into the private monologue of the enunciator with himself/herself.[10]

Some of the critical contributions explored above maintain that voice is all important in the essay film, and that only films with extensive voice-over are essays; some suggest that this feature is not absolutely necessary. The fact is that, while the author's voice is the literary essay's obvious, required prerequisite, the cinema is able to express authorial subjectivity at different levels. As Arthur rightly argues,

> since film operates simultaneously on multiple discursive levels – image, speech, titles, music – the literary essay's single, determining voice is dispersed into cinema's multi-channel stew. The manifestation or location of a film author's 'voice' can shift from moment to moment or surface expressively via montage, camera movement and so on. (2003: 59)

This complicates matters, but does not take away from the injunction that the essay film is the expression of a single, situated authorial 'voice' that enters into a dialogue with the spectator. If this dialogue can be achieved via purely visual means, in other words if the enunciator is able to convey an argument and enter into a dialogue with the spectator through images unaccompanied by commentary, we can call that an essay film. However, I argue that the spectator might not easily experience that film as an essay, in the same way in which she might enter into a dialogue with a film that uses both visual and verbal language.

The inscription of subjectivity in the essay film: voice-over, interpellation and the question of authority

Central to the essay film, the authorial presence can be achieved at different levels, and through various techniques. For instance, to borrow Bill Nichols' categorisation of the documentary, the enunciator is most evident in the 'expository' mode, in which we find a 'voice-of-God' commentary directed towards the viewer. Here,

> The authoring presence of the filmmaker is represented by the commentary and sometimes the (usually unseen) voice of authority will be that of the filmmaker him- or herself ... In other cases such as the evening news, a delegate, the anchorperson, will represent a broader, institutional source of authority. (1991: 37)

The enunciator is also evident, although in a different way, in Nichols' 'interactive' documentary mode, in which the filmmaker's presence in the film is apparent and synchronous to the filming, rather than superimposed in post-production. However, this mode frequently employs interviews, in which only the interviewee is seen; in these cases, 'the filmmaker is neither seen nor heard, allowing the witnesses "to speak for themselves"' (1991: 54). At times, 'Intertitles may provide the other half of the "dialogue" rather than a voice-off ... Although this tactic places the filmmaker "on screen", in the two-dimensional space of the graphic intertitles, a sense of absence remains"' (1991: 55).

The presence-absence of the enunciator is a key point of the essay film. The inscription of the author can be very direct, for instance by making the filmmaker's body visible and his or her voice audible. Other times, it can be more indirect, for example through the use of a narrator/spokesperson, or of intertitles, or of musical commentary, camera movements and the like. However, I have argued that one of the key features of the essay film is the direct address to the receiver; voice-over is the most simple and successful way of producing such an address.

It is necessary here to consider that, within documentary theory, the pervasive presence of a voice-over, a frequent and characterising marker of the essay film, has often been accused of producing an authoritarian discourse, and of superimposing a specific, particular reading on the pure truthfulness of the visuals. Stella Bruzzi, commenting on such widespread critical response, has argued that 'The negative portrayal of voice-over is largely the result of the development of a theoretical orthodoxy that condemns it for being inevitably and inherently didactic' (2006: 47). In other words, 'We have been "taught" to believe in the image of reality and similarly "taught" how to interpret the narrational voice as distorted and superimposed onto it' (ibid.). In particular, Bruzzi draws attention to the fact that Bill Nichols, in his categorisation, adopts a negative definition (the 'expository mode') for documentaries with prevailing voice-over and, chronologically and qualitatively, describes this mode as the oldest and most primitive. Within this category, as Bruzzi notices, Nichols includes documentaries with formal, open and poetic modes of exposition, hence very diverse films that are only held together by their adoption of the formal element of voice-over. Bruzzi is persuasive when she reminds us that voice, in documentary practice, is often and simply 'an economic device able to efficiently relay information', rather than used for 'telling people what to think' (2006: 50); and that voice can also be used as an ironic or a polemical tool.

The use of voice in an essay film can be all these things – it can be contrapuntal or ironic or polemical, as well as a means to convey information. It is also, first and foremost, a privileged tool for the author's articulation of his or her thought (in conjunction with sound and image), and hence a prime location of the author's subjectivity, as well as the main channel of the enunciator's address to the spectator. However, owing to its overwhelmingly negative reception in documentary studies, the use of voice-over remains a questioned technique.[11] Furthermore, such a blatant expression of authorial subjectivity obviously raises a whole series of issues, which can be only briefly touched upon here, and that go under the umbrella of the poststructuralist critique of concepts of authorship.[12] These factors potentially cast a shadow of authoritarianism on the essay film. And yet, I will claim the opposite; as Lopate reminds us, 'Adorno, in "The Essay as Form", saw precisely the anti-systematic, subjective, nonmethodic method of the essay as its radical promise, and he called for modern philosophy to adopt its form, at a time when authoritative systems of thought had become suspect' (1998: 282).

The accomplished essay film confounds issues of authority; and it is precisely because of its liberal stance that it is particularly relevant today, when the radical problematisation of the existence of objective, permanent, fixed viewpoints on the world has produced the decline of grand narratives and of the social persuasiveness of the myths of objectivity and authority. Unsurprisingly, for Lyotard 'the essay ... is postmodern, while the fragment ... is modern' (1984: 81). The essay is, in fact, a 'genre of absence' (Snyder 1991: 151), in which 'there is no truth, just truth-making' (1991: 200).

The place of the essay film

It is important to state one more time that heresy and openness are among the essay film's key markers. Its positioning at the crossroads of 'documentary, avant-garde, and art film impulses' (Arthur 2003: 62) suggests, as I have claimed, that we must resist the temptation to overtheorise the form or, even worse, to crystallise it into a genre. It being informal, sceptical, diverse, disjunctive, paradoxical, contradictory, heretical, open, free and formless, the essay truly is the postmodern 'matrix of all generic possibilities' (Bensmaia 1987: 92). The essay is a field of experimentation and idiosyncrasy, to the extent that we can accept Edgar Morin's comprehensive outlook: 'Talking of essay film, I would rather refer to the attitude of he who attempts (*essai* – essay, but also attempt) to debate a problem by using all the means that the cinema affords, all the registers and all the expedients' (Morin, in Maderna 1996: 4; author's translation).

I suggest, therefore, that we think of the essay as a mode, which is defined by the above-discussed textual commitments and rhetorical strategies; and explore the ways in which this mode is appropriated, manipulated, interpreted, modified and reinvented by filmmakers and videomakers. Experimentation and idiosyncrasy are intrinsic to a form that is always and necessarily unique and original. The first episode of Aleksandr Sokurov's television series *Dukhovnye golosa* (*Spiritual Voices*, 1995), for instance, is an essay that uses a fixed, single shot lasting approximately forty minutes, and extensive voice-over from the director himself, who muses about Mozart. Chris Marker's *Level Five* (1996) mixes instead documentary subject matter and fictional characters; its enunciator is principally embodied into a female narrator, who ultimately proves to be a computer image, an avatar. Almost completely devoid of voice-over, Jean-Luc Godard's *Notre musique* (*Our Music*, 2004) combines documentary and fiction, re-enactments of real events, imaginary figures and social actors; the enunciator is in the text as Jean-Luc Godard the director, but also uses various narrators and various visual means to formulate his line of reasoning. The first film has been alternatively bracketed as a television programme, as a documentary and as a video installation; the second as a documentary, as a fiction and as an essay film; the third exclusively as a fiction (but its fictional status is, in truth, problematic). Each embraces the textual commitments and rhetorical strategies of the essay film, but articulates them in infinitely diverse ways.[13]

To identify what essay is not might help to further enlighten my definition of essay film. Take the case of Harun Farocki; whereas his *Bilder der Welt und Inschrift des Krieges* (*Images of the World and the Inscription of War*, 1989) is truly and thoroughly an essay film, other works, such as *Ein Bild* (*An Image*, 1983), *Die Schulung* (*Indoctrination*, 1987) or *Die Bewerbungen* (*The Interview*, 1996) seem to me to be far better described as authorial documentaries. As we will see in more detail in the following chapter, *Images of the World and the Inscription of War* presents a narrator, a spokesperson of the enunciator, who expresses herself through extensive voice-over; her speech is the vocal part of a thought-provoking reflection articulated through words and images, sound and montage. The enunciator is also physically present in the text as Harun Farocki the filmmaker/researcher (who, however, is never fully in view); because of this double presence and this self-reflexive split, the essay's authorship is played in the interstices between narrator and enunciator. Interpellation is extensively used to involve the spectator in a dialogue with the film, which is simultaneously reflective and subjective, open and experimental.

Interpellation through written text: Harun Farocki's *Images of the World and the Inscription of War* (1989)

The other three films are nonfictions made for television. *An Image* is the record of the preparations and shooting of a photograph for German *Playboy*; *Indoctrination* is the examination of a week-long seminar on rhetoric and communication for executives; and *The Interview* looks at seminars aimed at preparing candidates for job interviews. None of the three films employs voice-over. All three reveal the personal position of their author on a topic, a position that can be inferred by a number of means through which the enunciator intervenes on the documentary material. The films' titles, for instance, and in particular the first two, are telling: 'an image' and 'indoctrination' add the depth of a commentary to the subject matter. The first attracts our attention to the disproportion between the photographer's painstakingly detailed preparatory work and the outcome of 'one image'; hence, to the constructedness of any image, to the hidden, elaborate process of creating a shot that must appear as natural as possible. The second title adds a definite spin on what we see: it is an appraisal that clarifies the position of the filmmaker, which is unambiguously critical. It also suggests that the author sees this seminar (and we ought to see it too), and the corporate mentality it stands for, as manipulation, brainwashing and frightening propaganda.

Other means are also employed by the director to convey his position in these films, especially montage; one could argue, for instance, that in *Indoctrina-*

tion Farocki selected only those moments of the seminar that were particularly telling, and that revealed the manipulation of the participants into espousing the logic of corporate business. As for *An Image*, the choice of focusing on the photographer and his assistants rather than on the naked model (as well as the decision to not show the final product of their efforts) conveys the filmmaker's ideological position. However, it is not easy to maintain that these films are essays. Despite the mythical goal of total objectivity that has accompanied the documentary for decades, it is important to acknowledge that, to use Bruzzi's words, 'all documentaries, because the product of individuals, will always display bias and be in some manner didactic' (2006: 36). All documentaries make an argument; even those that attempt to make their argument look like the pure observation of an unaltered reality – and yet, we do not call them all essays. *An Image*, *Indoctrination* and *The Interview* are documentaries, presenting factual images in a way that both informs us of certain realities and comments on them. They are quite overtly authorial; the sophistication of the films, the control of the image and the use of montage, all suggest a coherent, strong cinematic project and vision of the world. At times, the enunciator comes to the fore, by using a title, a cut, the juxtaposition of two shots; but we, the spectators, do not necessarily feel summoned and engaged in a continuous dialogue with a filmmaker/essayist.

Take now a very different and familiar example: the documentaries of Michael Moore, which have frequently been labelled as essays, for instance by Paul Arthur (2003). It is obvious that Moore's films are the product of an overt first-person author. Think, as an example, of *Fahrenheit 9/11*, which has a strong enunciator, unambiguously identified with the film's real author, who is by now a well-known public figure. This enunciator is embodied in the film in various ways, and most evidently through a narrator (Moore's own clearly identifiable voice-over dominates the film), but also via other means, including the use of irony (which is expressed, for instance, by contrapuntal musical commentary, the choice of humorous archival images and the use of sequences from fiction cinema). Moore is in the film simultaneously as enunciator, as narrator and as character – and all these figures directly identify with the extra-textual author. This seems to agree with one of the main stipulations of the essay. Moore occupies the image constantly, as voice, bodily presence or commentary; hence, we can easily agree that he is a strong enunciator, and that his film is very personal. However, there are two clear differences with the essay film. The first is that Moore does not problematise his authorship, which is not subjected to self-searching scrutiny; his subjectivity is accepted as a plain fact, and his self as a perfectly knowable entity. The second is that he does not present his subject matter as a subjective reflection on a problem, but as an objective investigation of factual events. Indeed, his is a work of reportage, in the tradition of the American 'muckraking' investigative

The enunciator embodied as investigative reporter: Michael Moore in *Fahrenheit 9/11* (2004)

journalism, which is 'hard-hitting in tone, often well rooted in fact, and at times brutal in its exposure of venality and corruption' (Fitzpatrick 1994: 1); a tradition in which frequently the journalist writes in the first person, and becomes a personality. His voice-over commentary is intended for a generic, broad audience; it is not a dialogue, in which the single spectator is called upon to participate in the reflection and in the construction of meaning in an idiosyncratic way that may well be different from that of any other member of the audience.

In *Fahrenheit 9/11*, spectators are asked to follow the facts, to watch and listen, and progressively discover an objective truth, to which the author holds the key. The film's rhetorical structure is that of journalistic exposé, in which the reporter investigates a topic and discovers scandal, corruption or controversy and aims to convince the audience of their historicity and factuality. The ambiguity, which may persuade critics to talk of essay, lies in the fact that, precisely the opposite of Montaigne's essayist, Moore 'pretends to discover things' together with the spectator. The text, however, is not open, but closed: at all times, the spectator is clearly told where to be, what to feel, how to react, what to find out, what to believe. For instance, contrapuntal music is used to induce us to laugh at George W. Bush's intellectual paucity; sentimental music is adopted to make us participate emotionally in the despair of families of the victims of 9/11. If we want to consider first-person journalistic reportage as essay, then *Fahrenheit 9/11* is an essay; however, if we think of an essay according to the lines explored above, it is not.

While basing my analysis on the parameters I have established here, in each of the three chapters that follow that form the first section of this book, dedicated to the domain of the essayistic in the cinema, I will test and problematise the boundaries of my definition of essay film. I will indeed always stress the necessity of its heresy, and try to keep the classification fluid; for the essay film, ultimately, is an open field of experimentation, sited at the crossroads of documentary, art film and experimental practices. As Corrigan has rightly argued, however, 'despite overlappings, this genre of filmmaking needs to be distinguished from a documentary tradition and an avant-garde/experimental one' (1995: 89). Although sitting at a crossroads, the essay film occupies its own place.

chapter two
THE METACRITICAL VOICE(OVER) OF THE ESSAY FILM: HARUN FAROCKI, FOUND FOOTAGE AND THE ESSAYIST AS SPECTATOR

'What kind of "I" is speaking to me through a film and how does a film in addressing me perceive me?' (Farocki, in Halle 2001: 61)

In both the introduction and in chapter one, I touched on the issue of authority raised by the presence of strong enunciators in the essay film and, in particular, by one of the form's main channels of expression and communication: voice-over.

Voice-over is an often-questioned technique, principally as a consequence of three related factors: the problematic role of voice in interpellation theory;[1] *cinéma vérité*'s rejection of the structuring and didactic functions of voice-over; and the predominantly negative response to verbal commentary which is found in documentary theory of the past twenty years. And yet, this rather compact critical position is not only reductive, but also unconvincing. Not all voices in nonfiction films can be equated; they do not all convey an omniscient and repressive meaning; and they do not all have the same function in the text. I will argue below that to reduce all nonfictional voice-overs to an imperialist, patriarchal and authoritative voice-of-God is controversial as well as counterproductive. Furthermore, it is time that we pay attention to the aesthetic values of voice-over commentary, as opposed to its cognitive possibilities. I concur with John Corner when he writes, a propos the need to analyse the production aesthetics of television documentaries, that sound in nonfiction, for instance modes of both informal and formal speech (the latter includes 'commentaries working essentially as read prose'), has 'an aesthetic density that requires more attention, in its local achievement, than documentary analysis has afforded to date' (2003: 98).[2]

In particular, I am here interested in examining the performance of the self in two essay films by Harun Farocki; through my investigation, I aim to highlight questions associated with the construction of authoriality, the issue of authority and the use of voice-over in the essay film. I will give consideration to voice, to the relationship between sound and image, as well as to other elements that conspire to inscribe subjectivity in the texts. I will consider how authorial subjectivity is played out in the interstices between enunciator and narrator; and will examine the position of both the enunciator and the receiver in the text. I will suggest that, while using extensive voice-over, Farocki in these two essays debunks his own authority, and conveys his personal discourse on the world without creating the illusion of omniscience. On the contrary, he succeeds in entering into a dialogical relationship with the viewer.

The trouble with the disembodied voice

In her critique of the negative reception of voice-over narration in documentary cinema, Stella Bruzzi argues:

> However varied the use of narration has been both before and after *The March of Time*, the overriding view is that the documentary voice-over is the filmmaker's ultimate tool for telling people what to think. This gross oversimplification covers a multitude of differences, from the most common use of commentary as an economic device able to efficiently relay information that might otherwise not be available or might take too long to tell in images, to its deployment as an ironic and polemical tool. (2006: 50)

Let us, indeed, consider some of the practical aspects of the use of voice-over, which respond, first of all, to economic and technical requirements, rather than to the filmmakers' supposed desire to superimpose an authoritarian meaning on the indexical traces of reality. Voice-over not only economically conveys information, but also offers a better quality of sound. In the context of his discussion of the poor quality of location sound as a marker of many documentaries, and especially of observational ones, in contrast to the clean sound typical of Hollywood narrative production, Jeffrey Ruoff recognises that voice-over, which 'has long been one of the stylistic signatures of documentary sound', is often used by documentarists in order to achieve 'maximum control over sound quality' (2003: 31). While noticing that recent North American documentaries 'have rediscovered the possibilities of voice-over narration, using personal, ironic, and interpretive commentary to counterpoint the synchronous images and sounds' (ibid.), Ruoff also observes that

> in Hollywood cinema voice-over is still considered 'the last resort of the incompetent', a view shared by many observational documentary filmmakers.

When Leacock and Pincus taught documentary filmmaking at the Massachu-
setts Institute of Technology in the 1970s, voice-over was not considered an
acceptable technique. (Ibid.)

The stigma continues to be attached to the device; indeed, it is common to see it
chastised even in contemporary scholarly writing. The often-repeated argument,
for instance, was phrased as follows by philosopher Jacques Rancière:

> 'Documentary' cinema in particular has always been caught between the am-
> biguities of cinéma-vérité, the dialectical turns of montage, and the imperial-
> ism of the voice of the master, usually *off*, that either lines the unfolding of
> heterogeneous images with its melodic continuity, or gives a step by step ex-
> planation of the meaning of the images' silent presence or elegant arabesque.
> (2001: 167–8; emphasis in original)

As encapsulated by the views of Rancière, Richard Leacock and Ed Pincus, voice-
over is problematic because it superimposes a meaning that presents itself as
unbiased and reliable, but that is ultimately partial, on the truthfulness and completeness of the image. In these accounts, the image is construed either as the
'real document' (alternatively because of its indexical photographic quality, or
because it contains the untampered voices of the interviewees), or as an aesthetically and communicatively superior and self-sufficient language.

The supposed deceptiveness and imperialism of voice-over commentary has
often been portrayed as constitutive of the device, a result of its inherent characteristics. In the late 1970s and early 1980s, a number of scholars identified the
source of voice-over's authority in its spatial positioning and functioning. For
Pascal Bonitzer, the superimposition of a commentary on the images censors
possible questions arising about the place and time of the voice's source, which
is radically *other*. Hence,

> the voice-off represents a power, that of disposing of the image and of what
> the image reflects, from a space absolutely other with regard to that inscribed
> in the visuals. Absolutely other and *absolutely indeterminate*. In as much as it
> arises from the field of the Other, the voice-off is assumed to know: this is the
> essence of its power. (1976: 33; emphasis in original)

Mary Anne Doane concurs with Bonitzer's opinion that voice-over derives its authority from its radical otherness, from its location outside the diegetic space, and
from its disembodiment: 'It is precisely because the voice is not localisable, because
it cannot be yoked to a body, that it is capable of interpreting the image, producing

its truth' (1980: 42). For Doane, the power of voice-over 'resides in the possession of knowledge and in the privileged, unquestioned activity of interpretation' (ibid.).

In his seminal book on the voice in fiction cinema, first published in 1982, Michel Chion defines this otherness and disembodiment by means of the concept of the 'acousmêtre': the presence in the film of an acousmatic voice which is not-yet-visualised (see 1999: 17–29).[3] The acousmêtre is always liable to be seen, and is perceived as being simultaneously offscreen and within the image; hence, it 'bears with the image a relationship of *possible inclusion*, a relationship of power and possession capable of functioning in both directions; the image may contain the voice, or the voice may contain the image' (1999: 23; emphasis in original). For Chion, the acousmêtre is everywhere; it is all-seeing, omniscient and omnipotent (adjectives which, I add, have often been associated with the classical 'voice-of-God' commentary of the documentary). Indeed, the word acousmatic comes from the name of a Pythagorean sect, whose followers listened to their unseen Master speaking from behind a curtain; and, as Chion notes, the 'interdiction against looking, which transforms the Master, God, or Spirit into an acousmatic voice, permeates a great number of religious traditions, most notably Islam and Judaism' (1999: 19). It is easy to see, then, how an invisible source of commentary becomes associated to an all-knowing, infallible Master or God.

While it is undeniable that an acousmatic voice is more evocative than an embodied voice, and that its suggestiveness can be explained, as all these authors did, resorting to psychoanalysis and to the role of voice in the formation of the self, it is hard to believe that spectators lose all their critical powers when listening to a voice-over commentary. Sarah Kozloff, for instance, pointed out that we are daily exposed to disembodied voices on the radio, on tape recorders, over public address systems, 'without pausing in awe: we do not, for example, take every anecdote told over the telephone as Truth' (1984: 48). We could, of course, reply with Chion that the power of the acousmêtre in the cinema is different from these more mundane examples, because the disembodied voice in film is always liable to become embodied, and engage with the image. However, while the possibility of embodiment is evident in fiction films, it is much less so in documentaries, in which voice-over is likely to remain disembodied. Chion, indeed, rightly distinguishes between the 'complete acousmêtre', which recurs in fiction cinema (to which his study is devoted), and 'remains liable to appear in the visual field at any moment' (1999: 21), and what he calls the commentator-acousmêtre, 'he who never shows himself but has no personal stake in the image' (ibid.). This second type, although Chion does not say it explicitly, obviously includes the documentary voice-over; it speaks, in fact, from the 'removed position of the picture-presenter' (1999: 50), and is for Chion more benign, and similar to the voice of Mother, enveloping the child as in a big veil.

Although retaining characteristics typical of sounds whose source is hidden, the voice of the 'picture-presenter' or 'commentator-acousmêtre' for Chion is not perceived by the audience as threatening; for Bonitzer and Doane, at the opposite, it is: 'In the documentary ... the voice-over has come to represent an authority and an aggressivity which can no longer be sustained' (1980: 46). Such unsustainability, for both Bonitzer and Doane, explains the proliferation of new documentaries, which reject voice-over and let 'reality speak for itself'. It is easy to see, then, that with such arguments we come back full circle to the myth of the documentary as the field of total objectivity, and to the rejection of voice as superimposition of a partial meaning on reality. Doane does recognise that the *cinéma vérité* solution only leads to further problems:

> Yet, what this type of film actually promotes is the illusion that reality speaks and is not spoken, that the film is not a constructed discourse. In effecting an 'impression of knowledge', a knowledge which is given and not produced, the film conceals its own work and posits itself as a voice without a subject. The voice is even more powerful in silence. (Ibid.)

From this opinion, it logically follows that, whether using a voice-over commentary or not, all documentaries aim to conceal their work, and promote the illusion of their objectiveness. The solution, then, is not to banish the voice but to construct another politics. For Bonitzer, this comes in the multiplication of voices and in emphasising the grain of the voice, hence generating a body not of 'imaginary cohesion but of dispersal, division, fragmentation' (Doane 1980: 48). Doane points out some of the risks of this new politics or 'erotics' of the voice-over, but ultimately agrees that we need to examine the spaces within which the voice in the cinema works, which are 'masked, one by the other, in the service of representational illusion' (1980: 50).

My problem with these and similar arguments is that they are based on the presumption that the documentary's system of signification is deliberate, programmatic deception. Their derivation from apparatus theory is self-evident. In this perspective, documentaries purposefully take advantage of the insidious power of the disembodied voice, or lack thereof (given that 'voice is even more powerful in silence'), in order to mask their constructedness, and impose a biased meaning as the Truth. Such an obviously untenable, and indeed preposterous, claim is in fact based on an account of voice-over that is incongruous. Examine, for instance, the two following claims:

> As a form of direct address, [voice-over] speaks without mediation to the audience, by-passing the 'characters' and establishing a complicity between

itself and the spectator – together they understand and thus place the image. (Doane 1980: 42)

The voice-over commentary and, differently, the interior monologue and voice-over-flashback speak more or less directly to the spectator, constituting him/her as an empty space to be 'filled' with knowledge about events, character psychology, etc. (Doane 1980: 43)

How to reconcile the first passage, which argues for the voice-over's ability to establish complicity with the spectator, a complicity on which a shared understanding of the image is achieved, and the second passage, which accuses the voice-over of filling the spectator's empty space with pre-established meanings?

It seems to me that such conflicting, inconsistent descriptions unwittingly urge us to acknowledge the existence of a range of historical and stylistic manners of articulating voice-over in documentaries. If we are to learn from Chion's work, a correct analytical practice has nothing to gain from taking all examples of voice-over as monolithic manifestations of authoritarian acousmatic sound in film, but should include consideration, for instance, of 'dramatic norms of performance, technical norms of recording' (Chion 1999: 50), including tone colour, auditory space and timbre; Roland Barthes would add the grain of the voice, which he defines as 'the body in the voice as it sings' (1977c: 188). We should furthermore consider what the voice actually says and how it says it; and we should not forget that the expression of meaning and of subjectivity in film is not the exclusive domain of voice-over.

And yet, voice-over remains a key site of the articulation of subjectivity in first-person nonfiction cinema, because it 'is constitutive of the narrative's subject – in the double sense "of what happens" and "whom it happens to" – because it asks the question of the knowledge and desire of this subject, of its/his *point of view*' (Chion 1999: 56; emphasis in original).

Found footage and the metacritical voice

As well as considering the idiosyncratic articulation of voice and subjectivity of each film, it is important to think of films historically. Types of voice-over are also the consequence of specific practices, for instance of voice casting, and are liable to be influenced by the productive, ideological and theoretical contexts within which they are made. Harun Farocki's works, for instance, are likely to be highly self-conscious about their use of voice-over. As Thomas Elsaesser clarified, in fact, the question of voice-over or, in more general terms, of 'who speaks' and 'who looks' in film, informed the debate on documentary that took place in

Germany in the 1970s, and that centred on *Filmkritik*, the journal that Farocki co-edited from 1973 to 1983. The separation of voice and image, a key feature of that avant-garde practice which in the 1970s aimed to challenge Hollywood's continuity system and its seamless suturing of sound and image,[4] was discussed in Germany in the context of the filmmakers' background in television; hence, 'in the context of the political-didactic function of voice-over commentary, or the strategy of the filmed interview when structuring a political cinema around long-term observation and an aesthetic of realism' (Elsaesser 2004: 146). Elsaesser's point is that the language of television is different from that of the cinema also in its use of sound; as the author argues, 'Sound motivates, focalises and cues the image on television in a way that both emphasises the material difference of the respective source, and precludes this heterogeneity from playing an oppositional role. The voice-of-God rules' (2004: 145). For Elsaesser, at the opposite, Farocki by 'allowing sound, voice, and image their autonomy' in his films, succeeded in opening up 'spaces of reflection and critical engagement, without creating the illusion of spatio-temporal unity, or of "voice-of-God" omniscience' (2004: 147). Indeed, we will see below how voice-over in Farocki is far from resembling a voice-of-God commentary, suturing the various elements in the text; and how Farocki uses voice in a distinctively self-reflexive manner.

The oeuvre of Harun Farocki currently spans over forty years, and includes work for television, documentaries and video-installations, as well as articles and books. The most extraordinary aspect of his work is, in my opinion, its pervasive and persuasive argument that all we have in this world are images – and that the world itself is an image, or a series of images, to be observed, read and deciphered. This impression is conveyed very powerfully by many of his films, through their use of still and moving archival pictures of various derivation, and their careful, repetitive, obsessive observation and investigation by means of verbal and musical commentary, montage and framing. Attention is always paid to the sources of those images – film, video or photo cameras, computers, satellites – suggesting that an unmediated vision of the world is, by now, impossible; but also investigating the specificities of the results produced by such machines for vision, and conveying the sense of the widespread culture of surveillance in which we live. Slowly but steadily, his films erase our experiential and phenomenological impression of being-in-the-world, and replace it with the uncanny recognition of the predominantly mediated nature of our experience. Farocki's interest in the growing sophistication of automated vision, and its relationship to surveillance and warfare, can be clearly seen, for instance, in his video installation *Eye/Machine I–III* (2001–03), in which we look through the eyes of various machines, including industrial equipment, simulators of various kinds, weapons and bombs, without ever having the solace of a vision that is 'only' mediated by Farocki's camera.

Farocki's images in this installation, as well as in many of his videos and films, may be collectively referred to as 'found footage', with reference to the artistic aesthetic of the found object, or *objet trouvé*. Found-footage filmmaking includes, of course, very different artistic practices and attitudes, ranging from avant-garde to parodic to essayistic cinema. It can make use of many types of images, from official archival material to 'ephemeral film' which, in US film collector Rick Prelinger's definition, comprises films made for local or temporary purposes, including educational, industrial and advertising films, home movies and travelogues, or films produced by religious groups, governments and unions (quoted in Zryd 2003: 56). Despite its diversity and variety, it is possible to detect in found-footage filmmaking a characterising interest, which could be defined as an inquisitive, deconstructive process. Found-footage practice is, indeed, one of appropriation and critique, in which images are extracted 'from the spatial-temporal and narrative continuity in which they were originally embedded and through which they acquired their original, intended meaning(s)' (Wees 2002: 3) and placed in new contexts, within which they retain their original meanings but also obtain new ones:

> Found-footage filmmaking is a metahistorical form commenting on the cultural discourses and narrative patterns behind history. Whether picking through the detritus of the mass mediascape or refinding (through image processing and optical printing) the new in the familiar, the found-footage artist critically investigates the history behind the image, discursively embedded within its history of production, circulation, and consumption. (Zryd 2003: 42)

The distinctiveness of this process of critical investigation of the image is particularly evident when we compare particular found-footage films, for instance Craig Balwdin's *Tribulation 99* (1991), or indeed Harun Farocki's films, with those documentaries in which 'the archive serves as visual evidence of history, with the role of found footage reduced to the textual authority of the documentary fact' (Russell 1999: 240).

Once in an interview Farocki agreed to talk of his cinema in light of the theory of the *objet trouvé*: 'Images and sounds that we find without already having been aware that they exist are like an *objet trouvé*' (in Halle 2001: 56). The interviewer, adopting in his question a terminology typical of discussions of found-footage film, thus describes Farocki's practice:

> to rely on the reconstruction of found (often familiar) images, re-establishing the order, space, and time of those images. This re-establishing of context invites the viewer to re-examine the familiar, to understand the image in a larger context of production. The reality of the image is both asserted and

> disrupted. And you as filmmaker are positioned ultimately not so much as a documentarist representing the real but as a metacritic of both the image and the society that produces those images. (Halle 2001: 55)

In Farocki's essay films, and especially the two that will be analysed below (as well as in many examples of found-footage films by other directors), voice-over commentary is one of the key channels of the re-examination of the archival and ephemeral images that constitute the visuals.

Indeed, generalising somewhat, one could argue that the voice-over of the essay film in general may be described as metahistorical and metacritical. Even those essayist filmmakers who produce their own footage rather than using archival material, in fact, by superimposing a commentary, distance themselves from their images and scrutinise them, almost 'finding' and presenting them anew, as pre-existing objects. It is significant, for instance, that in Chris Marker's *Sans soleil*, considered by many to be the ur-text of essay cinema, images are said to have been shot not by Marker, but by cameraman and traveller Sandor Krasna, who then sent them to the narrator as video-letters.

A recurrent role played by the voice-over in the essay film is to comment from a critical distance, to analyse and interpret the visuals. Such critical distance often parallels the positioning in the text of the filmmaker, who moves away from behind the camera, from her creative function, and becomes a metacritic – of the images, of the society that produces them, of her own text and of her role within it. In the metacritic activity of the essayist, indeed, the outer world is not the only object of analysis and appraisal; this activity self-reflexively extends to the act of production of filmic meaning.

Of course, meaning is not exclusively produced by the commentary, but by the interaction of voice and visuals. It is not my intention to underplay the importance of the image or, for that matter, of music and of other sound. My aim is, on the one hand, to demonstrate that not each example of voice-over should be seen as an authoritative voice-of-God; and, on the other hand, to offer a more productive description of the voice and of enunciation in some of Farocki's work in particular, as well as in the essay film in general.

Images of the World and the Inscription of War: the world as image and the director as its spectator

Images of the World and the Inscription of War is one of Farocki's films that most clearly establishes his argument on the world as image, and on the limits and dangers of both human and mechanical vision. Often described as a documentary essay, it is a flow of free associations, using both images and words, primarily on issues relating to vision, photography and measurement. One of its central topics is the story of US bombers flying over Poland in April 1944, and inadvertently photographing Auschwitz, resulting in photos buried in CIA files until the 1970s.

From the very first image, the film uses a female narrator (actress/director Ulrike Grote in the German version, director/actress/producer Cynthia Beatt in the English one), who utters an essayistic text superimposed upon a montage of mostly (although not exclusively) archival images. Some passages of the text that the voice recites have been the subject of controversy. In her analysis of the film, for instance, Nora M. Alter questioned Farocki's representation of women, and particularly of the unveiled Algerian women who were photographed for the first time in 1960 by the French army, in order to provide them with identity cards; of a suspected woman terrorist, and composite police pictures of what she might look like with different hairstyles and makeup; and of a Jewish woman photographed by a Nazi while entering Auschwitz. For Alter, Farocki's film is built around the concepts of in/ visibility and in/audibility, and its image track

Harun Farocki's *Images of the World and the Inscription of War*: Jewish woman entering Auschwitz

implies that the historical purpose of photography – whether scientific, forensic, or aesthetic – has been not only to record and preserve but also to mislead, deceive, and even destroy: that is, to aid yet obfuscate vision. In other words, to show the in/visible. Of course, this thematic aspect of the film itself is problematic (intentionally or not), since film in general – and, in particular, this film – is subject to the same visual regime as photography and hence must deceive and obfuscate, not only at the level of sight but also at the level of sound. (2004: 218)

The deception and obfuscation relate especially to the film's gender politics: for Alter, Farocki is not in control of his 'inscription (*Inschrift*) of the re/presentation of women' (2004: 219). While Alter appears to consider the image track as neutral, she identifies the soundtrack as biased and problematic: for the critic, the narrator unreasonably projects feelings onto the objectively blank stares of the women, who are therefore sentimentalised by the narrative.

Although this position is not unjustifiable, I agree with Kaja Silverman's defence of these sequences in her reading of *Images of the World and the Inscription of War* as a discourse on the distinction between camera and eye, a distinction which strongly echoes Lacan's theorisation of the gaze in *The Four Fundamental Concepts of Psychoanalysis* (see Lacan 1997). For Silverman, Farocki's film aims to demonstrate the dissociation of camera/gaze and eye, and the placement of the human subject within the purview of the camera/gaze apparatus; and to explore the role such an apparatus plays with respect to human subjectivity, especially through its memorialising and mortifying functions. Silverman argues, with particular reference to two stills of Jewish women, that 'To object to the commentary for imputing to these two photographs meaning which was not available to the camera/gaze, and which cannot be historically documented, is to overlook [a] crucial feature of [*Images of the World and the Inscription of War's*] interrogation of the visual field – its discourse on the human look' (1996: 154). The commentator, in fact, repeatedly directs our attention to the fact that the look has the ability to see things that escape the camera/gaze; and the point the film makes is that, although the look's 'truth' cannot be objectively verified, as it lacks temporal stability and formal coherence, the look can indeed be a site of resistance. The function of the comments on the Jewish and Algerian women, then, is to demonstrate the difference between the camera/gaze and the human look. Hence, the commentator 'attempts to apprehend and to make us apprehend something the photographs themselves cannot show: the subjective experience of being "inside" those particular bodies, as a camera/gaze, caught in a particular representational system, and embedded in certain material practices, was trained upon them' (1996: 159). The deficiency of the camera/gaze and the role of verbal (written or spoken) commentary in stressing the 'insufficient mimesis or pragmatic meaning of camera inscription' was also highlighted by Malin Wahlberg (2004: 24) with reference to another film by Farocki, the video *Ich Glaubte Gefangene Zu Sehen* (*I Thought I Was Seeing Convicts*, 2000).

For Nora M. Alter, however, it is not only the content of the speech that is problematic, but also its delivery. She criticises the use of a female voice-over narrator basically as an act of obfuscation of Farocki's biased gender politics. Her critique of the narrator makes passing reference to a different work by Kaja Silverman, *The Acoustic Mirror*. In this book, which is principally devoted to fiction films, Silverman, similarly to Bonitzer, Doane and Chion, discusses voice-over as placed in an *other* dimension, in a different order from the diegesis, and as transcending the body, the condition from which it gains its power. For Silverman, the voice-over of the traditional documentary is a voice which 'speaks from a position of superior knowledge, and which superimposes itself "on top" of the diegesis' (1988: 48). Voice-over presents itself as the enunciator, hence as the 'point of discursive origin' (1988: 51) and of authority. When voice-over 'preserves its integrity', i.e. remains in its separate order (disembodied), 'it also becomes an exclusively male voice' (ibid.).[5]

The disembodiment of the female voice in *Images of the World and the Inscription of War* is a key issue for Alter: 'Part of the problem in *Images of the World* is that Farocki's audible woman is never made visible: she is literally disembodied' (2004: 223). While being female, this voice is merely 'ventriloquising' for Farocki, the real enunciator, who through her conceals his lack of control over 'the problematic political tension between the in/visible and the in/audible' (ibid.). The problem is not only the lack of a body, but also the type of voice, which she describes in both the German and the English versions of the film as 'tonally objective and neutral' (2004: 218). This voice is coupled by the 'minimalist tinkling of a piano' (ibid.); indeed, 'the accompanying soft piano music acts in tandem with the female voice as a parallel suture: another way of seaming the movie together in terms of its seeming gendered content, or semés' (2004: 223).

Alter's negative stance is based on and shaped by her analysis of the components of the film's soundtrack, an analysis which is, however, untenable, based as it is on a misleading description of both voice and music. Take the English version of the film: Cynthia Beatt's voice is certainly unlike a traditional, stentorian commentary suitable for an expository documentary; but it is also the opposite of a reassuring, suturing feminine voice. Its timbre is calm and rather thin; its rhythm is regular; the voice is melodically flat, monochord, emotionally detached. In terms of auditory space, it was recorded with a close microphone; it is dry, without reverb, hence creating a sense of 'I-voice', which occupies its own space. The voice is superimposed on the images and comments and explains them; but it also follows the rhythm of the visuals, waits for them to move on before commenting, hence creating a 'space' in between image and sound. The combination of these characteristics produces an effect that could be described as Brechtian; there is in this film an unambiguous temporal, spatial and critical distance between voice and subject matter. This effect can be most evidently experienced in those sequences in which the voice seems to drag over the images, waiting for them to move on, and linking them with the drawn out chant of 'and... and... and...'.

Likewise, the music used in *Images of the World and the Inscription of War* is nothing like 'soft piano music', as described by Alter. It is a collage of music of Bach and Beethoven, produced in a mechanical way, and coupled to the images in a random manner.[6] Rather than allow us to listen to the music continuously, Farocki keeps interrupting its flow every few seconds, thus creating a thoroughly disjointed piece, which resembles a radical avant-garde composition. Hence, the fragmented music, mechanically produced and haphazardly matched to the images, produces a strong distancing effect – at the opposite of working in tandem with voice-over to suture the text.

My main interest here is to investigate the effect created by the use of this detached female narrator, and this disjointed music, in relation to the questions of subjectivity and authority in the essay film.

Commenting on the use of a female narrator in Chris Marker's *Sans soleil*, Bruzzi has argued that the use of a female voice-over in documentaries, because of its rarity in traditional, mainstream productions, often signifies protest and is contrapuntal: 'A female commentary is thus an overt tool for exposing the untenability of documentary's belief in its capacity for imparting "generalised truths" faithfully and unproblematically' (2006: 66). Bruzzi is, in my opinion, correct in thinking that a contrapuntal use of voice-over shows that 'documentary becomes a negotiation between the film and its subject, of which the narration is a constituent part' (2006: 72). Not only does the female commentator in *Images of the World and the Inscription of War* suggest a negotiation between the film and its subject, but also between the filmmaker and his film, and between enunciator and narrator. It is unreasonable to find it surprising that the voice-over in Farocki's film is not a fully-fledged, embodied female narrator, but only the ventriloquising of the director's voice. This is, after all, an essay film – the highly personal, subjective product of a strong (and, in this case, male) auteur. And yet, or precisely for this reason, it is no less than intriguing that an essayist like Farocki, who writes/films in the first person, and expresses his own, personal opinions, chooses to be embodied in the text by a female narrator. And I use the term 'embodied' here not by accident: even voice has, indeed, a body.

I propose that Farocki's negotiation with his text and distancing from his subject matter is part of a strategy of debunking his own enunciational authority. This strategy seems to me to consist of three parts; the use of a female narrator, hence of a narrator who can never fully coincide with the male enunciator, is its first component.[7] As we have seen, this narrator is further distanced from the text thanks to voice colour, timbre, and the auditory space it occupies. The second component is the use of music, which, in its radical disjunctive form, contributes to highlight the negotiation between the film and its subject, as well as between the filmmaker and his film.

The third component of Farocki's strategy is that he both inscribes himself in his text, and conceals himself almost completely. The filmmaker appears several times in the film, but his hands and, a couple of times, part of his head (but never his face) are the only visible parts of his body. His hands are often seen holding books, sifting through pages, photographs and documents; they always metonymically suggest Farocki's eyes, intently watching the images in those books. Through this strategy, Farocki tries to position himself in the text not as the enunciator (as the point of origin of the enunciation) or as a narrator (as the spokesperson of the author), but as a spectator, practically on the same level as the audience. Indeed, Farocki interpellates us directly only once; and he does it not by using his voice, which would strengthen his position as enunciator in the text, but indirectly, as a silent accomplice of the viewer, who by hand inscribes in a picture of a train transporting Jews to Auschwitz the following message, thrusting the audience into action: 'Prevent access!'

This enunciational 'self-debasing' is not unique to *Images of the World and the Inscription of War*; as Christa Blümlinger has argued, in fact, 'Although Farocki is not afraid of including

The essayist as spectator: Harun Farocki in *Images of the World and the Inscription of War*

his own image, he operates beyond narcissistic self-revelation. If he reveals his own body in these non-fictional films, then it is always in the context of the work conducted by the artisan, who happens to be a collector and editor of images' (2004b: 174). In *Images of the World and the Inscription of War*, I would describe Farocki's persona both as a researcher (he sifts through archives and carefully studies plans, drawings, photographs, books), and as a spectator (one who watches, rather than one who produces meaning as enunciating self).

Hence, Farocki constructs a paradoxical enunciator in his text. Through the use of contrapuntal voice-over, disjointed music and metonymic images of his hands, he fragments himself and inscribes his own subjectivity in the film in a disjointed and displaced manner, so as to debunk his own enunciational authority, and enter into a dialogical relationship with the spectator. On the other hand, he remains, of course, a strong enunciator; for instance, his hands at times cover the mouths or eyes of the women in the pictures he examines, thus operating an effective visualisation of the activities of framing and editing: 'This kind of manual reframing offers a visible and even pleading depiction of the manner in which historical photographs may be read' (Blümlinger 2004b: 174). Indeed, the gesture of framing images with his hands also attracts attention to Farocki's role as an artist of the *objet trouvé*, whose role is to recontextualise and reframe found images. The director, the editor and the essayist are all part of his persona in the film.

Furthermore, Farocki insists on choosing images that interpellate the spectator directly. Alter observes, again with reference to the same pictures of women, that they '"look back at us", implicating us in them in a political way' (2004: 220). However, not only the images of women but a very large proportion indeed of the images in Farocki's film have eyes – human, animal or mechanical – and stare, very often directly at the audience. This staring is a constant interpellation. I, the spectator, am looked at; I am called upon and, by answering, I am

A mechanical eye stares at the spectator in
Images of the World and the Inscription of War

implicated in the film. By adopting this strategy, *Images of the World and the Inscription of War*, as all essay films do, places the enunciator in a position of authority, that of he who summons the spectator, and asks him or her to answer the call, to take up a position in the text.

And yet, as we have seen, Farocki also subordinates himself to the images, hence contributing to create that extraordinary impression, conveyed by his film, that all that which exists is, indeed, images. There are only pictures in the world, nothing beyond them, as the world itself is a picture, or a series of pictures. All we can do is either view images, or produce images for others to view, including ourselves. Hence, we are all spectators of the spectacle of the images of the world. This is confirmed, for instance, by the fact that, as becomes evident in the course of the film, all we have of the Shoah is, indeed, images – photographs, drawings and aerial pictures. Even the rebelling Jews, whose story is told by the voice-over narrator, the Auschwitz resisters who succeeded in burning down part of a gas chamber, ultimately produced an image – that of a half-destroyed building, photographed by passing US bombers, and finally seen, interpreted and labelled only many years later.

By sidelining himself, Farocki creates interstitial spaces in which to play his subjectivity, successfully debunks his own authority, and empowers the viewer. He avoids fully embracing the discourse of the narrator, thus granting the spectator his or her autonomy from that discourse, and the right to problematise it. He establishes the fact that he does not produce his images, but that he is, like us, a spectator of the images of the world.

Images are all we have, and they interpellate us; but Farocki also insinuates that viewers may fail to answer their call, and may misread them. Misreading is, indeed, one of the main topics of the film. Because they were not asked to look for concentration camps, for instance, the allied military experts could not see the images of Auschwitz in the aerial photographs they were closely examining. Unguided by the indications of the filmmaker, the spectator of Farocki's film would also probably fail to see them and misread them. As Silverman put it, 'the disjunctive and oppositional relation between the camera/gaze and the look is often materialised [in *Images of the World and the Inscription of War*] through the disequivalence of photographic image and word' (1996: 159). It is the word that shows what the camera/gaze cannot see – and with 'word' here I mean the logical argument conveyed not only by the voice-over, but by the interplay of voice-over, image, sound and of enunciational and narrative strategies. The subjective 'voice' of the essayist, hence, may be questioned, disembodied, concealed and disjointed, but its dialogue with the spectator remains the quintessence of the essay film.

Workers Leaving The Factory: the artist enters the picture

In his essay on the 'Rhetoric of the Image', Roland Barthes (who based his considerations on the analysis of a magazine advert for a food brand) called 'anchorage' the verbal language's function of fixing the floating chain of signifieds in image-based communication: through the anchorage, the text guides both identification and interpretation (see 1977b). In the second case, the anchorage for Barthes has a repressive value, because it remote-controls the reader towards a meaning chosen in advance, repressing all other possible meanings.

It is obvious that the complex and sophisticated verbal (written or spoken) commentary of an essay film cannot be equated in either its finalities or its effects to commercial communication. At the same time, the commentary (as we have seen in the example of *Images of the World and the Inscription of War*) can aim to discover – and to a certain extent anchor – meanings that are not in the image, as produced by the camera/gaze, and that emerge instead from the human look. While it is true that the essayist wishes to put forward a certain interpretation of the visuals, it seems to me that the plurality of the meanings residing in the image is not only repressed but is, indeed, drawn attention to, preserved and explored.

This is particularly true of films that use archival footage and found images, which assess and reframe the meanings of those images by recontextualising them and subjecting them to verbal and non-verbal commentary. The archival image's status of indexical trace of the past is, in fact, challenged by the found-image film. As Wahlberg has argued, the 'image compilation questions the idea of the image-memory as directly correspondent to historical time' (Wahlberg 2004: 18). The recontextualisation of the found image, as documentary ready-made, reminds us that the image-memory, which tends to be treated as an incontrovertible and natural trace of the historical past, is itself a media construction. Wahlberg rightly suggests that, in some of Farocki's work,

> The significant use of sound and the inevitable social context of the film archive forces us to remember that 'the trace of the past' has less to do with essence, than with a complex production of historical time, where narration and reframing of media events rule out any preconception of the photograph as a window on the past. (2004: 19)

The role of the metacritical narration is, indeed, of paramount importance in reframing the image – and, of course, narration in cinematic terms is produced by a range of operations, both at the level of image track and of soundtrack:

> Images are transformed into image-memories by means of the moving gaze of a film camera, music, sound effects, text, or a narrator who interprets what we see, or suggests what the images fail to show. In this context of creative deconstruction and reframing, taken-for-granted notions of transparency, photographic realism, and narrative re-inventions of the past are being questioned. Here, the meaning of the trace cannot be separated from context, because the de-composition at hand posits the construction of montage and narration; the edges of the frame through which the world is transformed. (2004: 17)

As an artist of the found image, Farocki's role is that of an 'editor/filmmaker/ storyteller/historian', whose work is epitomised by the editing table, his 'metaphoric control desk' (2004: 18). Indeed, the critical/historicising voice of the found-footage essayist is never disjointed from a storytelling/narrative attitude, whether overt or implicit. It is this narrative aspect that I now wish to examine, with reference to another film by Farocki, *Workers Leaving the Factory*.

The video *Workers Leaving the Factory* is, like much of Farocki's work, 'less about the imprint as a trace of the past, than about images as signs, coded by the socio-historical realm of media culture' (2004: 19). Farocki takes as a starting point the inaugurating gesture of the cinema, Louis Lumière's *La Sortie des usines Lumière* (*Employees Leaving the Lumière Factory*, 1895). He notices that this scene has been repeated countless times in the history of the cinema, and compares and contrasts it with other scenes (both fictional and documentary) of employees exiting factory gates, or of events taking place just outside the gates (mainly, strikes). The images come from an array of sources, including fiction films (for instance, by Pasolini, Antonioni, Lang, Griffith, Bitomski), archival footage, documentaries, filmed theatre performances and industrial films, and span a period from the origins of cinema to contemporary days.

The first sequence: Lumière's *Employees Leaving the Lumière Factory* (1895), in Farocki's *Workers Leaving the Factory* (1995)

Farocki's film presents multiple arguments. One is that, although the first filmed scene is one of workers leaving a factory, cinema has never been drawn to the factory; when it is, it shuns its interior in order to concentrate on the characters' private lives. Another observation refers to the means through which the shot (the one in the Lumière film, and those in its countless re-presentations) creates the impression of a workforce – which seconds later gives way to a set of individuals going about their private business. The filmmaker also reflects on strikes and their representation in the media, and on how the area directly outside the factory gates tends to be portrayed as owned by the factory, rather than as a public space. Consideration is given to the symbolic meanings of the gates, and to the affinities existing between factory and prison, with reference to surveillance and containment. Farocki also deliberately 'links gestures which are symptomatic of Taylorism in work situations – and in the standardisation of filmic rules themselves – with the narrative gestures of such films' (Ernst & Farocki 2004: 267).

Unlike in *Images of the World and the Inscription of War*, there is no extra-diegetic musical commentary – the only music and sounds we hear are diegetic and belong to the excerpts that we are shown. The film, however, presents a voice-over commentary; the text is read by Farocki himself in the German version, and by Kaja Silverman in the English one. There exist other versions of the film, in which the translated commentary is read indifferently by a man or a woman. Other extra-diegetic voices, which offer alternative commentaries, are also present – namely, the original documentary voice-over in a 1956 British Pathé newsreel, showing the images of a strike at the Austin plant in Birmingham; and the narrative voice-over in Robert Siodmak's *The Killers* (1946), in which four men disguised as workers enter a factory to steal the payroll. These voices, which offer a commentary from a different historical, narrative and critical position to the one adopted by Farocki, and which also represent different traditions of voice casting, function of course as a mirroring of Farocki's own voice-over, whose framing and historicising functions are consequently highlighted. *Workers Leaving the Factory*'s commentary, thus, does not presume to be omniscient or incontestable; its partiality, as revealed by its declared idiosyncratic interests and personal line of reasoning, is self-evident.

What is more, the distance of the voice from its subject matter is clear, as it was in *Images of the World and the Inscription of War*. The voice-over is not in first person in the film, it is not close and emotional, and does not dominate the film; it presents itself as the voice of a critical observer of something pre-existing. Its relationship with the visual track is one of explanation and commentary. Indeed, the voice offers information on the images and contextual elements that help to identify and comprehend the sequences (the title of the film, its date and makers, its narrative context or historical references). At times, it puts forward explicit comments or idiosyncratic readings, makes connections, highlights parallelisms and offers reflections; when the critical musing becomes more evident, the montage often accompanies the voice by either slowing down the images or even by pausing them.

The persona that emerges from the commentary is, not unlike in *Images of the World and the Inscription of War*, that of a critical spectator. It is the voice of a cinephile who is also a narrator of the history of the cinema as seen through the recurrence of its first utterance; an intellectual observer of the cinema's complex relationship with modernity, history, society, power, production and the capital. Hence, in this film, the relationship between the voice-over and Harun Farocki, the director and film critic, is more direct and overt, especially in the original version of the film, in which the text is read by the filmmaker himself.

Despite being less concealed than in *Images of the World and the Inscription of War*, however, once again Farocki inscribes himself in the film not so much as a director but – as I have argued – as a critical spectator, as a historian of film, one who is located at a temporal and critical distance from the images. After all, 'Recycling found images implies a profound sense of the already-seen, the already-happened, creating a spectator position that is necessarily historical' (Russell 1999: 241). In doing this, Farocki presents himself not as a creator of images, but as a spectator of the images of the world; he places himself on the same plane as the audience, partly debasing himself, but truly raising the spectator to the level of creator of textual meanings. The dialogue of the essay film is thus established.

Of course, Farocki's self-inscription in the text is more complex than this. It fluctuates at least between the described position and that of a strong enunciator, of a creator of audiovisual meanings. This role is, throughout the film, probably more evident in the montage than in the voice-over. The activity of selection, manipulation, deconstruction, framing, reframing and repetition with variations, seems indeed to be mainly taken over by the editing; even though, at times, the voice dictates the rhythm of the montage and superimposes meanings that are not immediately apparent in the visuals.

Consonant with the self-reflexive tradition of essayistic cinema, the nature of the enunciator's positioning in the text is explicitly addressed by the voice-over commentary. This happens at the very end of the film, when the voice observes:

> If we line up one hundred years of scenes of people leaving factories, we can imagine that the same shot had been taken over and over, like a child who repeats his first word for one hundred years to immortalise its pleasure in that first spoken word, or like Far-Eastern artists who repeatedly paint the same picture until it is perfect, and the artist can enter the picture. (*Workers Leaving The Factory*).[8]

It is in this final commentary that Farocki openly reveals his enunciating stance, and tells his spectators where he is located in the film. The artist, says Farocki, enters the picture when, through innumerable repetitions, he made the picture perfect. Although the comment ostensibly refers to Far-Eastern art's affinity for repetition, an affinity which the cinema seems to have inherited, the fact that Farocki in this film has repeated the same image countless times should not be overlooked. He repeated it by replaying it with commentary, without commentary, at normal pace or slowed down, as well as in its infinite variations taken from other films – fictions or documentaries, reportage material or archival footage. The presence of the author is, therefore, in the repetitive, almost obsessive returns on the same image, on the same idea. These returns, which are effected from slightly different angles, each time with the advantage of added knowledge, through the adoption of a new perspective, via comparisons and contrasts, represent the inquisitive movement of the essayist's thought itself, which delves deeper and deeper into the subject matter, taking the spectator with it.

The performance of the self in *Workers Leaving the Factory*, hence, is played around two positions: that of a critical and informed spectator who, siding with the audience, observes and narrates the history of the cinema from a narrative, temporal and critical distance; and that of an artist/creator, who resides in the very heart of his text, and aims for no less than aesthetic perfection.

chapter three

THE MUSEALISATION OF EXPERIENCE: CHRIS MARKER'S DIGITAL SUBJECT BETWEEN ARCHIVE, MUSEUM AND DATABASE

'We are born in the museum, it's our homeland after all.' (Godard, in Godard & Ishaghpour 2005: 70)

Due to its decidedly self-reflexive nature and its metacritical attitude, the essay film is particularly inclined to explore the relationship between image and reality, between film and document, between audiovisual record and historical event. Essay films, in fact, often include archival material and found footage, and many of them are collage films, as is true, for instance, of the two works by Harun Farocki explored in the previous chapter. As a consequence, essay films pose searching questions about the cinema as repository of memory, as museum and as archive.[1] These questions, which are ever more relevant today, at a time when digital technologies are greatly transforming both the cinema and the archive, are also, as is widely accepted, central to Chris Marker's work.

This is, perhaps, unsurprising, given that Marker is one of the filmmakers most directly associated with the essay. As we have seen, one of the first uses of the expression 'essay film' was by André Bazin, with reference to Marker's *Letter From Siberia*.[2] Since then, Marker's intellectual and highly personal work has been and continues to be described by critics as essayistic. For Jonathan Kear, for instance, 'From first to last his films are cinematic essays on the passage of time and the mutable nature of historical memory' (2005: 49). Marker is not only one of the key figures working in this form; he is sometimes credited as the director who introduced it, for instance by Catherine Lupton, according to whom after his early literary endeavours Marker 'proceeded to bring to filmmaking the style and analytical powers of the literary essay, in a series of groundbreaking trav-elogues released in the late 1950s and early 1960s' (2006: 7).

One of Marker's key topics is the reflection on images, the media and their re-lationship with memory and with human subjectivity; an obvious example is *La*

Jetée (1962), that iconic and haunting investigation into the mysteries of remembrance, the power of images and the vertigo of time. As several critics have argued, Marker's conception of memory is indebted to the psychoanalysis of Freud and Lacan, and (via Hitchcock) to Proust. In line with Freudian psychoanalysis, memory in Marker's films plays a central role in the formation and the definition of the self; it is also, however, Proustian, in so far as an image of the actual present can activate, as a *madeleine*, an experience of the virtual past.[3] Because of his affinity with the topic of memory, Marker is an author whose work has much to do with the question of storing and accessing traces of events, artefacts, memories, records of all sorts – and the role of the cinema in such activity.

As Kear has argued, 'self-reflexivity and experiments with intermediality have been defining characteristics of Marker's cinema since the 1950s … so his style has become progressively more reflective upon the nature of the cinematic apparatus' (2005: 58). Marker's investigation into these topics has encompassed with increasing insistence a reflection on the digital media and their rapport with traditional cinema on the one hand, and with human memory and subjectivity on the other. Marker's work has always been akin to collage, to collating and combining different materials; the hypertext has *always already* been his ideal art form – it is not surprising that, after *Level Five*, he declared that he would no longer make traditional films, but would only work with the computer (see Lupton 2006: 205).

In this chapter, I wish to explore some of the ways in which new technology, the digital image and the hypertext have influenced Marker's conception of memory and the human subject, as well as of film and of the cinema as museum. This topic is, I believe, increasingly important in relation to the essay film and to subjective filmmaking and audiovisual production. The growth of digital technologies is often blamed for precipitating the death of cinema, as it is seen as a medium that, for many, shows far greater respect than video for human narrative and human history (see, for instance, Virilio 1994). On the other hand, it is also providing film essayists with an increasingly cheap, light and accessible medium that truly has come to embody the 'camera-pen' prefigured by Cesare Zavattini and Alexandre Astruc.[4] Much first-person, subjective and autobiographical audiovisual production is, today, made with DV cameras; and essay films, which historically rarely enjoyed proper theatrical distribution, have now become more easily accessible through DVD. Indeed, digital technology is offering new ways of maintaining, of reproducing and of accessing the memory of the cinema (as well as memory *tout court*); as Timothy Murray writes, digitality 'provides a catalyst for the revival of forgotten cinematic histories, for the reinvention of cinematic forms, and for the sharpening of theoretical reasoning' (1999: 4). Furthermore, digitisation has important repercussions for the archive:

> Images and sounds ... become calculable and can be subjected to algorithms
> of pattern recognition procedures, which will 'excavate' unexpected optical
> statements and perspectives out of the audiovisual archive. For the first time,
> such an archive can organise itself not just according to meta-data, but ac-
> cording to criteria proper to its own data-structure: a visual memory in its
> own medium (endogenic). (Ernst & Farocki 2004: 263).

Because of its characteristics of appropriation, repetition, layering, simulation
and retrospection, digitality offers new modes of thinking about, and of representing, memory, subjectivity and the museum, as I will argue through an analysis of Marker's work, and in particular of *Level Five*.

Marker's is a declaredly first-person, utterly subjective cinema; it is known
that, with reference to the documentary of interviews *Le Joli mai* (1963), a portrait of Parisian society after the end of the Algerian War, he rejected the label of
cinéma vérité, 'with its troublesome connotation of some general truth discovered through cinema' (Lupton 2006: 84), and cunningly rephrased it '*ciné, ma
vérité*' ('cinema, my truth'). Most of Marker's films present a voice-over reciting
extensive and allusive texts, alternating commentaries on history and society
and private musings and recollections; it is a voice that constantly shifts in linguistic registers, adopting now a poetic and now a prosaic tone, now an ironic
and now an erudite expression. These texts address the spectator directly and
involve her in the construction of meaning, hence complying with one of the
essay form's main requisites; in many cases, they do so by adopting the rhetorical structure of the epistle as happens, for instance, in *Letter From Siberia*; in
other cases, it is an authorial voice directly engaging the viewer in the essayistic
dialogue, as in *Chats perchés* (*The Case of the Grinning Cat*, 2004). Often, the
expression of authorial subjectivity is problematised and complicated by the
presence of multiple narrators, or by a narrator who functions as a screen for
the author, as in *Sans soleil*.

Such extensive use of voice-over raises, once again, the question of verbal
commentary in documentaries, and its corollary of the problem of enunciational
authority. For instance, writing mainly about Marker's *Le Tombeau d'Alexandre*
(*The Last Bolshevik*, 1992), French philosopher Jacques Rancière called Marker
a 'dialectical pedagogue', who uses voice-over to punctuate (and consequently,
in Rancière's mind, weaken) images that already 'speak for themselves', and that
would need no commentary (2001: 167–8). Rancière's negative take does not follow from the opinion that documentaries should be objective, and avoid adopting an overt stance (as is frequently the case in similar critiques); the author,
indeed, defiantly assigns the field of realism (of verisimilitude) to fiction cinema
rather than to the documentary. His judgement, rather, is based on the belief that

the cinema embodies the utopia of a language 'better equipped than the language of words to embrace bodies in movement' (2001: 167).

To accuse Marker of using an imperialist voice is, in my opinion, utterly unthinkable. Marker is better described as a filmmaker who, in his oeuvre, has given voice to as many people as possible – including real and fictional subjects, personal selves and others. His forms of address, his articulation of subjectivity through voice-over and through the relationship between voice and images, are simultaneously rhetorically sophisticated and morally humble. Indeed, in Marker, as Lupton writes, paraphrasing Raymond Bellour, 'the subject who addresses the viewer or reader through commentary, text and voice circulates freely through all the available personal pronouns – speaking in turn as you, he, she, we, they, one – but beginning and ending with "I". This "I" we take to be Marker himself, even if we accept that he is a fictional character, and so the function of the address is primarily self-portrayal' (2005: 77). And self-portrayal can often be a modest gesture, rather than a manifestation of arrogance and authority; as Marker himself has suggested, 'Contrary to what people say, using the first-person in film tends to be a sign of humility: "All I have to offer is myself"' (in Lupton 2006: 12).

In the case on which I focus below, that of *Level Five*, the reflection on authorial subjectivity and self-representation mixes and merges with Marker's contemplation of human subjectivity and of 'the possibilities of new media to create interactive archives of cultural memory' (Kear 2007: 129).

From the museum to the database

As Andreas Huyssen has noted, despite the pervasive sense of loss of historicity and memory that characterises our times,

> a museal sensibility seems to be occupying ever larger chunks of everyday culture and experience. If you think of the historicising restoration of old urban centres, whole museum villages and landscapes, the boom of the markets, retro fashions, and nostalgia waves, the obsessive self-musealisation per video recorder, memoir writing and confessional literature, and if you add to that the electronic totalisation of the world on data banks, then the museum … in this broad amorphous sense has become a key paradigm of contemporary cultural activities. (1995: 14)

Marker's essays are part of such a museal sensibility (in the same way other essay films are), and are, also, examples of (modest) self-musealisation. The whole history of cinema, of course, may be viewed in terms of musealisation; as Godard proposes in *Histoire(s) du cinéma: Une vague nouvelle* (1998), cinema is, in fact, *'le musée du réel'*.

If the cinema is the museum of the real, the special affinity of the essay film for the museum is exemplified by the fact that, as already discussed, many essays are archival films, which select, store, recontextualise and disseminate images of the past. Many essayist filmmakers should be studied, indeed, from the point of view of musealisation. A prominent one is Jean-Luc Godard; Antoine de Baecque, for instance, noticed that Godard's interest in the art museum is evident since as early as *Les Carabiniers* (1963), and that his conception of the museum, which was influenced by Malraux's *Les Voix du silence* (1947–65), is based on a comparative montage of images of artworks – as it is evinced especially in *Histoire(s) du cinéma* and in *The Old Place* (1999) (see de Baecque 2004: 118–125).[5] Godard's ideal (imaginary but also actual) museum is a 'museum-montage'. As I will argue below, montage is also central to an understanding of Marker's museum.

Not only do Marker's films overtly deal with the functioning of human thought and remembrance, and with the question of memory and its preservation at a thematic level, but they also investigate the specific ways in which each medium is capable of being a museum, of storing and of representing memory. By inscribing in the text forms of their author's subjectivity, his works are, of course, also a museum of Marker himself.

Marker's interest in museums and archives of all sorts is self-evident in his cinema and in his audiovisual work. Once again, a prominent example is *La Jetée*, which so succinctly and vividly articulates some of the filmmaker's main concerns, and which alludes to museums at least three times. Not only does the voice-over explicitly refer to the protagonist's memory as a museum, but also the underground camp in the film, in which the time travel experiments take place, is located, as Lupton notices, 'under the ruins of the Palais de Chaillot, once used as a storage space for Henri Langlois' Cinémathèque Française (the Cinémathèque itself would eventually be located here)' (2006: 94). Such a choice of setting emphasises the power of images, and especially of cinematic images, in shaping the unconscious and memory, as well as in providing an archive of past eras. Furthermore, the key scene of the penultimate encounter between the protagonist and the enigmatic woman in his memories takes place in a museum of natural history, teeming with stuffed birds.

An early example of Marker's investigation of the archive and the museum is his collaboration with Alain Resnais, *Les Statues meurent aussi* (*Statues Also Die*, 1950–53), for which he wrote the commentary. In an important sequence, commenting on Western culture's appropriation of African art, 'The contention that statues die once they are entombed in museums, no longer looked at as part of a living culture, is imaginatively reversed as an African statue in a display

The natural history museum in Chris Marker's *La Jetée* (1962)

case meets the gaze of a black woman museum visitor' (Lupton 2006: 36), and is magically resurrected by Resnais through a 'fluid repertoire of zooms, pans and sharp cuts to show objects liberated from their display case coffins and infused with life and movement' (2006: 37). The idea that the display is like a sepulchre until two gazes meet, the gaze of the visitor and the gaze of the artefact (or even the gaze of the artefact and the gaze of the camera), is simultaneously suggestive of the potential and of the limitations of the museum.

Indeed, *Statues Also Die* is an overt critique of colonialism and of its practice of transforming living, everyday objects in crystallised commodities and dead souvenirs – an accusation that can be made of the entire history of the museum, seen as one of the privileged sites of modernity. As Huyssen reminds us, in fact, 'A traditional society without a secular teleological concept of history does not need a museum, but modernity is unthinkable without its museal project' (1995: 15). The main argument of the critique of the modernist museum that has informed academic writing, and especially new museology, since the 1980s is the opinion that every display is both ideologically and scientifically suspicious, for at least the following reasons: because it 'means placing a certain construction upon history' (Vergo 1989: 3); because it institutionalises the taste of an elite as culture (see Bourdieu 1993); because it materialises culture, and contributes to 'structuring the modern way of seeing the world and comprehending the world "as if it were an exhibit"' (Macdonald 1996: 7); and because it is a 'symptom of cultural ossification' (Huyssen 1995: 13). According to the latter opinion, museums are in truth sepulchres of art, knowledge and experience, in which the objects gather dust and are de facto dead – an opinion that is espoused by *Statues Also Die*.[6]

In his work, Marker has often alluded to the shortcomings of museums and exhibits, while still presenting them as crucial loci of personal and public memory, and even nostalgia. It suffices to think of the already mentioned sequence of the natural history museum in *La Jetée*. Because of its special status, the natural history museum displays its unequivocal belonging to a bygone conception of knowledge and of its preservation and communication (as well as, in more general terms, life, history and the natural world), a position that makes it one of the most emphatic symbols of the human drive to preserve and catalogue – as well as of its obvious limitations and failures. This is due, in particular, to the fact that the natural history museum, with its ghostly practice of displaying animals that are embalmed or preserved in formalin, reveals more clearly than any other form of display its derivation from the *Wunderkammer*, the seventeenth century's cabinet of wonders, which was characterised by an indistinct mix of real and reconstructed remains, of factual and fantastic relics, of objects and artefacts.

Natural history museums are also highly problematic because of their participation in the creation of a national narrative. In fact, they traditionally helped, along with ethnology museums, to 'define the categories of the "human" as opposed to the "nonhuman"' (Zolberg 1996: 76); furthermore, in natural history museums 'the link between the collectors' salvage operation and the exercise of raw power, even genocide, is palpably there in the collection themselves: Madame Tussauds of otherness' (Huyssen 1995: 16). It seems to me that Marker's choice of using this type of museum in his film responds not only to its ability to suggest the metaphor of the 'embalming' of time; but also to the author's distinct interest in the obsolescence of the techniques of recording and of storing memory. As Lupton (2002) has convincingly argued, Marker's predilection for 'old-fashioned' technology and effects in his films, including *Level Five*, is a way of incorporating fragments of the recent past, of the forgotten pre-history of the present, 'into present constellations to create dialectical images', hence 'invoking a perspective from which our past has itself become history'. Although Lupton in her article refers specifically to computer graphics, the museum, the archive and the library are also technologies of memory and preservation; indeed, they obsolesce in the same way as other technologies do.

Marker also played a role in another early documentary by Alain Resnais, *Toute la mémoire du monde* (*All the World's Memory*, 1956). The nature of his participation, which is unspecified in the film's credits (where he appears as 'Chris "Magic" Marker'), is identified by André Bazin, and other sources after him, as the writing of the film's commentary (Bazin 2003: 44); other critics, however, limit Marker's contribution to a much lesser role, if not to a simple homage from the director to his friend (see, for instance, Lupton 2006: 43). *All the World's Memory* is an essayistic documentary on the Parisian Bibliothèque Nationale, which is seen, as the film's title suggests, as the repository of human memory, as the archive of all knowledge and remembrance. Indeed, the Bibliothèque is here presented in its three coexisting functions of library, archive and museum. There is little need to recall that Resnais, much like Marker, is a filmmaker chiefly concerned with the workings of memory, a director who in many of his works proposed true topographies of the human mind. Indeed, in *All the World's Memory* Resnais' exploration of the library, which is represented as a mysterious fortress, resisting the aggression of time and oblivion, is suggestive more of mental spaces than of a real building. Similarly to films such as *L'Année dernière à Marienbad* (*Last Year in Marienbad*, 1961) and *Providence* (1977), the architectures are unrelentingly explored by long, fluid and meandering tracking shots which, aided by Maurice Jarre's grave and reflective soundtrack, transform them into true mindscapes.[7] While offering a representation of the various levels of the library, from the cellars to the roof, and a record of its workings, the film draws parallels with the mechanisms of memory and the human mind. The camera slowly meanders through the corridors, up and down elevators, into underground rooms, as if mimicking the ways in which thought forms and progresses in the brain – or, even better, the ways in which a piece of information or the memory of an event are labelled and stored in a drawer of the mind's archive. Indeed, one of the main concerns of the film's narrative is that of showing us the process of tagging and of storing a book.[8]

The critique of the shortcomings of the modernist conception of the archive and the museum has developed over the past decades alongside the exploration of new models of storing and accessing knowledge, in particular those afforded by the computer; namely, the interactive database in its various incarnations, including the World Wide Web and the CD-ROM. Indeed, Eilean Hooper-Greenhill (1995 and 2000) foresees the birth of the post-museum, premised on a new relationship with the audience and on a stronger level of interactivity. Huyssen claims that, while audiovisual media can be used to great advantage by the postmodern museum, the museum itself cannot be replaced by the computer or the television, because 'it offers an alternative to channel flicking that is grounded in the materiality of the exhibited objects and their temporal aura' (1995: 33). For the author, it is the material presence of the objects that, while admittedly being augmented by the simulation of their spectacular display, guarantees them against simulation itself. In this sense, for Huyssen, who reminds us that the data bank is not memory, and even opines that it is incompatible with it, the museum is a bastion against the 'progressive dematerialisation of the world which is driven by television and the virtual realities of computer networking' (1995: 34).

Even though the data bank can never replace the museum, it can certainly aid it and complete it; furthermore, it offers new, successful metaphors and models to conceptualise the museum, the archive, and even human memory. As Vivian Sobchack has argued:

> It is no accident, for example, that in our now dominantly electronic (and only secondarily cinematic) culture, many people describe and understand their minds and bodies in terms of computer systems and programs (even as they still describe and understand their lives in terms of movies). Nor is it trivial that computer systems and programs are often described and understood in terms of human minds and bodies (for example, as intelligent and suscepti-ble to viral infection) and that these new computer-generated 'beings' have become the explicit cybernetic heroes of our most popular moving image fictions (for example, *Robocop*, Paul Verhoeven, 1987; or *Terminator 2: Judgement Day*, James Cameron, 1991). (2004: 137)

If information is not memory, the database is a bank of information that is avail-able for the 'creation' of memory, and that offers new metaphors to describe the human mind and experience. Marker is well aware of its potential, and used it to construct his own, portable audiovisual museum: the CD-ROM *Immemory*. Whereas for Huyssen the presence of the material object is essential to the expe-rience of the past, for Marker the image is more than sufficient. The same can be said for Godard, who reproduces the object's aura 'by resorting to slow-motion, freeze frames, stop-motion cinematography, commentaries and operatic music' (de Baeque 2004: 121). Indeed, one wonders whether the 'im' before 'memory' in the title of Marker's CD-ROM invokes the concept of 'immemorial', negates the possibility of memory, stands for 'image', or perhaps for 'immaterial' – or for all these concepts together. As Lupton noted, Marker obviously disagrees with those cultural theorists, for instance the already quoted Paul Virilio, who dif-ferentiate between older media, and especially the cinema, which respect and serve memory, and the new media, which undermine it. Marker shows how new media are, in many respects, closer approximations of the human memory.

> Marker makes a memorial virtue out of the fact that digital image manipula-tion distorts the representational and indexical qualities of filmed and pho-tographed images from the past … In the introductory text to *Immemory*, Marker contends that the virtual architectures of cyberspace, which permit non-linear, multi-directional navigation at the user's own chosen speed, are far closer to the aleatory, non-linear drift of actual human memory than the capabilities of older media. The CD-ROM format has allowed Marker to re-alise a mapping of the geography of his own memory more effectively than a film like *Sans soleil*, which can be seen as a prototype of this long-cherished

project, but one that remained limited by the linearity and fixed temporal rate of film. (Lupton 2002)

It is tempting to trace similarities between the waning of the (modernist) museum, seen as a medium to store and to provide access to memory and knowledge, and the obsolescence of film, which, with the predominant linearity of its narrative and montage, no longer appears to be the best medium to represent and investigate human memory, and is outdone by multimedia and the hypertext. *All the World's Memory*, similarly to other later films by both Resnais and Marker, attempted to overcome the limitations of the medium and to suggest and recreate the complexity of human thought. Its representation of memory as library and archive, however, was mainly based on the mobility of the camera, which produced a sort of internal montage, suggestive of a spatial and temporal stratification. In *Immemory*, the spatial and temporal stratification is achieved, instead, through the non-linear, multi-directional characteristics of the CD-ROM.

The exploration of memory, oblivion, records and human subjectivity also feature in Marker's 1996 essay film, *Level Five*. *Level Five* was shot on video and digital video and then transferred to 35mm, and it foregrounds a personal computer as one of its main 'protagonists'. It is a fiction based on a character named Laura and on her dead lover; but it is also a computer game; a documentary on the Battle of Okinawa; a homage to Alain Resnais' cinema; and an essay on historical and personal memory and on digital archives. Here, I want to give an account of Marker's reflection on the relationship between memory and the database, while also focusing on the performance of subjectivity in the text. Indeed, while being a museum of Okinawa, *Level Five* is also a film about human subjectivity, and about enunciation and the filming subject. I agree with Kear that 'The convoluted *mise en abymes* of *Sans soleil*, the discontinuous narration of *Le fond de l'air est rouge* and *Level Five*, serve to disseminate observations, to call into question the status of who speaks and what is said, and to both augment and complicate the perspective of the film' (2005: 57).

Level Five: The museum of Okinawa

A woman (Catherine Belkhodja), whose partner liked to call Laura after the character played by Gene Tierney in the film by Otto Preminger of the same title (1944), relentlessly speaks to the camera, actually addressing her dead lover, and simultaneously the screen of their computer.[9] While she mourns him, recollects their shared past and muses about death and oblivion, Laura endeavours to complete the task that had occupied him before his death – a computer strategy game on Okinawa, the last and most ferocious battle of World War Two. The bat-

Laura's compassionate gaze into the lens in Chris Marker's *Level Five* (1997)

tle, which lasted from late March to the end of June 1945, and claimed the lives of one third of the entire population, was particularly controversial for the Japanese army's use of civilians as shields against the Americans, and for the mass suicides of the locals, suicides which were instigated by Japanese propaganda and direct military orders (see Feifer 2001; Rottman 2002).

Laura navigates through the information stored by her partner, namely interviews with witnesses and commentators, among whom are Nagisa Oshima, Kenji Tokitsu, Ju'nishi Ushiyama and Shigeaki Kinjo; excerpts from documentaries, including two by Oshima, a film by John Huston and footage by Gérard de Battista and Yves Angelo; various information on the generals, the armies, the battle, the islands and the local populations; news coverage of the events; maps; and photographs. However, when she tries to play the game and reach level five, hence winning against the computer and changing the outcome of the battle, access is denied to her. If she insists, the system crashes: the computer will only allow history to repeat itself endlessly. Laura invokes the help of Chris, the 'wizard of montage', who 'enters the story at this stage', as Marker's own voice-over relates, in order to impose some order on the pieces of the puzzle. She also attempts to obtain a deeper understanding of the events, and especially of the horrific mass homicides/suicides, accessing an apocryphal double of the World Wide Web, the Optional World Link or OWL.[10] On OWL, Laura wears digital masks to access information and meet other navigators, and possibly her dead lover himself. Indeed, the status of both characters as virtual realities is suggested by the allusions to the strange circumstances in which Laura's lover died, and by her own disappearance at the end of the film. Laura, who controls the DV camera with a remote control, goes out of focus and vanishes as a digital image, apparently subsumed by the computer.

Level Five's reflection on memory and oblivion is complex, thanks to the density and multiplicity of the argument, to the use of multiple narrators, to the copresence and interaction of different media and technologies of memory, to the stratification of intertextuality. The film, on the one hand, enters into dialogue with two films about the death and resurrection of a woman, the loop of time, the elusiveness of perception and the death wish: Preminger's *Laura* and Hitchcock's *Vertigo* (1958). On the other hand, it explores themes and images from various films by Alain Resnais, and especially from *Last Year in Marienbad* and *Hiroshima mon amour* (1959), although affinities with other films, for instance *Muriel ou Le temps d'un retour* (*Muriel, or the Time of Return*, 1963) and *Je t'aime, je t'aime*

(1968), can also be found. *Last Year in Marienbad* is openly invoked by a reference to the table game played in that film, a game which, irrespective of the adopted strategy, always ended with an identical outcome. In *Level Five*, we see Laura playing a computer version of the 'Marienbad game'. The reference is both to the game of Okinawa, and the impossibility of defeating the computer at it, and to the Japanese strategy game, Go, in which one piece must be sacrificed in order to save the game – precisely as Okinawa was sacrificed in the hope of saving Japan. The correlation between *Level Five* and *Hiroshima mon amour* is profound, as both films explore the relationship between historiography and private experience, shared and personal history, official and private memory. In both *Hiroshima mon amour* and *Level Five* a woman, who mourns a dead lover, tries to grasp the magnitude of historical tragedy (respectively, Hiroshima's bomb and Okinawa's mass suicides) through her own experience of private loss, which she recounts to another person, a stranger/lover. Memory, oblivion, the tragedy and the necessity to forget, as well as the importance and struggle to remember, are at the core of both works, as is the realisation that the full comprehension of past horrors from our position in the present is impossible. *Level Five* truly is Marker's 'Okinawa, mon amour'.[11]

A key theme in *Level Five* is, unsurprisingly for a film on technologies of memory, the museum. As a matter of fact, the problem of the museum as representation of the historical past, and as a symbol of our memory of it, also figured prominently in *Hiroshima mon amour*, in which the French woman, Elle (Emmanuelle Riva) repeated that many times she had seen the Hiroshima museum, while her Japanese partner kept answering that she had 'seen nothing' in Hiroshima. The museum also featured literally, filmed by Resnais' camera. Similarly, Marker shows us images of the Himeyuri War Memorial, as well as of the Himeyuri Peace Museum, which displays the photographs of the 194 schoolgirls and 17 teachers mobilised as nurses during the Battle of Okinawa in 1945, only five of whom survived the carnage. He also shows the former Navy Underground Headquarters, several hundred metres of underground corridors and rooms, in which many sailors died (the holes of grenades used for committing suicide are signposted on the walls); the diorama of the caves of the horror; memorials where people pray for the rest of the souls of the dead; and reconstructions of battlefields displaying the debris of war. Marker alludes to a controversy linked to the Himeyuri Peace Museum, instigated by the choice of exhibiting, as representatives of all victims, the photographs of the young nurses who belonged to Okinawa's elite. Obviously, the controversy about Okinawa is much broader, and it involves the disagreement between Japan and Okinawa on the representation of the events and on the recognition of historical responsibilities, as well as the dispute between Japan and the United States on the respective national accounts of the war, and on the representation of the other – of the enemy.[12]

Japanese tourists visiting the caves of the horror at Okinawa in *Level Five*

The Japan International Cooperation Agency (2006) claims that each year 400,000 people visit the Okinawa Prefectural Peace Memorial Museum at Itoman. The websites of Okinawa's monuments and museums present them, as is only to be expected, as popular tourist attractions. Marker, indeed, in *Level Five* shows us Japanese visitors arriving on their buses at the sites, examining their tourist guides, taking pictures and smiling while being photographed before the monuments, looking intently at maps and displays, following their tour guide through corridors and tunnels, peering at the entrance of caves, wondering whether their images will be shown on American television, offering flowers, and praying before the memorials. The displays, both those at the actual sites of the horror or those that were reconstructed elsewhere, aim to convey some sense of the suffering; or else, to preserve the memory of the dead, through photographs, mementos or monuments.

The question obviously is whether it is possible to reach some understanding of past human experience, especially when highly traumatic events are involved, through mass tourism and through the visit to the museum. The vast literature on the musealisation of the Holocaust, with its critique of the risks involved in the representation of the Shoah, is a case in point. Marker's observation of the Japanese tourists is non-judgemental; indeed, he presents the museums and memorials as sites in which at least a trace of experiential knowledge can be attained. With reference to the small museum in Mabuni, for instance, he remarks that its displays are able to convey the sense of chaos and destruction; however, he also notices that something is missing: the smell of the battle. On this occasion, Marker explicitly makes the connection between museum and film as technologies of memory, and argues that only in the case of the birth of an 'odorama' cinema, hence through the addition of smell, would true war films be possible – however, as he remarks, no spectators would be able to view them.[13]

Our attention, hence, is attracted to the rift between past and present and, especially, between experience and the representation or memento of it. As Lupton noted, 'This acknowledgement of historical distance between past and present registers a contemporary shift in cultural perceptions of World War Two at a moment when the fragile burden of remembrance is palpably shifting from survivors to public museums, archives, recordings, and broadcasts' (2003: 59).

And yet, while acknowledging the helplessness of our technologies of memory, *Level Five* re-establishes the need to remember and to represent, and produces its own museum of Okinawa. Rather than using linear montage and linear narrative, however, Marker adopts the model of the database. *Level Five* is like a data bank, storing a vast range of fragments of information on Okinawa: direct witness accounts; footage and documentary images; books; comments and interviews; maps and aerial pictures; scholarly writings; sounds, voices, songs. Bewildered by all the data, Laura hopes that Marker will sort out the information by applying his montage skills. While he agrees to intervene, Marker (who never becomes fully embodied in the narrative, but remains a voice-over) does not reorder the data, but stacks it, combines it, layers it, and moves it around as pieces in a puzzle, or indeed in a computer game, thus exploiting the computer game's ability to provide 'a framework to break up narrative structures which ordinarily produce continuity' (Spielmann 2000: 23). The montage is guided by the characteristics of the database; the information is ordered according to pre-established criteria ('witness accounts', 'media' and 'commentary', and so on) but is explored idiosyncratically, following association and contiguity, anticipation and delay, repetition and return, searching and branching out, rather than an exhaustive linear pattern with a clear beginning and a logical end.

In a sense, Marker is making the database structure of his customary style of montage even more explicit than usual. As early as 1958, André Bazin had already defined Marker's montage practice as 'horizontal', 'as opposed to traditional montage that plays with the sense of duration through the relationship of shot to shot. Here, a given image doesn't refer to the one that preceded it or the one that will follow, but rather it refers laterally, in some way, to what is said' (2003: 44). Such horizontality can be seen, in a sense, as the branching-out style of the data bank. Marker's use of digital technology 'inscribes the discourse of memory on multiple registers of time, space, and national identity that are simultaneously available on the screen of cinematic representation' (Murray 2000: 118). The result is achieved by accumulation, co-presence and stratification; images, ideas and words are allowed to form patterns of meaning and to sediment in our memory as an archive of Okinawa.[14]

It is significant that the two models of musealisation gestured by Marker are the Internet and the computer game. Both are based on ideas of interactivity, unlike older media such as film, which is generally seen as unable to produce reciprocity, if not through mechanisms of projective identification of the spectator with the camera and with the characters. In *Level Five*, Marker constantly attracts attention to the interactive capabilities of the computer and of digital technology. Laura constantly speaks to her workstation; her image is often seen on the computer screen, digitally altered in multiple ways; in order to explore OWL she must wear a mask, an interface between brain and computer, strongly reminiscent, among other things, of the wired eye patches worn by the time traveller in *La Jetée*. When on OWL, she wears digital masks; she is frequently seen imparting commands to the processor, and interacting with the game. The interactivity, however, has limitations: the computer does not know how to respond to the unpredictable commands that Laura inputs; Laura's communication with the world through OWL is limited to encounters with men who attempt to seduce her, or with enigmatic figures whose claims go unaccounted for; the game can be manipulated in a very limited way and its outcome is frustratingly fixed.[15] In other words, the database gives access to information that seems unlimited but, ultimately, is not; and information is, in any case, not experience. It is, however, also true that the database structure and the computer game bring into play 'a complexity, intricacy and heterogeneity missing from more straightforward representations of historical events' (Kear 2007: 134).

It is interesting that Marker, in order to construct his own personal museum of Okinawa, while using new media (digital video, the computer) and adopting a database structure for the montage, still chooses to make recourse to a film, endowed with a narrative (even though a very fragmentary one), rather than making a CD-ROM like *Immemory*, and allowing the user to freely interact with his work. Going against the frequent claim that, unlike the new media, film imposes its own rhythms and teleological narrative onto the spectator, who is, therefore, a captivated and passive user, Marker draws attention to and intensifies the interactive capabilities of the cinema, via the relationship established between the spectator and Laura, as we will see below. It seems to me that *Level Five*'s argument is that at least a trace of experiential knowledge can be achieved via the mediation of a subject (the enunciating subject); and that the cinema allows for such subjective mediation of experience through narrative, through the embodiment of the enunciating subject in a narrator, and through the direct address to the audience, which creates a strong sense of reciprocity. Marker's museum of Okinawa, his 'Okinawa, mon amour', is indeed filtered through the personal loss and mourning of a fictional character, Laura. The fact that she was named after a famous film is clear recognition of the medium's ultimate success as a powerful technology of memory and museum of experience. Ultimately, the film *Level Five* is, I would argue, more poignant and successful at conveying a sense of (mediated) experiential knowledge than the CD-ROM *Immemory*.

It is not my intention to suggest, however, that Marker celebrates film over digital video or the CD-ROM as a medium that is more respectful of human history and experience on the basis of its technological characteristics. While he distinguishes between different media by reason of the specificities of their apparatus, he uses all of them and is able to bend their characteristics to his advantage. At the same time, he somehow distances himself from all of them, by adopting graphics and special effects with a quaint, anachronistic look, which work as a commentary on the transitory nature of our technologies of memory, including each embodiment of the museum, of the archive, and of the cinema.

Ultimately, Marker's attitude towards all media, old and new, is humanistic in a somewhat veiled and distinctive way; their correct use depends on human responsibility. Take his reflection on image, on representation and on simulation. All media, Marker shows us, can produce a fake:

> When Marker introduces the formal system of the game in order to explain the structure of media (in particular hypermedia), he also refers to related examples (from the history of documentary film and photography) of images made up for the camera or otherwise 'manipulated' so as to prove the 'reality' of facts that have never existed. (Spielmann 2000: 21–2)

Marker's reflection goes beyond even the question of the intentional fake, to include the problem of a reality which is induced or generated by the simple presence of the media. A telling example is the montage of grainy black-and-white footage of a woman from Saipan jumping to her death from a cliff, and of a caped man jumping from the Eiffel Tower in 1910; both seem to have second thoughts an instant before jumping but, noticing that they are on camera, they are compelled to go ahead and kill themselves. Marker also compares their behaviour to that of suicidal Okinawans, who behaved as if the camera-eye of history was observing them and pushing them to their death. This sequence, in my opinion, does not 'implicate [Marker's] own media in the drive towards death itself', as Murray has argued (2000: 104); on the contrary, it contends that the difference is made by the attitude of the human eye behind the camera (the enunciating subject), and by the eye that watches the images (the embodied spectator).[16]

Laura's eyes, for instance, are not indifferent; they are deeply compassionate. Her empathetic gaze mirrors the neutral gazes of other faces in the film, faces which look at us and interpellate us – those of the still oblivious Okinawan children and young girls, who gaze at us from photographs taken shortly before their death. Thanks to the mediation of Laura's eyes, we are compelled to look at them not with indifference or neutrality, but with her same deep concern, compassion and tenderness. As Sarah Cooper has argued, 'Laura embodies the position from which a viewer might begin to relate to others' pain in Marker's film, in which her suffering is no less palpable than that of the people of Okinawa but is a conduit to this pain rather than its equivalent' (2008: 159).

The address of the digital subject

Laura, our mediator, is, however, an unusual protagonist, an elusive character. Although she speaks for much of the screen time, while looking directly at the spectator, baring her soul and sharing her feelings as in a confessional, it is ul-

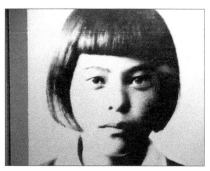

Photo of one of the schoolgirls killed at Okinawa displayed at the Himeyuri Peace Museum in *Level Five*

timately her virtuality that stands out. Indeed, Laura is not a fiction film's classical, round character, not only because she is a reflection of and homage to at least two other cinematic characters – Preminger's Laura and Resnais' Elle – but also because she is often shown as a digital image, in the act of morphing, appearing or vanishing. Laura is best seen as an avatar, which can be described as a stand-in, a graphic representation of the computer user. The avatar can simply be a two-dimensional icon that represents the user on the Internet, for instance in forums and chat rooms; or even a three-dimensional, anthropomorphic model used in computer games. In the second case, the avatar not only has a gender and a precise physical form, but also a personality.

The avatar is a virtual embodiment of the user; hence, its status and function is intermediate, in between human being and computer. In *Level Five*, Laura the avatar can be seen as Marker's digital self-representation (indeed, the first image of the film, a male hand – obviously Marker's – using a mouse, is soon replaced by a female hand, Laura's). Laura speaks for Marker, while at the same time maintaining her own gender, personality, history, opinions and reactions. As Marker's avatar, she is one of the sites of the director's subjectivity, which is split among various narrators. Far from presenting an 'imperial voice', which superimposes its meaning on the images, *Level Five* offers a multiplicity of voices: Laura's, Chris's, the computer's and the interviewees'. While the witnesses can claim a direct or, at least, a near-experiential familiarity with Okinawa's tragedy, the other voices, and especially Laura's and Chris's (those in which Marker's subjectivity is more directly sited) can approach this knowledge only indirectly. The two figures are, however, quite distinct. Chris admits that he has by now become so Japanese that he embraced the national phenomenon of memory loss and forgetfulness. Laura, instead, although fearful of oblivion, is constantly in touch with her painful memories. Her form of address, the confessional or love letter, is warm, passionate, intense and in the present tense; we stare into her eyes, and are asked to share her pain with her.[17] On the other hand, Chris's address to the spectator is that of a voice that, being disembodied, and located in the now of the story, after the end of the events (not only those of Okinawa, but also of Laura's life), narrates from a position of knowledge and with participation – but also, inevitably, from afar.

Laura, hence, is not a simple narrator; she is an avatar who, while having her own personality and physical shape, is a site of the author in the text, and who mediates between the enunciating subject and his subject matter.[18] As Bellour noticed, in fact, Marker both identifies with her and uses her as a medium: 'He films her before his own computer, in his own room of working life; through her he concentrates on a new dialogue with the machine-memory henceforth destined to include all words and images, and to renew our view of creativity and its exchanges' (1997: 118). Machine-memory is the expression that Bellour uses to name the computer; but the cinema is also machine-memory.

While, on the one hand, Laura is Marker's avatar and one of his narrators, she is also, at least occasionally, the spectator's avatar, particularly when she plays the game and interacts with the computer (and we do with her, through a subjective camera); thus, she is a representative of the spectator in the narrative. Indeed, her incomplete knowledge and understanding of the events places her in a position similar to ours – like her, with her and via her, we navigate through the information, we discover and accumulate facts and figures, and move deeper and deeper through the levels of the game.

If Laura is both Marker's and the spectator's avatar, both narrator and narratee, where is she positioned? Where is her address? The question of the address is, of course, multilayered, as Bellour reminded us: 'For an address is as much a destination as a mode of discourse, it is a physical or moral quality as much as an informational sign (for instance, the digital or literal expression representing a site of memory in a computer)' (1997: 113). Laura's mode of discourse oscillates between the confession and the video-epistle; her quality is that of a caring, concerned spectator who wants to understand and to share, as much as possible, a traumatic past, but also of a player who wants to interact with the narrative/history and change its teleological outcome; her informational address is that of a site of memory in Marker's computer. Her position in the film's rhetorical structure fluctuates between that of a spokesperson for the enunciator and that of a representative of the spectator. Because of her intermediate status, she is an ideal mediator, in between enunciator and receiver. Because of her virtual nature, she is an instrument of interactivity – both that of the director with his subject matter, and that of the spectator with the film. As Cooper has argued, 'It is Laura's occupation of a space between fictional character and documentary voice-over that permits her to work through her own traumas while remembering suffering that is not her own' (2008: 160).[19] Indeed, as with the spectator's, Laura's 'relation to the fate of Okinawa is remote and mediated' (Kear 2007: 131).

I have argued that the essay film's most characteristic strategy is interpellation, which establishes the address of the enunciator as a dialogue with the spectator. *Level Five* not only utilises the address on an ongoing basis, through Laura's gazes into the lens and her epistolary communication with the audience; it also creates an avatar who allows enunciator and spectator to interact. Laura is constantly interpellating us; her tender, plaintive speech, to borrow Lupton's description of *Letters From Siberia*'s voice-over, 'uses the intimate and seductive address of the personal letter to draw the viewer directly into the scene' (2006: 54). Such a letter is addressed 'to her absent lover as viewer or perhaps also to her viewers as distant discursive lovers' (Murray 2000: 119). The spectators are, perhaps, absent; but they certainly are not distant. Laura, in fact, speaks directly to the camera, which is placed, as we are constantly reminded, in lieu of the computer screen. And, obviously, the spectator is also to be found at this site, because he is, as always, at the address of the camera.

At this address, we find a work that is simultaneously film and computer game, digital image and electronic image, window onto the world and inserting effect. As Edmond Couchot reminds us, in fact, while the cinematic apparatus works as a window onto the world, 'the electronic screen does not function like a window, it does not inscribe onto a wall, it does not carry the look of the inside towards the outside; it inserts, on the contrary, the outside in the inside, in a centripetal and violent movement, at the place of the spectator. It acts by way of an inserting effect' (quoted in Spielmann 2000: 33). Many would argue that the inserting effect highlights the circularity and self-referentiality of new media's image, which no longer refers to an outer reality but only to itself; with the outcome that the spectators no longer reach out of themselves. However, as I have already suggested, Marker uses the characteristics of the new media to his advantage, to create a representation of the self-exploratory action of memory, which rummages through the images and information stored in its database in order to create its own memory, its own narrative of the past. Multimedia, hence, can be seen as liberation from film's linearity, from its linear representation/reconstruction of memory; however, it is still through the relationship between the spectator and the avatar/narratee that an almost-experiential understanding of history is reached. Despite its multimedia or intermedia aspect (see Spielmann 2000), *Level Five* is still cinema; an essayistic cinema of the address, of the encounter between the experience of the author, the experience of the film and the experience of the spectator. A cinema that is dialogue among strangers, and yet also loving exchange, as in the lesson of *Hiroshima mon amour*; it is not by chance that Laura repeats Elle's famous phrase, '*c'est la première fois que je parlais de toi à un autre*' ('this is the first time I've spoken about you to another') – an other-lover, an other-spectator.

With *Level Five*, Marker, whose essayistic work always adopted a 'horizontal' montage, shows one of the routes that are open today to the essay film to actualise the negotiation of the spectator with the text: namely, to take as a model the interactivity offered by the database and by digital technology. Such interactivity takes place, via the text, between the embodied spectator and the enunciating subject; it is the latter, in fact, that mediates the experience, and constructs museum/texts in which a knowledge and understanding of history can be achieved. As in Sobchack's already quoted passage, today 'many people describe and understand their minds and bodies in terms of computer systems and programs', but, she adds, 'they still describe and understand their lives in terms of movies'. It is still at the cinema that we are submerged in the lives of others, that we have the chance to attain some sense of the human experience behind the historical events, and reach level four – although never the fifth, experiential level, which cannot be attained via any technology of memory.

chapter four
PERFORMANCE AND NEGOTIATION:
JEAN-LUC GODARD PLAYS JEAN-LUC GODARD

'I think of myself as an essayist.' (Godard 1972a: 171)

While broadly belonging to the realm of nonfiction, the essay film is an experimental, hybrid, self-reflexive form and, consequently, an erratic and inconsistent one. Its instability is also determined by other characteristics. The essay film systematically employs the enunciator's direct address to the audience; my argument is that it interpellates not a generic, broad audience, but an embodied spectator, for the purpose of directly involving her in the construction of textual meaning. In order to do this, the essay must embrace openness and uncertainty; it must leave questions unanswered, and accept and nurture the ultimate instability of its meaning. Open and fluid by both choice and ethos, the essay film articulates its rhetorical concerns in a performative manner, by integrating into the text the process of its own coming into being. Performance, as a result, plays a key role in essayistic cinema.

In the course of the previous chapters, I have more than once employed the expression 'performance of subjectivity', with reference to the essay films' enun-

ciators and their activity of self-representation in the texts. However, the use of the term 'performance' in the field of nonfiction cinema is far from being unproblematic; while being pertinent to the documentary in many ways, performance as a concept, as a practice and as an object of study is still very marginal in critical and theoretical writings on nonfiction film. The idea itself of performance, in fact, is in apparent contradiction to the established understanding of the documentary as distinguished from fic-

Unanswered questions and unstable meanings:
Jean-Luc Godard's *Notre musique* (2004)

tion precisely by the absence of elements of acting and staging. Performance, which is never devoid of a sense of fabrication, disguise, ingenuity and excess, seems quite simply to negate the documentary's (actual or alleged) claims to un-mediated truthfulness, to being an untampered indexical trace of real events and real people. And yet, having recognised the performative nature of all social iden-tities and human practices, we do accept that performance is intrinsic to social life. Judith Butler's ideas on the performance of gender (see 1993; 1999) are only one noteworthy example of this perspective; we can, indeed, extend the concept beyond gender, to the entire social sphere. For Erving Goffman, for instance, in-dividuals perform within the context of everyday life in order to provoke specific, desired responses from others; hence, performance is 'all the activity of a given participant on a given occasion which serves to influence in any way any of the other participants' in a social action (1959: 26). When an individual repeats such performance, we can talk of a part; a series of parts constitute a social role.[1] As Richard Schechner put is, 'All social behaviour is actually the performance of "strips of behaviour" that have already been behaved and are, therefore, "twice behaved"' (quoted in Martin 2006: 10).

Performance is at the very core of nonfiction cinema. It is directly relevant, as is most obvious, to the practice of re-enactment and dramatisation, which involve the repetition and re-presentation of events that are expressly staged for the camera.[2] In many cases, and particularly those in which no direct witnesses exist, events are recreated in radically inventive ways. Performance is relevant even to events that are faithfully reproduced on the basis of evidence and wit-nesses' accounts. At times, they are replayed by the same people who experi-enced them, by the 'real protagonists'; often, professional actors are employed to embody them. It is evident, however, that even in the former case, which in terms of faithfulness and reliability would appear to be the least artificial and most realistic, amounts indeed to a performance. A staged event is always a re-presented event; even the subject who plays himself is doing it for the second time, for the sake of the camera and of an audience – his behaviour is, quite literally, twice behaved.

Performance is also relevant to those documentaries that do not make use of re-enactment. It becomes directly visible in interviews, for instance; but also in any other instance of the documentary presentation of a subject, given that, once again, that subject is, more or less self-consciously, performing for the camera. The nonfictional actor always actively participates in the construction of mean-ing, and produces a self-representation through an engagement with the camera, with the filmmaker and with the audience.

In his extensive work on nonfiction, Bill Nichols tackled issues of perform-ance very sparsely; he introduced the term 'social actors' to refer to those subjects who appear as themselves in documentaries (see 1981: 181–5). Social actors are so important to nonfiction that 'Documentary film raises in acute form the persistent question of what to do with people, how to represent them, or, how to represent the human body as a cinematic signifier' (Nichols 1987: 9). Because they are the documentary's primary referent, the performance of social actors by professional actors for Nichols is troubling, because 'Fictive performance would depart from the indexical compact that grounds the reception of documentary' (1987: 17). Documentary, hence, reveals a desire 'for performance that is not performance, for a form of self-representation that approximates a person's normal self-presentation … In documentary we have the desire for performance stripped of the training, rehearsing, and directing that normally accompany it' (Nichols 1991: 121). Nichols calls this performance a 'virtual performance', which is rather 'the everyday presentation of self' (1991: 122). When performance does appear to be acting proper, it signals for Nichols a manifestation of excess (see 1991: 144). Nichols does not discuss performance overtly in his categorisation of documentary modes; however, he introduces a 'performative mode', which he identifies with contemporary, postmodern documentary production – the latest mode in his periodic categorisation:

> Performative documentary puts the referential aspect of the message in brackets, under suspension. Realism finds itself deferred, dispersed, interrupted and postponed … Performative documentary clearly embodies a paradox: it generates a distinct tension between performance and document, between the personal and the typical, the embodied and disembodied, between, in short, history and science. (1994: 96–7)

Stella Bruzzi has clarified the importance of performance to all nonfiction. She has redefined the performative documentary as one that 'uses performance within a non-fiction context to draw attention to the impossibility of authentic documentary representation' (2006: 185). Hence, the performative element functions as distancing device, and is actualised either by the intrusive presence of the director, or by a self-conscious performance of the 'actors'. This amounts to 'the enactment of the notion that a documentary only comes into being as it is performed, that although its factual basis (or document) can pre-date any recording or representation of it, the film itself is necessarily performative because it is given meaning by the interaction between performance and reality' (Bruzzi 2006: 186). Bruzzi rightly considers recent performative documentaries (including those of Errol Morris, Nick Broomfield and Michael Moore) not as utter novelty, but as the latest embodiment of those many forms of nonfiction in which the filmmakers self-reflexively express their unease about what documentaries are and do. Essay cinema, I add, is an essential and leading component of this self-reflexive tradition.

For Bruzzi, performance is relevant not only to performative documentaries, but to all documentaries, which are in fact 'performative acts, inherently fluid and unstable and informed by issues of performance and performativity' (2006: 1). While it is certainly true that all documentaries 'are a negotiation between filmmaker and reality and, at heart, a performance' (2006: 186), my argument is that issues of performance and performativity are especially relevant to and evident in the essay film. Because of its hybridism and experimentalism, and its generic instability, the essay film, in fact, foregrounds and problematises issues of performance; and, on account of its openness and reflexivity, it articulates its concerns in an eminently performative manner.

Performance in and of the essay film

In one of the rare scholarly contributions on acting performances in documentary cinema, Thomas Waugh reminds us that the classical documentary tradition, as can for instance be evinced by a 1940 text by Joris Ivens (see Ivens 1940), took the notion of performance for granted; indeed, 'semi-fictive characterisation, or "personalisation," as Ivens called it, seemed to be the means for the documentary to attain maturity and mass audiences' (Waugh 1990: 67). Waugh notices that little or no difference is found between documentary and fiction, either in the terminology used to describe acting, or in the practice: 'Documentary performers "act" in much the same way as their dramatic counterparts except that they are cast for their social representativity as well as for their cinematic qualities, and their roles are composites of their own social roles and the dramatic requirements of the film' (ibid.). One of the elements that qualifies the social actors' performance is the requirement of not looking into the lens, of performing unawareness of the camera – corresponding to the stipulation of 'acting naturally'; this is what Nichols would call the virtual performance, the everyday presentation of the self. Based on whether the social actor acknowledges the camera or not, Waugh proposes to distinguish between a 'representational performance', in which the documentary borrows the code of narrative illusion and naturalness from fiction cinema; and a 'presentational performance', whereby the awareness of the camera is performed, a code that for Waugh the documentary absorbed from documentary still photography.[3] This second tradition includes the variants of aural presentation, partly inspired by the radio, such as the interview, the monologue and choral speech. Although – as Waugh aptly shows – the two traditions historically intersect and alternate, and despite some notable exceptions, in classical times 'the presentational style predominated only in the documentary vernacular of the commercial newsreel (as later in its descendant, television journalism), or in specialised forms like the still rare campaign film' (1990: 71); representational performance ruled instead in the classical documentary. Waugh also notices that representational performance continued during the *vérité* wave, and that American direct cinema carefully eliminated all looks at the camera in order to preserve the illusion, thus denying that even 'the most noninterventionist camera instigated palpable performance on the part of the subjects' (1990: 73).[4]

In what ways, if any, does the essay film differ from a more traditional documentary in terms of performance? Essays are open and fluid textual structures, searching for their own rules and specifications – in other words, they are intrinsically performative acts. It is, then, logical to deduce that the essay will use performance self-consciously, and naturally tend to the presentational style of acting. In other words, performance is likely to be used by the essay film in a way that highlights the distance between the film and its subject matter. We should perhaps even talk of Brechtianism; we would be authorised to do so by the fact that the essay film developed at a time and geographical location that was influenced, particularly around the year 1968 and after, by Brechtian theory.[5] Furthermore, as I have argued in the previous chapters, the essay film's relationship with the evidence, the fact and the archive is one of complexity and interrogation. This is a characteristic that the essay film shares, for instance, with documentary theatre, 'a genre that can invite contemplation of the ways in which stories are told – a form of Brechtian distancing that asks spectators to simultaneously understand the theatrical, the real, and the simulated, each as its own form of truth' (Martin 2006: 12). I propose, similarly, to think of performance as a lens through which we can understand the truthfulness of the filmic, the real and the simulated in the essay film.

With the aim of examining more closely questions of performativity and performance in the essay film, I will focus below on the expression of enunciational subjectivity, on the presentation and representation of the authorial self, and on the establishment of a dialogue between filmmaker and spectator through performance. The essayistic cinema of Jean-Luc Godard in which the filmmaker 'plays' himself provides a fascinating case study. Godard is an ideal choice not only because of the central role that performance always plays in his work, but also because his essay films integrate the process of their own coming into being in an especially visible and deliberate manner. As Godard once suggested, commenting on his *Deux ou trois choses que je sais d'elle* (*Two or Three Things I Know About Her*, 1966):

> Basically, what I am doing is making the spectator share the arbitrary nature
> of my choices, and the quest for general rules which might justify a particu-

lar choice. Why am I making this film, why am I making it this way? ... I am constantly asking questions. I watch myself filming, and you hear me thinking aloud. In other words it isn't a film, it's an attempt at film and is presented as such. (1972b: 239)

My analysis will engage not only with the parameters of Godard's and his actors' performances, but also with the ways in which performance and performativity fit into the films' overall communicative strategy.

Godard, essayist and actor

Widely regarded as an essayist director, as much as or even more than Harun Farocki and Chris Marker, Godard has often described himself as one, as in the following passage, noted in part in chapter one:

As a critic, I thought of myself as a filmmaker. Today I still think of myself as a critic, and in a sense I am, more than ever before. Instead of writing criticism, I make a film, but the critical dimension is subsumed. I think of myself as an essayist, producing essays in novel form, or novels in essay form: only instead of writing, I film them. Were the cinema to disappear, I would simply accept the inevitable and turn to television; were television to disappear, I would revert to pencil and paper. (1972a: 171)

Bordwell notes that, between 1959 and 1967 (the date of release of *La Chinoise*), talking of Godard's cinema in terms of essay was already a critical cliché (1985: 312).[6] Jose Mouré, however, is right to point out that, despite 'the narrative ruptures, the quotations and the moments of reflection or social critique', Godard's early films remain fundamentally narrative, and that it is 'only since 1968, with the political films, that works begin to appear which are fully inscribed in the essay form' (2004: 34; author's translation).[7] For Moure, Godard's post-1968 essayistic films no longer present true narration, but at most a situation; they are made up of very diverse audiovisual materials; they are inspired by the documentary format; and utilise intellectual montage techniques.

One additional, fundamental characteristic must be added. Writing about Godard's video-essays, and specifically *Six fois deux – Sur et sous la communication* (1976), *France/tour/detour/deux/enfants* (1977–78), *Scénario du film 'Passion'* (1982), *Soft and Hard* (1986), *Puissance de la parole* (*The Power of Speech*, 1988) and *Histoire(s) du cinéma*, John Conomos (2001) has argued that 'Perhaps the most recognisable textual trope of Godard's art is the *mise-en-scène* of direct address: Godard's self-reflexive voice questioning the work at hand, its fictionality and cultural or production features'. I agree, and suggest that we take the defining characteristics of Godard's essays to be the direct address to the viewer, the director's self-analysis, the simultaneous probing of a philosophical argument and of the film's rhetorical structure, and the stylistic hybridism.[8]

Furthermore, I argue that performance holds a privileged role in Godard's essayistic cinema, and that it is, along with montage, the most evident site of the negotiation between filmmaker and film, audience and film, film and meaning. It is important to remember that performance is a fundamental component of all Godard's work, including his most narrative and less essayistic films.[9] The influence of Brechtian epic theatre on Godard's cinema is self-evident, not only in the fragmentation of an elliptical montage, the partition of the film into tableaux, the use of captions, the overt socio-political commentary, the lack of synchronisation between voice and image; but also, specifically, in the sphere of performance, as seen for instance in the frequent use of character asides and direct addresses to the camera; and, especially in the later work, in a theatrical, vaudeville-like acting style.

Bart Testa has suggested that, in the *nouvelle vague*'s early period, which of course includes Godard's first films, the relationship between actor and film style was not integrated. Actors behaved as if they were stars in a classically constructed film, but the screen space was not constituted to respond to them; for instance, 'the actor persistently quotes a star, or famous classic performance, in order to behave like a star and thus, foregrounds the fact of playacting' (1990: 95).[10] Furthermore, 'The films of Godard … deploy acting composed of quotations' (ibid.); this characteristic, evidently, continues well beyond *nouvelle vague* times, and indeed intensifies in later work. For Testa, Godard's attitude to performance does not mean that his style asserts itself against the actors; his approach, on the contrary, 'opens a space for performance that moves in an opposite direction: the editing may interrupt the acting, but it never controls its significance; the camera contains, then elides over performance, and this allows performance to rediscover itself across the interruptions' (1990: 121). Furthermore, we should add that Godard, after the *nouvelle vague* period, moved away from the figure of the Author who exerts total control over the making of the film, by renouncing his authorial stamp and sharing it not only with co-authors, but also with the actors as authorial figures, who are collectively responsible for the production of meaning. This position obviously owes something to Brecht's theorisation, in which the entire group of artists and performers, as well as the audience itself, become the producers.

Godard frequently acted in his own films: his first appearance dates back to his second film, the short *Une Femme coquette* (1955), but his voice was already audible in his first short, *Opération béton* (*Operation Concrete*, 1954). In his first feature, *À bout de souffle*, he is the informer who recognises Poiccard and identifies him to the police; his voice is also heard several times, thus inaugurating Godard's habit of inscribing himself in his films both visually and aurally – through the image of his body and the sound of his voice, which are at times synchronised, at times disjointed. Subsequently, Godard performed frequently in his films, either as a fictional character or as the 'Director'. He appears extensively in his most recent essay films, for instance in *Histoire(s) du cinéma*, in which he adds fragments of 'his own life, by his continual presence: he is the artist working on his own editing, offering his own interpretation, his own choice of archival material, using his own voice, either a seemingly whispered voice from beyond the grave or an assured voice speaking with oracle-like certainty' (de Baecque 2004: 122). In his investigation of the ways in which Godard's voice is present in his oeuvre, in the form of recitation, ventriloquism, diction or through apparatuses, Roland-François Lack has argued that Godard used his voice 'to play novel and sometimes subtle variations on the old trope of cinematic self-reflexivity whereby the director's material presence in a film disrupts narrative illusionism' (2004: 314). I suggest that voice does much more than this, at least in some of Godard's work, where it becomes one of the main channels of the film's essayistic drive, as well as a site of performance and, therefore, of negotiation.

Especially in his most overtly autobiographical work, including *Numéro deux* (*Number Two*, 1975), sections of *Six fois deux*, and especially episode 2b, *Jean-Luc, Soigne ta droite* (*Keep Your Right Up*, 1987), *King Lear* (1987) and *JLG/JLG – autoportrait de décembre* (*JLG/JLG: Self-Portrait in December*, 1995), Godard inscribes his self-reflexivity and paints a self-portrait.[11] He appears here as the Artist, the Filmmaker, the Old Master or even the 'old fool isolated in his Swiss retreat', as the press has often construed him (Temple & Williams 2000: 11). Frequently, his self-portrait amounts indeed to humorous parody or caricature, especially of himself as a reclusive figure. In *Numéro deux*, for instance, he appears surrounded by machines in his studio,

> barely visible in the darkness in the top right-hand corner of the frame. The majority of the screen is taken up by a large video camera which films Godard as he speaks, the resulting image played back simultaneously on a television screen in the bottom right-hand corner of the frame. Godard appears here as a kind of cyborg identity, his organic body connected up to a circuit of machinery and electronic transmission through which the sound of his words and the image of his face are made available to the spectator. The studio, as he points out, is like a kind of factory in which he is at once the worker and the boss, and a part of the machinery. (Morrey 2005: 115)

In *King Lear*, he is Professor Pluggy, an expert in visual signification: 'Pluggy, who appears with dreadlocks made of electrical cables and connector leads, is a deliberately self-mocking caricature of Godard. The character plays up to an image generated by the media of Godard as an eccentric hermit working away on impenetrable projects in his remote Swiss grotto' (Morrey 2005: 169).

My contention is that, in these films, Godard plays with the multiplicity of the I, as directly suggested by the title of his most personal film, *JLG/JLG: Self-Portrait in December*. *JLG/JLG* is declaredly a self-portrait; hence, a film whose pact with the viewer is that it offers a truthful self-representation of the director.[12] Such a pact is confirmed by the audiovisual presence of Godard in the film. As Nora M. Alter suggests, 'The overlapping of the iconic presence of Godard (as author/director/actor) with an aural track of speech indexically pointing to the author/director induces the spectator/reader/listener to (mis)believe the veracity of the autobiographical claim: We see and hear him, ergo the information presented must be true' (2000: 79). And, indeed, we mis/believe, as Godard himself keeps attracting our attention to the rift between the man and his representation. As he once says in the film, we live in language, and

> When we express ourselves we say more than we want to. We think we express the individual but we speak the universal. 'I am cold.' It is I who say I am cold, but it is not I who am heard. I disappear between these two moments of speech. All that remains of me is the man who is cold, and this man belongs to everyone.[13]

Interestingly, during Godard's recitation of this passage, we can read on his notebook, which is shown throughout the film, 'I am a legend'. If all that remains of Godard is the man who is a legend, and who belongs to everyone, one is prompted to wonder whether this is the core of Godard's self-representation in this film (and in all his autobiographical films).

More often than not, Godard frames himself in a dim light, or even in semi-darkness, with the camera positioned either behind him or at his side; when he is shot in daylight, the camera is always placed at some distance. His image, therefore, remains intact, almost ungraspable, only alluded to – as that of a man who disappears between the moment of the utterance and the moment of reception; or, perhaps, that of a legend. Godard may here be constructing his own artistic immortality: towards the end of the film, he announces: 'If there is any truth in the mouth of the poets, I shall live.'[14] Alter comments: '*JLG/JLG* threatens to become a traditional creation or insurance of Godard's own immortality' (2000: 88). Several commentators, indeed, were critical of the film and its self-pitying tone, and especially of its ending; Jacques Morice, for instance, has argued that 'the language of sacrifice in the film implies a desire for sainthood or martyrdom on Godard's part' (quoted in Morrey 2004: 207).

Other critics presented textual evidence against this interpretation, at the aim of saving Godard from the accusations of immodesty. Before I review their arguments, and add my own, I should say that I see no contradiction whatsoever between the impulses to self-effacing and to self-celebration, which actually coexist in the film. Self-portraiture is, by default, an immodest act. The drive to produce a representation of one's self is always related to questions of self-promotion, self-fashioning and self-celebration. Godard is too familiar with the history of art to ignore this fact and this tradition, and to believe that it is possible to produce a thoroughly modest self-portrait.

Morrey proposes that 'if Godard's body is largely absent from his self-portrait, it is precisely because he seeks to avoid the perils of self-mythologising by constantly questioning the possibility of self-representation' (ibid.). Indeed, Godard's body does not claim any representational priority over other objects in the frame, and is often sidelined or only partly visible. Furthermore, his performance is rather parodic; throughout the film, Godard 'plays up the notion of the eccentric hermit, exaggerating his "autism" through incoherent mumbles and grumpy growls' (Morrey 2004: 208). Marie-François Grange noticed that he plays the misunderstood and bankrupt genius in the scenes with his blind assistant editor (in Morrey 2004: 208). We should add that he plays other parodic roles, for instance those of the misogynist and/or old fool, who cannot remember the name of his cleaning lady; and of the old womaniser with Cassandra, a scantily- dressed young woman from the 'Cinema Centre Inspectors', whom he pushes away, placing his hand on her rear.

Most importantly, as Morrey notices, 'the (often rather wooden, perhaps deliberately so?) acting of his fellow players serves to underline a sense of Godard's identity as performance. Indeed, in the opening shots of the film, over a photograph of the director as a boy, Godard describes the assumption of identity as a process of learning a role by heart' (2004: 209). The performances are, without a doubt, deliberately 'wooden' – or should we say Brechtian; and presentational, as is so typical of Godard's cinema. It is useful to transcribe the whole passage to which Morrey refers, a passage that is whispered by Godard in an 'I' voice, recorded very close to the microphone and with no reverb, thus producing a sensation of intimacy, of zero distance between the voice and our ear:

> Cast the roles, start the rehearsals, settle the problems concerning *mise-en-scène*, perfect the entrances and exits, learn your lines by heart, work to improve your acting, get under the skin of your character, have the role of ... do

a rehearsal or the final dress rehearsal, do the opening night, be – as the case may be – a success, a triumph, or on the contrary a failure, a flop.

The suspension coincides with a shot of a blown-up picture of Godard as a young boy. This passage produces several layers of meaning. It does refer, as Morrey suggests, to the boy's assumption of an identity; but also to Godard himself as an actor, who is about to take up the role of JLG; and to Godard as a director, who has to take care of the actors (including himself), *mise-en-scène*, opening night and public assessment. Hence, the passage suggests that Godard is aware (and we should be too) that each identity is constructed and performed; that Godard's own identity, which will be investigated in the film, is that of the Director, the Maestro, who is the origin of the entire filmic discourse, from planning to direction to the presentation to the public; and that his self-portrayal in this film (as well as in life) can only be a performance. Indeed, Godard's whisper is deep and studied, so much so that Kaja Silverman rightly describes it as 'an actor's exaggerated breathing' (2001: 18).

In her analysis of the film, Silverman shows how the 'authorial identity' established by the opening sequence is immediately undermined and problematised by the subsequent voice-over, which changes tone, becomes 'orphic' and relegates the authorial role to the youthful self. Silverman goes on to successfully demonstrate how Godard in his film ponders the meaning of his own authorship, metaphorically tries to kill himself as author, and describes himself instead as receiver (of images and words), as well as a mirror that reflects what is projected onto him. However, she also shows how Godard is ultimately unable to commit authorial suicide; and claims that the death of the author is 'better understood as an ongoing process than as a realisable event' (2001: 34). Silverman's analysis is, in my opinion, correct; but there is even more in the film, there are even more Godards. We could say that Godard's identity is expressed in his film as 'a fiction in process, as a fictionalising of the self', and that *JLG/JLG* offers us 'a continual circulation or variation' of selves (Dior, quoted in Morrey 2004: 209). Indeed, the film's title itself, *JLG/JLG*, as I have already noted, suggests the multiplicity of the I. My argument is that this multiplicity is negotiated by filmmaker and spectator through performance – it is Godard's performance of different roles and the differentiation of the acting registers which materialise and articulate the possibility of different identities, while also reflecting the conception that identity ultimately consists of role-playing.

This method becomes, if possible, even more evident in the essay film *Notre musique*, which employs an ample spectrum of performances. Communicative negotiation is, I will argue below, both *Notre musique*'s subject matter and its textual strategy. It is through performance, or the variation in registers of acting performances, that the film's ethos of unreserved openness and instability is fully realised, and comes to fruition for its embodied spectator. Written and directed by Godard, with art direction by Anne-Marie Miéville, *Notre musique* was first presented at the 57th Cannes Film Festival.

Notre musique: performance and negotiation

At the onset of my discussion of *Notre musique*, I wish to devote some attention to its categorisation as essay. Because it is such an unorthodox work, *Notre musique* allows me to further refine, as well as challenge, my definition of essay film. Indeed, one is tempted to see Godard's film as a fiction with essayistic moments; this is because there are several imaginary characters, which are central to the story, as well as a rather recognisable plot, which is framed within a tripartite, Dantesque organisation of the subject matter. However, I argue that *Notre musique*, similarly to Marker's docufictional *Level Five*, complies with all the requirements of the form, thus showing not only how generic hybridism is indeed a marker of the essay film, but also how the presence of fictive elements does not impinge on the communication of an essayistic argument.

'Hell' is a ruthless ten-minute archival montage of fictional and documentary images of war, death and destruction. Partly reminiscent of *Histoire(s) du cinéma*,[15] it boldly mixes fragments of newsreels, war documentaries, essays like Resnais' *Night and Fog*, and feature films as diverse as *Bronenosets Potyomkin* (*Battleship Potemkin*, 1925), *Aleksandr Nevskiy* (*Alexander Nevsky*, 1938), *Les Anges du peché* (*Angels of the Streets*, 1943), *Fort Apache* (1948), *Kiss Me Deadly* (1955), *Zulu* (1964) and *Apocalypse Now* (1979). In 'Purgatory', the most extended and most complex section of the film (as is typical of painted triptychs), Jean-Luc Godard arrives in postwar Sarajevo to lecture on 'The Text and the Image' at the European Literary Encounters, where he will meet a number of noted authors and artists. Two young women also attend: Judith Lerner (Sarah Adler), an Israeli journalist from Tel Aviv, and Olga Brodsky (Nade Dieu), a Jewish Israeli of Russian origin, both of whom are wrestling with the Israeli-Palestinian crisis. Judith, who has come to see a place where 'reconciliation is possible', tries to arrange an interview with Olivier Naville (Simon Eine), a French ambassador who gave shelter to her grandparents in Vichy France in 1943, and asks him to comment on the Israeli-Palestinian conflict from the point of view of his past resistance to the Nazis. She then interviews Palestinian poet Mahmoud Darwich, who argues, referring to the Israelis, that 'The world cares about you, not about us; you've brought us defeat and renown'. Olga attends Godard's lecture; she visits the collapsed Mostar Bridge; and talks to her uncle, translator Ramos Garcia (Rony Kramer), about suicide. The Encounters are over; somebody delivers to

Godard Olga's DVD of his masterclass. Back at home, some time later, Godard receives a phone call from Ramos, informing him that Olga, who threatened to blow herself up in the name of peace in a cinema in Jerusalem, was shot down by a marksman; however, as it turned out, she only carried books and not a bomb in her bag. In 'Paradise', Olga arrives on the shores of a lake, guarded by US marines. She walks by some young people, sits next to one of them, and shares an apple with him.

This outline of the film's plot is, to an extent, deceptive, not only because it does not fully account for the film's richness (many are the characters and situations I did not describe, and will not have the opportunity to discuss below), or for its fragmentation, which undermines the wholeness and teleology of the plot; but also because it does not reflect the film's documentary drive, which is an essential feature of *Notre musique*. I refer not only to the filming of Sarajevo, which, as Ginette Vincendeau noticed, demonstrates the director's 'prescience and talent to document key places at key moments' (2005: 70), and for Michael Witt is 'at times strongly reminiscent of Rossellini's *Germany Year Zero*' (2005: 28); or to the presence of real-life figures (including Mahmoud Darwich, Spanish author Juan Goytisolo and French authors Pierre Bergounioux and Jean-Paul Curnier); but also to many elements of the fictional plot itself. For instance, the European Literary Encounters are an event 'organised annually since 2000 by the André Malraux Cultural Centre in Sarajevo, in which Godard took part in 2002' (Witt 2005: 28), with a masterclass on the same topic as the lecture in *Notre musique*; in the staged interview of Mahmoud Darwish by Judith, 'he repeats his own lines from a real interview with an Israeli journalist' (2005: 29); Juan Goytisolo recites lines from his own poem about the revelation of the 'better fate' of the dead, and Mahmoud Darwich's texts are quoted by other characters;[16] when she visits the Mostar Bridge, Olga meets architect Gilles Pecqueux, who was at the time supervising the rebuilding of the bridge (which, however, was never realised), and who talks to her about the meaning of the restoration. These and other elements, although mixed with and somehow disguised by the fiction, are of actual documentary nature, in so far as they are re-enactments of factual events and people. There also are several instances in which the camera purely captures the presence of shelled buildings, the beauty of Sarajevo at night, the bustle in a market at daytime or, simply, trams passing by.[17]

Stylistic eclecticism and the attitude of frequently crossing the border between fiction, documentary and experimental filmmaking are characteristics of the essay film, and *Notre musique* truly confounds boundaries. An even more emblematic feature is the direct address to the audience, and the establishment of a dialogue between filmmaker and spectator. In terms of direct address, a female voice-over in 'Hell' utters a sparse, poetic text, adapted from Montesquieu's

De l'esprit de lois: 'And so, in the age of fable, there appeared on earth men armed for extermination.'[18] That Godard feels the need to use a voice-over in the only segment devoid of his actors, of narrators who can address the audience on his account, is significant of his desire to communicate with the spectator. In *Notre musique*, indeed, many are the instances of overt or partly disguised direct address. In 'Purgatory', several characters appear to be speaking to themselves, and of course to the audience. Examples occur in the segment set in the Sarajevo library; or when Olga looks directly into the lens for several seconds, all noise disappears, including her voice, and on her lips we read what seems to be the French equivalent of the exclamation: 'I don't give a damn!'

The most obvious and relevant example of direct address is Godard's own performance at his masterclass, in which he lectures to a public of young people, the representatives of the real audience in the text. This sequence ends with a close-up of Godard's face in semi-darkness, staring speechless into the lens, and into the spectator's eyes. In the rest of the episode, the characters' lines are very often literary or philosophical quotations; because they are taken out of their contexts – and do not always receive replies from other characters – they function as open questions that are ultimately addressed to the spectator. The spectator is, therefore, constantly urged to listen, reflect and respond, both emotionally and intellectually, to a text that opens and never solves problems, that incessantly formulates questions dialectically. Indeed, the entire film is built on dialectical oppositions: death/life, darkness/light, real/imaginary, people who act/people who tell

Godard's lecture in *Notre musique*: shot/reverse-shot

stories, criminals/victims and, as Godard argues in his lecture, shot/reverse-shot.

Taking this structure one step further, to its ultimate consequence, one should add the binary director/spectator. The spectator is situated by the film in a dialectical position to the director's, as his other, and is therefore asked to answer the questions raised by Godard, and actively participate in the creation of filmic meaning.[19] This is in keeping with Godard's self-positioning in *JLG/JLG* as spectator, reader, receiver, as well as a mirror who reflects back that which he received, as we saw above (see also Silverman 2001). The mirroring, the 'stereo', as Godard defines this structure in *JLG/JLG*, also takes place between director and spectator; Godard, after all, said just this when he stated in an interview that 'The camera is the true reverse-shot of the projector' (in Frodon 2004b: 21; author's translation) – and the subject who films is the reverse-shot of the subject who views. It is, after all, the recognition of the reciprocity of all communication:

> The distribution of roles in the enunciation as described by Benveniste is not merely a system of social rules; it is found in every use of language. Every speaker bears within him two polarities, that of sender and receiver and that of enunciation and statement. He rests on a scission. Or, rather, he does not 'rest' (implying a paradoxical stability); he functions by virtue of this schism. 'The individual is a dialogue', Valéry used to say. Communication is thus a 'dialogue of dialogues'. (Lejeune 1977: 30)

Communication and the address to the spectator become the film's very textual strategy. *Notre musique* not only places dialogue (between factions, between people, between different political or theoretical positions) at its narrative and philosophical core, but also postulates the dialogue between filmmaker and spectator as its main goal and subject matter. This is immediately established by the film's very title which, with its allusion to 'us' and its appeal to common, shared ground ('our music'), summons the spectator and asks him or her to feel bound to the subject behind the camera. Such a desire for a close relationship was confirmed by Godard himself, when he ironically commented: 'There was a time when we said we made films for 200,000 potential friends; today that number would certainly be lower' (in Frodon 2004b: 22; author's translation).

A further, constitutive feature of the essay film is that it must introduce and muse about a philosophical problem or set of problems and, once again, it is easy to see how *Notre musique* fulfils this requirement; it does so not only through narrative material and the characters' philosophising, but also linguistically, by means of montage. Rather than producing a seamless, sutured text, Godard relentlessly disjoints the binary elements of cinematic language – shot and reverse-shot, image and counter-image – letting meanings clash and emerge from oppositions.[20] In Godard's own words, the rapprochement of two images 'provokes a question or introduces another response in the form of a question, so that we don't just say the same things over and over again' (in Witt 2005: 30). The intellectual probing is articulated through antitheses, which shape the film's macrostructure itself – hell and purgatory, purgatory and paradise, hell and paradise. *Notre musique* is simultaneously philosophy *through* the cinema and *of* the cinema, because the clashing is also linguistic: 'Hell' is a rhythmic montage of relatively short shots, 'Paradise' proceeds through observational, slow tracking shots, while 'Purgatory' is stylistically eclectic. Elements of the concepts that are verbally introduced by the characters are also split and made to collide: 'We consider death two ways: the impossible of the possible and the possible of the impossible'; 'Killing a man to defend an idea is not defending an idea. It's killing a man'; 'Not a just conversation, just a conversation'. It is Godard himself who clarifies this methodology of thought and connects it to the language of cinema. In his lecture, in fact, he discusses the shot/reverse-shot structure: truth has two faces – Vichy France and French Jews; Nazi Germany and Israel; Israel and Palestine. The film calls for transition, meeting, dialogue and reconciliation: languages (French, Spanish, Hebrew, Serbo-Croatian, Arabic and English) are constantly translated for the characters, and for us; all characters speak more than one language; intellectual exchange between people from different backgrounds is achieved; the planned reconstruction of Mostar's destroyed Old Bridge has obvious symbolic meanings, which are implicit in its ability to link not only people, but also ideas and instances in time.

The accent is placed on the structure of exchange itself, and on the difficulty of the process; the key topic of *Notre musique* is, in other words, communicative negotiation. In Francesco Casetti's definition, communicative negotiation, 'the process through which every addressee personalises the sense of what is being communicated, makes it his own' (2002b: 18), is less about reaching an agreement, a compromise between the parties involved – something which would ultimately result in a 'closing down' of the meaning – and more about establishing a framework for communication. *Notre musique* does just this: it explores frameworks for communication; not for nothing is it set in public places, the vast majority of which are sites of movement, mixing, exchange and encounter – an international airport, a taxi, an embassy, a hotel hall, a library, a street market, a conference room, a bridge. The film, however, not only talks of social, political, philosophical, literary and emotional communication, and proposes more or less successful instances of it in a setting encouraging reconciliation (postwar Sarajevo), and within a situation propitious to inter-cultural exchange (the Literary Encounters). It is also, as I already argued, an essay film that creates the conditions of its own communicative negotiation, and takes it as its subject matter as well as textual strategy.

Casetti rightly noted that the notion of negotiation allows us to think of the filmic text, on the one hand, as containing a series of proposals that the addressee relates to and transforms into resources ('opportunities for information, entertainment, strengthening of current relationships, definition of identities') and, on the other, as a terrain within which the encounter with the addressee is 'already prefigured and outlined' (2002b: 19). Overflowing with resources that can be appropriated by the audience, *Notre musique* also sets up the rules of its own encounter and exchange with the spectator, as I have argued above. What I will suggest below is that it is through the actors' performances that the spectator negotiates with the film's meanings and structure. This happens in the central instalment, 'Purgatory'; 'Hell', indeed, is the absence, the negation of communication (which is replaced by violence), and 'Paradise' is the overcoming of the need for (the purgatory of) negotiation, and its replacement with effortless communication, one that does not need any words (the segment is completely devoid of dialogue).

Godard could have chosen to philosophise directly on communicative negotiation (for instance, by means of voice-over, which he is never shy of using), or else to make his argument exclusively through montage, or via a combination of the two. However, he prefers to enact it. The meaning of this choice is self-evident: negotiation is a performance. Indeed, the extreme fragmentation and diversity of 'Purgatory' correspond to a differentiation in the types of performance. The variations in acting style and rhetorical structure are bewildering, and coexist within a segment that now adopts an (almost) traditional fictional approach, now an anti-realist, even grotesque tone, now a documentary eye. 'Purgatory' begins with a dialogue between two actors (a representational performance, which sets the tone of a fiction film); moves on to a piece of anti-realist theatre (the sequence in the semi-destroyed library, an intensely presentational performance that summons the spectator on a Brechtian stage traversed by poets, translators, children and Native Americans in traditional costumes); then to an interview (presentational); a lecture (presentational); and finally a series of dialogues (representational). Further complications, even within the same sequence, are numerous. Take the interview with Darwich, which is ostensibly a fictional moment, for the interviewer is a character in the fiction, but whose presentational nature is highlighted by the status as social actor of the interviewee, a writer playing himself; and, especially, by a woman who, after introducing Judith to Darwich, exclaims in English: 'Ok folks, it's your play', and signals to somebody to start filming – a cameraman subsequently appears behind Darwich.

Godard's desire to cover all types of performance that enact communication is evident: dialogue, monologue, interview and lecture are all forms of address between two subjects, for they all imply a subject who talks to another, even if at times an absent one (for instance the monologue, which is nevertheless always in-

The semi-destroyed Sarajevo library in *Notre musique*: a Brechtian stage

tended for an audience). Godard sets up all these forms as dialectical, open questions, as interpellations that solicit an answer, one which is not proposed and is, therefore, allowed to emerge somewhere else, namely in the position occupied by the spectator.[21] *Notre musique*'s various performers site the spectator as receiver of a series of questions, interpellations or stimuli; the lack of answers in the film places the spectator in an empty, free position. Because it is genuinely empty, and not filled with prearranged meanings and responses, this space is in the singular – no uniform/prevalent spectatorial position is prearranged by *Notre musique*. The film constantly emphasises that essayistic communicative negotiation is a structure based on the interaction between two embodied subjects, and that the receiver's response is, therefore, open and unpredictable; it is the product of the

negotiation of a single, embodied individual with the text. Godard takes care to reinforce this concept verbally: the French ambassador tells Judith that, while the dream of the State is to be one, the dream of the individual is to be two. This line not only draws attention to the political (resistant, revolutionary) implications of dialogue, but also to the fact that the 'us' in *Notre musique* is formed by an 'I' and a 'you', the filmmaker/essayist and the spectator, real partners engaged in communicative negotiation.

A genuinely free position: a place for the spectator at the table of Godard's film

It is of particular relevance that Godard in his self-representation privileges the lecturer over the filmmaker. In his review of *Notre musique*, Jean-Michel Frodon has suggested: 'There is Jean-Luc Godard as the teacher, one of the film's characters who, like the others, brings his own background and identity to the role, but there is also, though not exactly in the same style, Jean-Luc Godard the filmmaker' (2004a: 18; author's translation). For Frodon, Godard the director emerges from certain statements made by various characters. While this is certainly true, I wish to focus on Godard the character, played by Godard the filmmaker. His choice to lecture, to be a performer before an audience, a speaker engaged in a situation of communicative negotiation, rather than a director behind a camera,[22] is important – so much so that his masterclass is placed almost exactly at the central point of 'Purgatory', and of the entire film. This is not to say that Godard takes his performance very seriously, and shows no self-irony in it; indeed, the opposite is true. Humorously, many of his young listeners shortly lose interest; they begin to shuffle in their chairs, to talk and giggle, or even laugh out loud at a time when a joke was not made – it is not exactly the image of an absorbed public. It is a representation that, once again, draws attention to the fact that communication, especially of a reflective text, is not a straightforward act, but the result of a (difficult) process of negotiation for each single receiver with the text. This negotiation is personal, and may or may not be successful.

When, at the end of the class, one of the attendees asks him whether he thinks that new DV cameras will save cinema, Godard disengages; he remains silent, his perplexed face, half-hidden in the semi-darkness, staring in the void for long seconds, until the audience is heard leaving in the offscreen space. The sequence amounts to a gag on Godard's well-known opinions on the importance of watching films in 35mm and on the death of cinema; on his gruffness; and on his disconnection from young audiences. I argue, however, that to simply note the self-irony in this sequence, as many reviewers have done, is not to say very much, and it is certainly to say too little. The sequence is significantly more important than a gag, or an instance of self-awareness. Jean-Luc Godard is here as himself, the world-famous director and intellectual whose opinions have international resonance; at the same time, he is playing (and playing with) his stereotypical and media-constructed persona, while also attracting our attention to the rift between the two representations, by means of the dimness of the lighting. He is doing, actually, even more: he is performing the ethos of his film. My point is that, had he answered the question, he would have closed down the dialogue. There would only have been one speaker here, the one with not only all the questions, but also all the (right) answers. Faithful to the content of his lecture, and to the rhetorical structure of his entire film, he chooses instead to let the question hang;

he wilfully does not fill the void, does not close the space, or framework of negotiation, opened up – through his performance – by his act of communication.

At the end of 'Purgatory', we learn that communication has, indeed, taken place. At least one of the attendees, Olga, did engage with Godard's lecture, and responded to it, so much so that she made a digital video (a pun? or recognition of the inevitability of change?), which she then asked somebody to deliver to Godard. The video, somehow inspired by Godard's lecture – by Godard's film – testifies to the fact that she has made the text her own: the cover of the DVD is significantly decorated by a picture of her face and not of Godard's; and her film is entitled *Notre musique*. As a model receiver in a communicative situation, she negotiated the meaning, and went through the difficult process of making the object of communication her own.

This, however, ultimately proves that the essay film is a performative, highly open and unstable form, and that it produces unpredictable results, which depend on the embodied receiver's idiosyncratic and independent process of appropriation of the text. It also proves that *Notre musique*, hailed by most reviewers as an optimistic film (with some surprise and relief, given Godard's generally bleak take on contemporary society), is a far less hopeful text than it has generally been depicted. If Olga's final choice of self-demise was in any way precipitated by Godard's lecture, we know for sure that he did not wilfully urge his young audience to suicide. *Notre musique* might include some instances of optimism, but is also framed in between the hell of large-scale, indiscriminate and unwarranted death and suffering, and a paradise guarded by armed marines, and containing exclusively young people, who are probably happier here than they have ever been on earth (is this Dante's circle of the 'violent against themselves', although relocated to Paradise?).

It is significant that Godard's character does not, and probably never will, watch Olga's film; conceivably suggesting that, in the particular communicative negotiation between essayist director and spectator, it is the spectator who has the last word – the director only asks questions. And, perhaps, he does not even know exactly what questions he has asked. When the French Ambassador enquires of his former classmate, author Pierre Bergounioux, whether writers know what they are talking about, 'No. Of course not' is his answer. Bergounioux adds that people who act do not have the ability to express themselves adequately about what they do; and, conversely, those who tell stories do not know what they are talking about. Asked in an interview whether all shot/reverse-shots are fecund, once again Godard chose not to fill the space of the embodied receiver and, meaningfully, answered: 'I do not know! I only pose the question' (Godard in Frodon 2004b: 20; author's translation).

part two | **personal cinema**

chapter five
FIRST-PERSON FILMMAKING:
HISTORY, THEORY, PRACTICES

'The film is like a diary, a notebook, or the monologue of someone who seeks, just as one does before a lawyer or a psychiatrist, to justify him or herself in front of a camera that is almost accusing.' (Godard 1985: 221; author's translation)

The films that will be explored in the second section of this study are best seen as belonging to the field of essayistic cinema; they should, however, be considered as distinct from the essay film proper. One of the reasons for this distinction is their obvious autobiographical content. Whereas essay films are necessarily subjective and personal, but may not be autobiographical, diaries, notebooks, travelogues, letters and self-portraits always are, though not necessarily with the same degree of intensity.

Their autobiographical nature is key to an understanding of these forms. As will become clear in the course of my discussion, while the representation and performance of the self are pertinent to all the films examined in the previous section of the book, they are even more decidedly relevant to the ones that will be investigated in the following chapters. In these films, the author often becomes the true hero of the text, and its focal point; everything is overtly filtered through his or her sensibility and point of view, to the extent that, at times, the films compellingly approximate the confessional style. They are, indeed, more decidedly private than essay films are; and, for this reason, they are also more ephemeral – so much so that some of them were not originally meant for theatrical release, but were intended for exclusively personal use.[1] Their foregrounding of autobiography and their expression of authorial subjectivity position them in between three traditions: that of the personal cinema of the avant-gardes; that of auteur and art cinema; and that of the first-person documentary.

Although examples can be traced in other filmic traditions, diaries, notebooks and self-portraits are forms of personal filmmaking that prospered in the domain of the avant-garde, independent and experimental cinema of the late 1960s and 1970s, especially in North America. This cinema, often overlapping with the home movie, was characterised by a strong autobiographical vein, and placed the author at the centre of textual concerns. Noteworthy examples of this approach include the work of Andy Warhol, which reaches peaks of first-person expression in films such as the lost *The Andy Warhol Story* (1967); the auto-biographical and introspective cinema of Maya Deren; films by Stan Brakhage, with telling titles such as *An Avant-Garde Home Movie* (1962); *Sincerity I* (1973); *Sincerity II* (1975); *Sincerity III* (1978); *Sincerity V* (1980) and *Confession* (1986); Jonas Mekas's diaries;[2] or, again, Carolee Schneemann's autobiographical trilogy, *Fuses* (1967), *Plumb Line* (1971) and *Kitch's Last Meal* (1978).

The second tradition to which these films relate is the first-person documentary. With this expression I refer to autobiographical nonfiction in which the director comes to the fore and places himself or herself at the centre of attention; documentaries that foreground their director's life, experiences or body. One of the outcomes of the avant-garde and political autobiographical cinema that emerged around 1968 was a movement of autobiographical documentary, which 'rejected the myth of the objective camera of US Direct Cinema and endorsed a politics of experience. The majority of these documentarists have produced their films in the United States, where the most complex development of the autobiographical documentary has occurred' (Lane 1996: 38). For Jim Lane, this movement was influenced by the autobiographical nature of the American avant-garde, by reflexive European films, such as those of Godard and Rouch, and by a reaction against the observational documentary of direct cinema (see Lane 2002: 11–12). Examples include, among many others, the films of Ross McElwee, per-haps the most prominent representative of this tradition, with *Charleen* (1980), *Backyard* (1984), *Sherman's March* (1986), *Six O'Clock News* (1996) and *Bright Leaves* (2003). The first-person documentary has been studied not only in dedicated scholarly works (see Katz 1978; Lane 2002; Renov 2004) and in histories of documentary cinema, but also from within critical discourses on specific historical embodiments of nonfiction. The first-person documentary, in fact, is often linked to ethnographic nonfictional practices and to counter-cinema (third, feminist and diasporic).

Indeed, biography and autobiography are important and often-debated aspects of ethnographic work, and ethnography, as is well known, frequently crossed paths with filmmaking. The adjective 'ethnographic' has also been used as a synonym of autobiographical nonfiction cinema. Catherine Russell notes that the ethnographic mode of self-representation is pervasive in the 'new au-tobiography' in film and video, and argues that a first-person film or video that explores not only the immediate subjectivity of its maker, but also his or her implication in social and historical discourses, is ethnographic:

> Autobiography becomes ethnographic at the point where the film- or video-maker understands his or her personal history to be implicated in larger social formations and historical processes. Identity is no longer a transcendental or essential self that is revealed, but a 'staging of subjectivity' – a representation of the self as a performance. In the politicisation of the personal, identities are frequently played out among several cultural discourses, be they ethnic, national, sexual, racial, and/or class based. (1999: 276)

It is important to note that, although being expressions of the first-person documentary, the cinematic forms I set out to explore resist being fully assimilated into it; in fact, they deeply challenge the documentary format. They confound the conventions of documentaries that replicate the structures of fiction, and 'present' reality in narrative ways; these films take non-narrative forms as their models.[3] They are, therefore, interstitial and experimental; and, like the essay film, they refer to pre-existing artistic practices, relating to the fields of literature (and of paraliterature) and the fine arts. While it is true that much cinema pays homage to and finds inspiration in literature especially, these are not, however, forms of adaptation, but filmic appropriations of the textual structures and discourses first introduced and developed by other arts.

The third tradition to which these films relate is that of the art film, as it developed in Europe especially in the 1960s, at a time when the filmmaker 'became' an auteur, took up a central position in both textual and extra-textual discourses and, reconnecting to the experiences of the historic avant-gardes, as well as learning from the novelties introduced by Italian neorealism, attempted to produce a personal, private, idiosyncratic vision of the world.

The rationale to include these cinematic forms in a study of essayistic cinema is, thus, their belonging to a first-person, authorial and experimental tradition which engages with rhetorical structures and discourses of a literary or fine-arts nature, and in which the camera is used 'as a pen' (or a paintbrush) to produce a personal and reflective discourse. As in the essay, strong enunciators, who overtly identify with the extra-textual authors, and who speak in the first person, characterise these films. Each of these forms is, however, quite distinct, for it employs particular rhetorical structures to articulate the relationship between enunciator, text and audience. In general, and unlike the essay, they do not seek a one-to-one dialogue with an embodied spectator, but fashion themselves as private monologues (or, better, as dialogues with the self, or with an intimate partner), and thus only allow the spectator in as an overseeing and overhearing third party. As will become clear from my study, however, this monologic, self-centred structure always hides a dialogical attitude, which seeks the relationship with an audience.

Having already engaged with questions of filmic autobiography and of filmic subjectivity in the introduction , and with the history and theory of the essay film in chapter one, I now wish to briefly explore some of the theoretical roots of the personal cinema that is in focus in the second section of this study. While each of the three ensuing chapters will offer an in-depth engagement with the theory and practice of the diary, the notebook and the self-portrait respectively, both in film and in other arts, here I want to concisely examine the emergence of ideas around and about first-person cinema.

Special attention will be paid to early theories of film connected to French cinematic impressionism, to Cesare Zavattini's ideas of a cinema in the first-person, and to Pier Paolo Pasolini's theorisation of a cinema of poetry. Of course, other instances of the history of film theory could be considered here, and especially the writings of practitioners of avant-garde film and of ethnographic cinema (for instance, the surrealists, Rouch and Mekas). It seems to me, however, that these three theoretical gestures are essential to an understanding of the emergence of first-person practices. French theorists such as Ricciotto Canudo, Louis Delluc and Germaine Dullac introduced the concept of the expression of subjectivity in film; Zavattini pioneered the idea of an autobiographical documentary cinema; and Pasolini produced an early attempt at theorising an ideology of a personal and subjective use of the camera in art film.

The roots of first-person filmmaking: at the intersection of counter-cinema, avant-garde and auteur film

The contemporary phenomenon of exponential growth of personal expression in film and, especially, in video, is exemplified by the success of television auto-documentaries (for instance, the BBC series *Video Diaries* (1990–92) and *Video Nation* (1999)) and by the increase in the 'personalisation' of television, with reality programmes that offer the audience the impression of watching somebody's real life in real time. More relevantly, this phenomenon finds full expression not only in the increased production and importance of first-person documentaries made for the cinema and for television, but also in the boom of autobiographical videomaking, of personal blogs, including video blogs (or vlogs), and of candid cameras, new forms of digital expression that frequently display strong autobiographical content, and whose distribution is made possible by the Internet. The homepage of Vidblog.com, an online portal and community of videobloggers, thus welcomes its visitors:

A video blog is the new hot way for people to stick their personal lives on the internet! Not just simple words, static pictures, or grainy audio. They invite you to join them where-ever they go; meet their friends, their family, go on vacation, fall in love, and all vicariously from the comfort of your home computer.[4]

The tagline of YouTube, the popular portal that, in its creators' words, 'is empowering [people] to become the broadcasters of tomorrow',[5] is – tellingly – 'Broadcast Yourself'.

Although video blogging was made possible by the spread of digital cameras in terms of production, and by podcasting as regards distribution,[6] its origins, at least at the level of precognition, are to be found in the personal cinema championed by the European new waves. Unsurprisingly, videobloggers frequently cite François Truffaut's famous 1957 visionary passage:

The film of tomorrow appears to me as even more personal than an individual and autobiographical novel, like a confession, or a diary. The young filmmakers will express themselves in the first person and will relate what has happened to them. It may be the story of their first love or their most recent; of their political awakening; the story of a trip, a sickness, their military service, their marriage, their last vacation … and it will be enjoyable because it will be true, and new … The film of tomorrow will not be directed by civil servants of the camera, but by artists for whom shooting a film constitutes a wonderful and thrilling adventure. The film of tomorrow will resemble the person who made it, and the number of spectators will be proportional to the number of friends the director has. The film of tomorrow will be an act of love. (1987: 25).[7]

As I have suggested when discussing the history of the essay film, ideas on a personal and subjective use of the camera emerge very early in some strands of European film theory.[8] In 1920s France, intellectuals and artists influenced by poetic impressionism and by naturalism, such as Delluc, Dullac and Canudo, urged filmmakers to transform reality according to the image of their dreams, and to access the secrets of inner life (see Agel 1971: 9). These ideas accompanied and mirrored the development of a poetic, avant-garde and authorial cinema that, in the field of nonfiction, found expression in French modernist documentary filmmaking, with films such as Alberto Cavalcanti's *Rien que les heures* and Jean Vigo's *À propos de Nice*. These texts both evoked a poetic reality, and concerned themselves with the expression of subjectivity. The interest of this moment in the history of film theory, in view of an understanding of first-person cinema, resides in its nature as an early attempt to describe the articulation of subjectivity in film. While the subjectivity talked about by these theorists clearly belonged to characters, its expression was nevertheless seen to be mediated and conjured by the sensibility of the filmmaker, who was presented as a true auteur:

> The neo-symbolist conception of film art which characterised impression-ism privileged the importance of the artist's vision and imagination, and the impressionists believed that, for film to evolve into a genuine art form, the filmmaker must transform the material reality before him or her in some rev-elatory fashion. (Aitken 2001: 81)

While aiming to strengthen the credentials of the new art, which was still fight-ing for recognition, these theories opened up the possibility of an authorial, idi-osyncratic and highly subjective use of the camera, both in fiction and in nonfic-tion cinema.

The most lucid and assertive early prediction of the private cinema to come is, however, to be found three decades later, in Cesare Zavattini's theories, as well as in some of his practical experiments.[9] Best known as a theorist of Ital-ian neorealism, as well as the author of many neorealist screenplays, in writ-ings spanning from the early 1950s throughout the 1960s Zavattini developed pioneering and radical ideas on the need and opportunity to use the camera for a personal, autobiographical, first-person cinema. His interest in the expression of the filmmaker's subjectivity may appear to be in contrast with his faith in the absolute objectivity of the lens, and in the cinema's ability to record reality, which finds expression in passages such as the following, originally written in 1951: 'The cinema has by now come to represent an almost scientific contribution to our knowledge of life' (1979c: 83; author's translation). Nevertheless, for Zavat-tini the technology is never independent of the filmmaker; the 'subject behind the camera' is, indeed, central to the discourse of the cinema: 'The story will be replaced by man in his entirety, ready, and at the same time disarmed before the facts, like a reporter,' he wrote in 1950 (1979b: 75; author's translation). This centrality translates into a decidedly autobiographical and first-person concep-tion of the cinema: 'We should not talk on behalf of others, but in the name of ourselves ... For this reason I believe that it is actually necessary to be autobio-graphical, that it is necessary to use the first person' (quoted in Fortichiari 1992: 66; author's translation). It is a cinema that directly engages with reality, to the extent that it comes very close to reportage, as well as to counter-cinema.

At 66 years of age, Zavattini led the filmmakers' protest at the 1968 Venice Film Festival, and invoked a cultural festival free of the conditioning of the mar-ket. In the same year he set up the *Cinegiornali liberi* (Free Newsreels), which followed his own *Cinegiornali della pace* (Peace Newsreel) of 1963. The *Free Newsreels* fulfilled the prophecy of a cinema made by ordinary people in total freedom, using lightweight and inexpensive technology, and apt to communicate its makers' personal thoughts and opinions, as well as to document events big and small. This was, for Zavattini, a way to continue and to perfect the unfinished project of Italian neorealism; but this intuition long preceded 1968. In interviews and writings of the early 1950s, for instance, Zavattini stated in 1950, thus anticipating Truffaut:

> The camera must be placed in the hands of young people; the camera, I said, not a screenplay. And these young people, as they come out of their homes, must report everything they see, anything that strikes them. Some will film people; some just windows; others will turn the camera onto themselves. (1979a: 71–2; author's translation)

While deriving from the sphere of influence of neorealism, Zavattini's contribution moves beyond it. His conception of first-person cinema is shaped simultaneously by the exigencies of the autobiographical and the political. These influencing factors combined to produce a counter-cinema that places the director at its centre, and makes her accountable for its discursive engagement with reality.

Pier Paolo Pasolini's concerns, in his 1965 essay on the 'cinema of poetry' (see 1988), were different. Pasolini's essay, which engaged head-on with the then emerging field of the semiotics of cinema, intended to both propose elements of an analysis of the language of film (which he described as an irrational, pre-morphological fact, akin to the language of memory and dreams), and to propose a theory of auteur filmmaking. It is this second aspect that interests me here. Pasolini's discussion of a cinema of poetry coincided with an investigation of the representation of subjectivity in film. It is the director's subjective vision that is at stake, a vision that coincides with his personal style. In a move that remains somehow puzzling, Pasolini tackles the question of authorial vision by introducing the idea of a 'free indirect point-of-view shot', which is proposed as the equivalent of the literary free indirect discourse. It is, in other words, a shot in which the subjective vision of the character and the subjective vision of the director fully coincide and merge. The process of integrating the director's point of view and that of his character is, for Pasolini, a stylistic operation – because the cinema, lacking a *langue*, is not capable of effecting a naturalistic, mimetic reproduction of a character's vision (in the way in which literature is able to reproduce a character's speech). It is through a radical display of his idiosyncratic style that the director can fully embrace a character's vision of the world, and make it manifest.

As John David Rhodes has rightly argued, in Pasolini's account subjective vision and style are inextricably connected to social class, so much so that his essay 'theorises a necessary link between style, subjectivity and class consciousness' (forthcoming). The 'free indirect point-of-view shot' is, indeed, only possible when the character belongs to the same social class as the director.[10] In this way, Pasolini's essay both proposes the cinema of poetry as a 'unique vehicle for the representation of class consciousness in the cinema' (ibid.), and reveals itself to be the outcome of Pasolini's attempt to 'theorise a dual allegiance to formal experiment and to social referentiality, or realism' (ibid.).

Pasolini's convoluted but provocative argument is the manifestation of his desire to theorise modern narrative art film, as it was developing in the 1960s;[11] and specifically, as Rhodes has suggested, his own modernism, always heretically situated in between experimentalism and realism. What interests me here, from the perspective of a study of first-person cinema, is Pasolini's equation of art film with the expression of authorial subjectivity, even if mediated by the narrative pretext of a character's vision. In this, Pasolini's argument recalls and reconnects with the intuitions of the authors of French cinematic impressionism. The cinema of poetry is, therefore, a key step in the establishment of a filmic practice in the first person, one which places the expression of authorial subjectivity at the centre of the textual discourses.

Zavattini's tutelage of reportage-filmmaking in the first person, with its counter-cinema undertones, and Pasolini's investigation of the personal cinema of poetry, with its ideological underpinnings, respectively prepare and comment on the *naissance* in the late 1950s of a personal and autobiographical cinematic practice. I refer to the cinema of the Parisian *nouvelle vague*, with its theorisation of the personal 'cinema of authors', and its later evolution into more radical and engaged avant-garde practices that spread in the 1960s, both in Europe and in the US. Pasolini's and Zavattini's ideas could, indeed, be seen as representative of two parallel but distinct forms of personal expression in film: the auteurist narrative art cinema, and first-person and autobiographical nonfiction respectively.[12] While often being pitched against one another, including by filmmakers working within the two different traditions, these two forms certainly have much in common, and especially their emphasis on the possibility of personal expression in a medium so strongly shaped by its indexical realism, its bulky technological apparatus, and its association with the industry and the market. It is the theoretical, ideological and artistic background of cinema in the first-person that will be in focus in the second section of the present volume.

In the following three chapters, I will address the specific histories and characteristics of diaries, notebooks and self-portraits respectively. While exploring the category of the diary film at large, with a view to understanding its rhetorical and communicative structures and tracing its history and incarnations, chapter six takes particular interest in a series of television documentaries by Aleksandr Sokurov, as an exemplification of the diary's interest in and treatment of the question of time. Chapter seven focuses on the notebook film, investigates its relationship to the travelogue and its nature of groundwork for future films, and focuses on the case study of Pier Paolo Pasolini's filmed notes. Chapter eight is an examination of the filmic self-portrait, *vis-à-vis* the structure and tradition of the self-portrait in the fine arts and in literature; the chapter also offers an analysis of Michelangelo Antonioni's penultimate film, an 'occasional documentary' on the restoration of Michelangelo's *Moses*.

While being persuaded of the opportunity of studying these films within the confines of the formats that I will more accurately describe over the following pages, I also wish to immediately recognise and flag their constitutive hybridism. Their ability to cross boundaries, to confound generic issues and to experiment with and merge linguistic forms is, ultimately, the essence of and the reason for their enduring fascination.

chapter six

THE DIARY FILM: ALEKSANDR SOKUROV'S *SPIRITUAL VOICES* AND THE FEELING OF TIME

'With a documentary, we are never trying to be objective. As soon as any object appears on the screen, all objective criteria vanish, yielding their place to the absolutely subjective dictatorship of the filmmaker's will.' (Sokurov, in Sedofsky 2001: 3)

Born at the end of the Middle Ages, established by the end of the Renaissance, as a result of this epoch's interest in individuality and the inner self,[1] finally constituted as a literary genre in the nineteenth century, and currently in a phase of deep transformation and great expansion, the written diary is a multiform practice that takes many shapes (ledger, logbook, spiritual journal, pillow book, private diary, travelogue), and that accounts for the diarist's relationship with themselves, with others and with their epoch (see Lejeune 2003; 2005).

While autobiography and memoirs are written at considerable temporal distance from the narrated facts, the diary is composed simultaneously with the events, or after a minor interval, and does not anticipate its own ending and closure. The quintessential work-in-progress, open and unstable, instantaneous and discontinuous by nature, the diary mixes high and low, both in stylistic registers and in subject matter: 'because this is a type of writing exempt from all rules, from any effective limit, the diary can accommodate anything and everything. Anything can give rise to a diary. The diarist can open his text to his laundry bills, newspaper clippings, fragments and drafts of texts he is working on, almost anything, in the end' (Didier 1976: 187; author's translation). Because it may include these and other types of verbal and non-verbal materials (for instance, poems, photographs, letters), the diary is a highly heterogeneous text (see Lejeune 1998). As a literary genre, it is not a draft, and is without drafts – even if no diary is ever published without some alteration (ibid).

The diary has frequently been dismissed as 'a practice caught in the banality of everyday existence' (Langford & West 1999: 6); or extolled for the same reason: 'The interest of the diary is its insignificance' (Blanchot 2003: 185). Repository of the everyday, like the essay the diary resists categorisation:

> The diary, as an uncertain genre uneasily balanced between literary and historical writing, between the spontaneity of reportage and the reflectiveness of the crafted text, between selfhood and events, between subjectivity and objectivity, between the private and the public, constantly disturbs attempts to summarise its characteristics within formalised boundaries. The diary is a misfit form of writing, inhabiting the frontiers between many neighbouring or opposed domains, often belonging simultaneously to several 'genres' or 'species' and thus being condemned to exclusion from both at once. (Langford & West 1999: 8–9)

Such in-betweenness can be seen from at least two perspectives: that of the diary's 'insignificance', and hence of its association with marginal subjects, identities and discourses (for instance, of women's, gay, diasporic and resistance writing of all sorts); and that of its tendency to cross generic boundaries and merge with related forms, such as the travelogue, the notebook, the chronicle.

Among the most important critical discourses surrounding the diary are: questions of subjectivity, identity, authorship; the diary as practice of everyday life, and its relationship to temporality; its role as (or unreliability as) historical document, record and aide-mémoire; and its relationship to fiction writing. In the light of the present study of cinematic diaries, two aspects are particularly relevant: the communicative structures of the diaristic, and the issue of temporality. The first topic is a necessary introduction to a comparison between the textual strategies and commitments of literary and filmic diaries, and to a definition of the field of the diaristic in cinema. The second issue – time – will be of particular relevance when analysing the chosen case study.

Dear diary: authorship and readership

In diaries, authorship is always in focus; at all times, a diary refers to the writing subject, who blatantly and persistently speaks in the first person, and who includes – along with the record of facts and events – her own impressions, ideas, sensations; her self-analysis; and her reflection on the act itself of composing a diary: 'the diary, a text that talks of itself, looks at itself, and interrogates itself, is often constituted as a diary of a diary' (Rousset 1986: 155; author's translation). The unvarying formal precondition of such a protean genre consists, indeed, in 'maintaining the enunciatory voice, which remains the same from start to finish, which says I and can only say *I* and *now*' (Rousset 1986: 218; author's translation; emphasis in original).

Such overt and continuous presence obviously raises questions of authorship, identity and subjectivity. Several scholars, for instance, note that, in psychoanalytical terms, the diary, on account of 'the calming effects of the periodic repetitiveness with which we find refuge in it, represents the maternal protection, the artificial paradise, the regressive intimacy' (Battistini 1990: 182; author's translation). In this sense, the subjectivity promoted by the diary appears to be of a narcissistic and regressive kind. In the diary, 'The "I" is what's on the inside' (Didier 1976: 89; author's translation) – hence, by offering their authors an opportunity to turn inward and to focus on their solitude, diaries also become a centre and an anchorage for the individual, against the threat of dispersion generated by the external world: 'The diary grants the person identity, unity, and harmony. It's the promise of an I' (Girard 1963: 537; author's translation). This may explain why diaries are seen as particularly relevant today, when, 'in these times of "liquid modernity", to use Zygmunt Bauman's expression, marked by schizophrenia and by the end of meta-narratives, it is more difficult than in any earlier epoch … to furnish one's identity with unity and coherence' (Mazierska & Rascaroli 2004: 35).

Promising wholeness and harmony, the diary, however, also leads to a proliferation of subjects: at the level of textual figures, because 'The diarist constructs for him/herself a double identity: as writer, and as the matter of his/her writing' (Didier 1976: 116; author's translation); and at the level of linguistic registers, because 'the variety of the diary's linguistic expression also multiplies the writing self' (Langford & West 1999: 9).[2] This aspect introduces the question of the communicative structures of the diaristic: who is the 'I' of the diary? Who is the recipient?

'As in autobiography, what defines the diary is the unity of author, narrator and character' (Didier 1976: 147; author's translation); in other words, one of the main prescriptions of the autobiographical pact as described by Philippe Lejeune (1996), with all the complications inherent in the splitting of the authorial identity into three figures. According to Girard, at least three are versions of the diarist: the one who writes and says 'I'; the ideal subject, the model and utopia the diarist aspires to be; and the character, the persona and mask he wears for others (see Girard 1963: 543–5). Thus, the subject experiences a sort of 'double consciousness', a sense of otherness: 'It is a paradox that the process whose frequent goal is to establish self-continuity involves at its heart a dislocation from the self, a turning of subject into object' (Culley 1985: 10). It is safe to argue that no diary contains an authorial wholeness, a 'self' in any total sense; but one that is always 'to some degree a fiction, a construction' (1985: 12).

While the narrator says 'I', and talks of him/herself as a character that identifies with the author, the identity of the reader is uncertain – in some cases, it has even been denied, and the diary described as a text without an addressee. As Margo Culley wrote, however, 'The importance of the audience, real or implied, conscious or unconscious, of what is usually thought as a private genre cannot be overstated' (1985: 11). This is because the 'act of writing itself implies an audience and this audience will be the vehicle of preserving the life-record (through the act of reading)' (1985: 8). Hence, an addressee always exists, and all diarists postulate indeed an 'intimate reader' (see Rousset 1986).[3] After all, 'Intimism is solitary in appearance only. The theme of the other, which is a significant contribution of existentialism … amounts to one outcome of an analysis that is directed inwards. Rooted in their solitude, intimists are constantly in the presence of the other' (Girard 1963: 565; author's translation).[4] The identity of such an 'intimate reader' can be conceived in different ways: for instance, the diary itself can be the addressed other, often seen as a forever-available and sympathetic friend and confidant; as an anthropomorphised object ('dear diary', 'my poor diary'); or as a fictional, personified receiver (for instance, Kitty in Anne Frank's diary). In all cases, the addresser is an alter ego of the narrator – and the diary is, ultimately, self-addressed; it is a form of 'autocommunication' (Rousset 1983: 438). As a result, because the 'I' and the 'you' (the 'dear diary' as other) are the same, this dialogical structure barely conceals the inner monologue.

Ostensibly private, written in solitude, self-addressed and monological, to the extent of attracting accusations of narcissism and self-indulgency, all diaries – it is frequently claimed – are in fact implicitly written for an audience; and diarists secretly wish for their diaries to be read and published (see Mallon 1984; Taylor & Taylor 2003). Besides, an 'other', an implied reader, is always projected into the text; such other is 'the possible reader of whom the diarist, even if he has no intention of publishing his diary, remains always more or less uncomfortably conscious' (Didier 1976: 113; author's translation). A reader is implied by both functions of the diary: the psychological dimension of the diarist's search for another who listens and understands; and the literary dimension of the creation of an image of oneself, and of a text capable of seducing a reader (see Lejeune 1989: 22).

Because of the above-described communicative structure, the reader of a diary, who is only apparently excluded by the personal, self-addressed discourse, but is indeed positioned in the text as an implied reader, will feel let into the private monologue of the diarist with herself. The position of the reader oscillates, therefore, between that of confidant and that of voyeur (see Lejeune 1989). The reader will identify with the diarist as author (as well as character). Hence, the diary establishes a true pact of complicity with the reader; and its reader can easily experience the diary as a text (also) about himself/herself.

The pact of the diary with its reader is not only one of complicity, but also of sincerity. Its textual commitment to truthfulness is associated with the diary's immediacy, which is a promise of reliability, because it 'hinges on what has been called the "autopsy principle", the claim to truth based on the assertion: I was there, and I saw it with my own eyes' (Agnew 1999: 50). It is, furthermore, linked to the diary's quotidian dimension, with its aura of genuineness: the thoughts of all diarists must be kept 'within the circle of everyday life and must not wrong its truth. Thus sincerity represents, for the diary, the requirement it must attain but not surpass' (Blanchot 2003: 183). Of course, it is the pact itself that creates the effect of sincerity, and that asks the reader to believe in the truthfulness of the diarist's account.

The readership promoted by the diary, a fragmentary form that often includes the inconsequential, the banal and the uninteresting, is also distinctive because of the type of engagement it requires – so much so that for Lejeune diary readers are a 'new race': 'curious and patient, they like to slip into the life of another, they learn how to read between the lines, and they know that a diary is like a fine wine: it takes time for all of its aromas to develop' (in Lejeune & Bogaert 1997: 13; author's translation). Furthermore, because the diary is a paratactic structure, in which 'there is no subordination to suggest that one idea or event is more important than another' (Hogan 1991: 101), the reader is actively engaged in the process of assigning a hierarchy of significance to the narrated facts, and reconstructing a biography from the text.

Bound to time

Although an erratic genre, the diary obeys at least two rules: it must say 'I', and it must say 'now'. Temporality is an all-important marker of the form, and for various reasons; perhaps the first is that the blank pages of the diary stand for the emptiness of time, waiting to be filled:

> The uniform durations, provisionally blank, are seen by the diarist both to require filling (by experience in life, by inscription on the page), and also to facilitate it. They function as isochronic containers that in the uniformity, specificity, and seriality of their temporal dimensions make it possible to reckon fullness, and hence to 'realise' it: to embody it palpably on the page. The date makes fullness necessary and makes it possible. (Sherman 1996: 34–5)

Diaries are fragmentary, never-finished texts in progress, whose 'shapes derive from their existence in time passing' (Culley 1985: 19).[5] Composed at a short distance from the events (immediately following them – or else after a few hours or, at most, a few days), diaries produce an effect of immediacy, one that 'conveys to the reader a direct and apparently unmediated insight into the life and times of its author' (Agnew 1999: 50). Such immediacy distinguishes the temporality of the diary from that of other autobiographical writing: while the autobiographer, in an attempt to dominate time, imposes a teleological design on contingency and inscribes a profound meaning onto disconnected events (a meaning that often resembles a narrative of predestination), the diarist adapts and surrenders to the unpredictable and variable rhythm imposed by the everyday (see Battistini 1990: 183–4). Furthermore, diary writing is a systematic, continuing practice; 'the daily repetition of the act of diaristic inscription roots this mode of writing in everyday existence' (Langford & West 1999: 9). In fact, because they are 'periodic in creation and structure, incremental repetition is an important aspect' of diaries (Culley 1985: 19).

Through contingency and repetition, daily, calendar time is inscribed into the form:

> The diary – which seems so removed from rules, so responsive to life's impulses and capable of all liberties, since thoughts, dreams, fictions, commentaries on itself, important or insignificant events are all suitable for it, in whatever order or disorder one likes – is however subject to a seemingly negligible but formidable law: it must respect the calendar. That is the pact it signs. The calendar is its demon, inspirer, composer, provocateur, and guardian. (Blanchot 2003: 183)

Because of its affinity for immediacy, contingency and the calendar, the diary is linked to a personal and private time, to time as it is humanly experienced; thus, it appears to be better suited to produce micro-history than macro-history. However, diaries grant the reader a vision of the diarists' times as well as of their private lives. Furthermore, because of their role as aide-mémoire and record of events, as well as for their structure, which is organised chronologically according to subsequent dates, diaries sharpen our consciousness of time: 'whether we are mapping out next week's appointments, planning our social life or even secretly recording memories of the recent past, diaries force us to see things in terms of a timescale. If there is one defining trait shared by all diaries ... it is the significance of time, no matter how discretely conveyed, as a framework against which to chart experience' (Heller, quoted in Mazierska and Rascaroli 2004: 35). If temporality shapes diary authorship, it shapes its readership too:

> The text created in a continuous presence but now fixed in time, must be re-created by a reader in a new, continuous present. The reader's consciousness of time passing may be, in part, what makes reading the journal a compel-

ling experience. As the journal pages construct continuity out of the apparent discontinuity created by time passing in the writer's life, the act of reading may generate a parallel process for the reader. The participation of the reader means that the writing act has indeed succeeded in defying time; and the text, in turn, grants the active reader the conviction, 'they wrote, therefore, I am'. (Culley 1985: 24)

Time is relevant to diaries in at least one more way. Open-ended, limitless and interminable, the diary's only necessary conclusion is the death of its author. 'The diary is a record of death. It records the death of others, the diarist's own progress towards death and, even when it seems to broach other subjects, death always remains the diary's true centre, its sole concern, because what it is founded on as a literary genre is the inscription of meaning' (Didier 1988: 145; author's translation). Hence, while apparently excluding a teleological approach to temporality, the diary in fact always tends towards the final event that will retrospectively inscribe meaning in the contingency of everyday time.

Diary-making after literature

The concept of life writing has of late expanded well beyond literature and literary theory, and has become an object of interest for disciplines including anthropology, cultural studies, history, philosophy, psychology, sociology, art history and visual studies. Within such a context of renewed and expanded attention, the diary has even gained the status of the epitome of art; and an artist's oeuvre is now often described as his or her 'diary'. This is because

> Art, like a diary, is inherently individual, in a sense representing artist's thoughts at particular moments in time. Most works of art are given a date to register the significance of the time when they were made, and the majority of retrospective shows are organised chronologically, inviting us to witness the different stages of artists' lives unfurl as revealed through the development of their work. Art can thus be a metaphor for a diary. (Heller, quoted in Mazierska & Rascaroli 2004: 34)

As a consequence, in recent decades 'the boundaries between the diary and other forms of art became blurred. The term "diary" is now often applied to works which are mainly or even purely visual, for example photographs by Christian Boltanski and Darren Almond, Emma Kay's and Jeremy Deller's maps made from memory, paintings by John Baldessari, appliqué quilts and video productions by Tracey Emin' (Mazierska & Rascaroli 2004: 33–4).

Furthermore, the practice itself of keeping diaries has evolved; thanks to the Internet and new technologies, diary writing has today transferred online. The World Wide Web hosts a proliferation of online diaries or blogs, which by now constitute a recognisable and ever-expanding subculture. Electronic diaries, of course, differ from traditional ones in more than one way, and at least in terms of the used interface, which, among other effects, causes blogs to be 'perpetually revisable' (Sorapure 2003: 4); in terms of their interactivity – blogs are not only public, thus challenging our 'conception of diary writing as a private act' (2003: 9), but also entail constant interaction with and feedback from their readers; and in terms of use and reception – for instance, readers usually start from the most recent entry rather than the opening one (entries are presented in reverse chronological order). Furthermore, online diaries encourage a random form of reading, and promote navigation via their links to other blogs and websites.

Even more relevant to cinematographic diaries are the so-called videoblogs or vlogs, which present regular entries consisting of embedded videos, or video links accompanied by supporting text and images. Vlogs can be collaborative, or else single-authored, and may be seen as an evolution of diaristic television programmes. Well-known examples of such programmes are the BBC series *Video Diaries*, created in 1990, which involved members of the public who were given camcorders, training and assistance from the programme's production team, and asked to film their own diaries, which were then edited and screened; and the series *Video Nation*, started in 1999. Since 2001, these video diaries have been accessible on the BBC website.[6] Televised diaries challenge the traditional private dimension of the written journal, and raise questions of authorship (given the intervention of the producers and broadcasters in the managing and editing of the material), as well as ethical issues (even though diarists are usually granted a veto on the screening).

The confessional camera: history and practice

A New Yorker of Lithuanian descent, Marie Menken is sometimes credited as the filmmaker who introduced the diary form to the cinema (see James 1992: 151), undoubtedly on account of the ordinariness and 'intimism' of her subject matter in shorts such as *Glimpse of the Garden* (1962) and *Notebook* (1963) – which, however, do not present a diaristic structure. It is indeed thought that the diary, intended as the tendency to shoot everyday, ordinary occurrences and subjects, emerged in the 1960s from women filmmakers as diverse as Menken, Chantal Akerman, Storm de Hirsch, Sue Fredrich, Marjorie Keller, Yvonne Rainer, Amalie Rotschild, Carolee Schneemann and Claudia Weill (ibid.), as well as from the personal portraits of Stan Brakhage, such as *Window Water*

Baby Moving (1959), documenting the birth of his first child, *An Avant-Garde Home Movie* and *Dog Star Man* (1961–64) (see Lane 2002: 13). The cinematic diary became common in the 1970s within North American avant-garde practices, with such exponents as Andrew Noren, Robert Hout, Howard Guttenplan, Ed Pincus, Jonas Mekas (see James 1992: 151) and Warren Sonbert (see Sitney 1979: 360). However, it must be noted that Man Ray was already using his camera from 1923, in Paris, to take entries of everyday occurrences and places, which together form his diaristic (and occasionally avant-garde) *Home Movies* (1923–38). Other pre-1960s European examples, although in a completely different vein, include Humphrey Jennings' documentary *A Diary for Timothy* (1946), distributed by the British Ministry of Information, which records the final stages of World War Two in the form of a diary kept for a newborn child (the commentary, by E. M. Forster, was spoken by Michael Redgrave).

The diary makes its appearance in film theory as early as 1950. In the previous chapter, I briefly explored the role of Cesare Zavattini's articles of the 1950s and 1960s in the establishment of an autobiographical cinema, a cinema in the first person. Zavattini's own literary works were always extremely autobiographical, all 'forms of primary egocentric writing', in his own words (quoted in Fortichiari 1992: 65; author's translation), and akin to genres such as the diary especially, but also the letter, the autobiography and the self-portrait. The interaction between diary and cinema in Zavattini's mind came to assume paramount importance: 'Diary and cinema represent the components of a radiograph of existence, observed through a screen that magnifies its contours; the diary performs the function of a camera pointing at reality and producing an instantaneous analysis of the facts' (Fortichiari 1992: 72; author's translation). Some of his diaristic projects were, indeed, cinematographic, or at least implied a filmed component; for instance, *Diario di un uomo* (*Diary of a Man*, 1962) and *Diaro di una donna* (*Diary of a Woman*, 1963), which were never realised, were conceived as film-books that would faithfully record each moment of an ordinary person's day. Already in 1950, when promoting the opportunity to film spontaneously, without scripts, in order to stop betraying 'the immediacy and freshness of the camera' (Zavattini 1979a: 71; here and below are author's translation), and for the purpose of eliminating the gap between the idea and its cinematic realisation, Zavattini called for a diaristic cinema: 'I think of the diary as the most complete and most authentic expression of the cinema. It is obvious that, for diary, I mean something new: not an actual written diary, but all that is knowledge of ourselves and of others – an immediate, not a predetermined knowledge. We must have a great faith in reality' (ibid.). The diary, broadly described as 'the attempt to subject to the [spectator's] judgement oneself, the others and everything worth telling' (1979a: 72), is for Zavattini a film without a screenplay – thus a spontaneous, unplanned film; it is instantaneous and simultaneous to the events, annulling the gap between the conception of the film and its realisation. It is also comprehensive, as it includes all the instants of a person's day, even the most insignificant ones (see 1979: 39), because 'there isn't a day, an hour, a minute of a human being that does not merit being communicated to others' (1979c: 82). It follows calendar time, the time 'of the watch, which marks the hours of the so-called marginal life' (1979b: 75), showing us the *'real duration'* of human time (1979b: 76; emphasis in original). Finally, it is an itinerant, nomadic film, shot in the streets, along the road (see 1979a: 72). It can be argued that Zavattini's conception of the cinema, at least from the year 1950, if not before,[7] becomes thoroughly diaristic; and that the diary comes to represent the type of cinema he promotes – the complete realisation of the unfinished project of Italian neorealism: 'We are, in other words, close to the truly free artistic forms, to the diary intended as attitude, as chronicle of daily thoughts, and as most direct means of self-knowledge' (1979b: 75).

Another filmmaker, critic and theorist for whom the diary (initially a substitutive practice adopted to 'keep in touch' with the camera (see Mekas 1978: 190–1)) becomes privileged form of expression, is Jonas Mekas. The Lithuanian-born filmmaker emigrated to the United States in 1949, and became the father figure of the New American Cinema, not only through his filmmaking and critical writings, but also for his role in the establishment and direction of key institutions such as *Film Culture* magazine (1955), the Film-Makers' Cooperative (1962) and the Film-Makers' Cinematheque (1964), which eventually grew into Anthology Film Archives, hosting a famous collection of avant-garde films. Mekas is by far the most renowned filmmaker-diarist, especially thanks to works such as *Walden* (1969), *Reminiscences of a Voyage to Lithuania* (1972), *Lost, Lost, Lost* (1975), *Zefiro torna* (1992) and *As I was Moving Ahead, Occasionally I Saw Brief Glimpses of Beauty* (2001). However, his entire oeuvre can be defined as diaristic. One of his most quintessential diary-projects, inaugurated in January 2007, is the Internet-based *365 Films*, consisting of daily entries of digital films, of an average length of five to ten minutes each, which can be downloaded in MP4 format for computer or iPod viewing.[8] *365 Films* is a sort of refined vlog – an Internet video diary – which, through its calendar structure and graphics, makes the temporal dimension of diary-making fully tangible. For Mekas, the filmed diary form is not substantially different from the written one. The reflective process at work in the written diary, due to the distance of its composition from the events, is for Mekas already implicit in the filming; furthermore, writing a diary is not simply reflecting, because in the process of writing 'It's all happening again, and what one writes down is more true to what one is when one writes than to the events and the emotions of the day that are past and gone' (Mekas 1978: 192).

Jonas Mekas's online diaristic project, *365 Films* (http://www.jonasmekas.com/)

Jonas Mekas is a genuine film diarist – one for whom shooting entries is an everyday, life-long practice. Another diarist of equal assiduity is, in France, Joseph Morder, who started making films at the end of the 1960s and has so far produced some eight hundred autobiographical films (sometimes mixing documentary and fiction), in Super8, 16mm, Super16 and video – his best-known work is, probably, *Mémoires d'un juif tropical* (1988). His monumental diary, initiated in 1967, is a work in progress of which only some sections are intended for public screenings. In the US, another prominent diarist is Ed Pincus, 35mm whose *Diaries* (1982) cover his life and times from 1971 to 1976, including footage and records of his family life, his loves, his colleagues and his travels. Other North American authors whose work is often defined as diaristic include Ross McElwee, and George Kuchar, with his work-in-progress *Weather Diaries* (1986–). In Britain, Derek Jarman had a strong affinity for the diary format; the author of several written journals, Jarman also adopted the form in some films in between avant-garde and autobiography, such as his 35mm diary testament *Blue* (1993), and the collage of twenty years of Super8 home-movies, *Glitterbug* (1994). Both Wim Wenders' *Lightning Over Water* (1980) and *Tokyo-Ga* (1985) have diaristic and, especially the second, travelogue elements within them, and have been described as diaries by Wenders himself. In the first, the German director arrives in New York to spend some time with Nicholas Ray, who is dying from lung cancer, and to make a film with him; in *Tokyo-Ga*, he arrives in Japan in the spring of 1983, to see whether anything remains of the world that Japanese director Yasujiro Ozu chronicled in his films.

Moving beyond the sphere of the documentary and of avant-garde nonfiction, there are two prominent diarists who merge fiction and autobiography: Italian Nanni Moretti and Hungarian Márta Mészáros. Moretti made several 'autofictional' diaries, the most famous of which are *Caro diario* (*Dear Diary*, 1993) and *Aprile* (1998), reconstructed chronicles of both private events and public affairs (see Mazierska & Rascaroli 2004: 31–43). Moretti's interest in diaries also extended to his activity as producer, with *I diari della Sacher* (*The Sacher Diaries*, 2001), a series of films by several directors, based on actual written diaries coming from the national archive of Pieve Santo Stefano in Italy. Márta Mészáros made a whole series of diaries – *Napló gyermekeimnek* (*Diary for My Children*, 1984); *Napló szerelmeimnek* (*Diary for My Loved Ones*, 1987); *Napló apámnak, anyámnak* (*Diary for My Father and Mother*, 1990); and the prequel, *Kisvilma: Az utolsó napló* (*Little Vilna: The Last Diary*, 2000) – in which she chronicled personal and public life and manifested her political dissent.

Other cinematic diaries (the list is far from complete) include: Alain Cavalier's *Le Filmeur* (2005), which condenses into 101 minutes eleven years of daily shooting (from 1994–2005); Erik Bullot's three 16mm filmed diaries of the first three years of the life of a child: *Le Calcul du sujet* (*Calculus of the Subject*, 1997–2000), *Oh oh oh!* (2000–02) and *La belle Étoile* (*Under the Stars*, 2004); David Perlov's *Yoman* (*Diary*, 1983), a political, professional and personal diary produced over ten years of shooting; *Gina Kim's Video Diary*, by Gina Kim (2002), a coming-of-age journal combining video performance art and private home-movies; Dominique Cabrera's *Demain et encore demain* (*Tomorrow and Tomorrow*, 1997), which exploits the diary format to explore questions of identity and social roles; John Smith's *Hotel Diaries*, an ongoing series of videos made in hotel rooms, all of which relate personal experiences to contemporary world events – works in the series include *Frozen War* (2001, shot in Ireland), *Museum Piece* (2004, shot in Germany), *Throwing Stones* (2004, filmed in Switzerland), *BandB* (2005, filmed in England), *Pyramids/Skunk* (2006–07, filmed in the Netherlands) and *Dirty Pictures* (2007, Palestine); and Vincent Dieutre's *Leçons de ténèbres* (2000), shot in DV, Super8 and 35mm, in between diary, travelogue and self-portrait, a gay man's confessional journey through night-time Utrecht, Naples and Rome.

Two controversial films that recently brought the format of the diary to public attention are Andrew Jarecki's *Capturing the Friedmans* (2003), and Brian De Palma's *Redacted* (2007). The first, a documentary about a case of paedophilia and sexual abuse in New York, included much home-movie, diaristic footage shot by the family of the accused, Arnold Friedman, while he awaited trial. *Redacted* is based on the real-life gang-rape and murder of Abeer Qasim Hamza al-Janabi, a 14-year-old Iraqi girl, by US soldiers in March 2006. The film, which disturbingly challenges the borders between documentary and fiction, draws from and re-constructs soldiers' war home-videos, online blogs, security cameras, television footage, insurgents' videos and images posted on YouTube.

Film diary, diary film:
communicative structures and textual commitments

> No matter how I film, fast or slow, how I expose, the film represents a certain actual, historical period. But as a group of images, it tells more about my own subjective reality, or you can call it my objective reality, than any other reality. (Mekas 1978: 193)

The film diary has not received extensive theoretical attention; writings on specific diary films, and especially Jonas Mekas's work, constitute the existing critical framework for this form. The film diary is sometimes described as belonging to the family of the essay: 'Diary filmmaking, autobiographical filmmaking, and personal videos can all be subsumed within what Michael Renov has described as the "essayistic impulse" in recent film and video' (Russell 1999: 277) – a stance with which I agree. However, the communicative structures and textual commitments of the diary significantly differ from those of the essay proper, and need to be studied separately.

Some scholars have attempted definitions; for instance, Jim Lane, in his study of American autobiographical nonfiction, uses the term 'journal entry documentary' to describe not all types of filmed diaries, but a historically and stylistically specific manifestation of this form, and precisely:

> a type of autobiographical documentary that involves the shooting of every-day events for a sustained period of time and the subsequent editing of these events into a chronological autobiographical narrative. Events appear along a diachronic chain as if they are occurring for the first time in the present tense. For the most part these events show people, including the documentarist, interacting with each other instead of speaking about those events in the past tense, for instance, in formal interviews. (2002: 33)

For Lane, the journal entry documentary – examples of which include Ed Pincus's *Diaries*, Mark Rance's *Death and the Singing Telegram* (1983), Ross McElwee's *Sherman's March*, Tom Joslin and Peter Friedman's *Silverlake Life: The View From Here* (1993) – is characterised by having been shot over a significant period of time, and by its adoption of a chronological narrative: 'The documentarist establishes an intricate relation between direct and indirect address that hinges on the discursive effect of the chronological passage of time. Events appear as cinematic entries that later were organised in a sequential order that creates an unfolding of the present tense. A singular macronarrative emerges from this approach' (2002: 49). The journal entry documentary is further characterised by the lack of delay between the event and its recording; by a focalising autobiographical self; by the collapsing of the roles of author/narrator/protagonist and the variations in the levels of narration; and by an attention to the cinematographic apparatus: 'In many cases the documentarist comes out from behind the camera to pay close attention to the recording apparatus' (2002: 45).

In a paradigmatic contribution on the diary film, an essay devoted to a study of Jonas Mekas's *Walden*, David E. James introduced the crucial distinction between 'film diary' and 'diary film'. Film diary is, James suggests, the practice of filming regularly, of producing footage of one's life, for purely personal purposes: 'It is a private event (the coded or locked diary) where consumption, especially consumption by others, is illicit: a pure use value' (James 1992: 147). When the film diary is open to others, it becomes a diary film, which exists within 'an economy that privileges the completed artifact as a whole, the moment of projection, the spectating public, and, in some form or other, exchange value' (ibid). The diary film is edited from the film diary; while the film diary is private and provisional, the diary film has 'its own justification and its own telos' (1992: 149). James also distinguishes between the diary film proper and the fictional one; the latter includes such films as G. W. Pabst's *Tagebuch einer Verlorenen* (*Diary of a Lost Girl*, 1929), versions by Jean Renoir and Luis Buñuel of *The Diary of a Chambermaid* (1946; 1965), Robert Bresson's *Journal d'un curé de campagne* (*Diary of a Country Priest*, 1951), Godard's *Vivre sa vie* (*It's My Life*, 1962) and *David Holzman's Diary* (1967), by Jim McBride – all of which for the author can be compared to novels written in the form of diaries. James furthermore discusses some important features of the diaristic in film, by comparing them to the corresponding characteristics of the written form. For the author, the film diary differs in terms of temporality and subjectivity from the literary journal. In the written diary, a gap typically occurs between the events and their recording; the opposite is true in film, which 'cannot escape the present and the present tense, for filming can only capture events as they happen' (1992: 153).

Filmed diaries are also characterised for James by a dispersion of authorship, while the written diary requires single authorship. This is because the subjectivity of the author cannot be easily inscribed in the film: 'The film diary must go to greater lengths to include the author (shooting mirror images or shadows, or have some other person handle the camera); otherwise authorship must be inscribed in style' (1992: 154). Finally, James discusses editing as a practice that somehow betrays the film diary; post-production modifies chronology, and adds music, voice-overs and captions, which 'substantially inflect the visuals' (ibid.). For James, 'what is essentially at stake in the film diary lies in the moment of shooting' (1992: 155). Post-production adds a new layer of temporality to the film diary: the review of the traces of the past and the commentary imposed on them reveal the present situation of the autobiographer and, while adding explanations and clarifying the present perception of the past, also 'register the unbridgeable gap between then and now' (1992: 164).

James' comments on post-production are convincing when it comes to Mekas, who in some cases (and especially for *Walden*) worked on images that he filmed at least a decade before their inclusion into a diary film; indeed, 'Memorialisation and loss are the defining characteristics of Mekas's diary films' (Russell 1999: 281). In those cases in which the temporal interval is much shorter, however, the notion of the registration of an unbridgeable gap is, undoubtedly, less pertinent. While, obviously, some time always elapses between shooting and editing, the gap, at least to a degree, is akin to the one between the experiencing of events and their subsequent recording in literary diary practice. There does, however, exist an obvious, constitutive difference at the level of temporality between literary and film diaries: the written form reorders, reports and comments on the author's memory of the events; the filmic form reorders, reports and comments on indexical traces of reality.

The filmic diary is twice in the present: it offers both the 'now' of the recorded images (because images are always in the present tense), and the 'now' of the reflection and commentary on them. In different diary films, one of the two 'nows' can prevail to a point – if the reordering through editing does not attract attention to itself and its own temporality, and presents the entries as in the dimension of 'today', the 'now' of the filming will dominate; in those cases in which the post-production intervention more explicitly attracts attention to the temporal gap between filming and editing/commentary, the 'now' of the post-production will prevail. In all circumstances, however, at an ontological level, it is the simultaneity of the shooting with the events and, therefore, the indexical quality of the entries that differentiate the filmic diary from its literary counterpart.

While for James the true filmic diary is, to some extent, the act of filming, of recording (the 'film diary'), it is incorrect, in my opinion, to see the editing and post-production as a betrayal or compromise of the genuine item. In view of the fact that the diaristic is always a form of reordering and reorganisation, albeit instantaneous and unprocessed, I argue the opposite: it is the editing and the post-production that make a diary out of a set of audiovisual 'notes'.[9] Furthermore, the purity and innocence that James argues for the film diary, which is made never to be edited or screened, verge on the romantic – one should not forget, in any case, that even the most private written diaries, as was argued above, are composed with a readership in mind, because the act itself of writing always implies an audience. Similarly, the act of switching on a camera immediately produces a (future) audience, even if an 'intimate' one.

James' analysis of authorship in filmed diaries, then, is useful and convincing; however, the problems of the dispersion of authoriality and of the difficulty of the author's inclusion in the images should, in my opinion, be played down. Of course, authoriality is always more dispersed in film than it is in literature; and the narrator's voice, which in written diaries says 'I' from start to finish, can only be suitably reproduced in film through a persistent voice-over. However, as was clarified above, also in the written diary we witness a multiplication of the writing self, and no diary contains a self in its wholeness. Furthermore, even when images of the director are not included, or when a cameraperson filmed those that are present, I claim it is the textual commitments and the pact with the spectator that establish the diary as the product of its author. Even though some images of Mekas in *Walden* were not taken by him, for instance, *Walden* is utterly and undoubtedly a project of Jonas Mekas – it is his diary, because Mekas presents it as such. In Mekas's own eloquent words, at the presentation of *Diaries, Notes and Sketches* in 1969:

> The diary form, traditionally, belongs in the narrative end of art. And the clearest dividing line of the narrative from the non-narrative, if there is one, traditionally has been the protagonist: in the narrative there is a protagonist, and the non-narrative forms have only the creator's, the artist's presence, or ego. And it's through me that every detail is presented, day by day, and you gain more and more knowledge about me as we go further and further. Of course, most of the time, I am there only indirectly, for those who can 'see' me. (2003: 13)

The instances of circulation/dispersion of authorship, in other words, do not take away from the compelling impression that the film is the product of Mekas's work. It is the overall pact with the spectator, the authorial declaration, 'this is my diary', that truly shape the reception of the film. Take the extreme example of Derek Jarman's *Blue*. The film contains no images of the director; indeed, no images at all. It presents an unchanging blue screen, against which music, sounds and the voices of three different actors are heard: John Quentin, Nigel Terry and Tilda Swinton. Jarman's voice, broken by pain, is also heard at the end of the film.

Yet, despite the dispersion of his authoriality onto four narrators, it is unquestionable that *Blue* is Jarman's diary – of his illness and therapy, his memories and thoughts, his reactions to the conflict in Bosnia, the death of some friends and his physical decline.

In spite of an unquestionable authoriality, however, as established by the textual pact, it is true that, in diary films, the presence of images of the diarist unavoidably imply a split subjectivity, and attract attention to the apparatus, to the technology: 'The image of the filmmaker, when it appears in a diary film, refers to another cameraperson, or to a tripod that denotes an empty, technologised gaze' (Russell 1999: 280). In the example of *Blue*, conversely, it is not the images of the filmmaker, but their absence – especially in the context of a complete lack of images – that reduces the subjectivity to the pure properties of the apparatus, producing a sort of zero degree of the subject.

In conclusion, I argue that it is important, as in the case of the essay film, to resist overtheorising the form – partly because the diary film emerges from avant-garde practices, and is hence a field of freedom and experimentation; partly because it is a marginal genre, which borders and often merges with other neighbouring forms, for instance the essay, the notebook, the home-movie, the autobiography, the travelogue, the self-portrait; and partly because, while deriving from the literary genre, it is also always in dialogue with other, visual, audiovisual, and now even online diaristic forms. It is, however, safe to say that a diary film is a film in which the camera has been used to 'take notes' of both private and public events, notes which have then been organised by the editing into a diaristic structure.

As is true of the literary genre, the diary film can be a repository of everything, of the banal as well as of the momentous; it integrates public and private; it is capable of accommodating and not reconciling different stylistic registers, from the banal to the sublime; it makes a record of time passing; it reorders events and records details; and is reflective and self-reflexive. As its literary counterpart, it is a strongly subjective art form, in which the enunciator says 'I' and talks to a 'you' that is himself or herself (as in a confessional); even when no voice-over or written captions are used, the first-person authoriality is established by the pact with the spectator: 'this is my diary'. Such a pact is one of reliability and sincerity, even though, of course, 'The confessional mode is a testimonial discourse with no necessary validity beyond the viewer's faith in the text's authority' (Russell 1999: 279). The spectator will take the diary to be the faithful record of events and of the author's emotions and ideas, and will paradoxically identify with the addresser, and feel let into the intimate dialogue of the author with herself.

Furthermore, it is important to note that, in this form, the desire to express one's subjectivity merges with the idea of the liberation of the medium from the constraints of mainstream production and distribution, because the diary film was born from 'private' (home-movie) and avant-garde practices. Super8, video and digital video are often adopted; the form is hybrid, the language transgressive, or at least independent from the traditional codes of both fiction and non-fiction cinema.

No room for aesthetics:
Sokurov's *Spiritual Voices – From the Diaries of War*

Aleksandr Sokurov is probably most famous for his fictions; but he is also the author of many outstanding, authorial, highly personal documentaries, which include travelogues such as *Elegiya dorogi* (*Elegy of a Voyage*, 2002); portraits such as *Moskovskaya elegiya* (*Moscow Elegy. Andrei Tarkovsky*, 1987) and *Uzel* (*Dialogues with Solzhenitsyn*, 1999); essays like *Hubert Robert. Schastlivanya zhizn*; and several diaries, like the series of St. Petersburg, which includes *Peterburgskiy dnevnik. Otkritie pamyatnika Dostoeskomu* (*The Diary of St. Petersburg: Inauguration of the Monument to Dostoevsky*, 1997), *Peterburgskiy dnevnik. Kvartira Kozintseva* (*The Diary of St. Petersburg. Kozintsev's Flat*, 1998) and *Peterburgskiy dnevnik: Mozart. Rekviem* (*The Diary of St. Petersburg: Mozart. Requiem*, 2004), or *Dukhovnye golosa. Iz dnevnikov voyny. Povestvovanie v pyati chastyakh* (*Spiritual Voices: From the Diaries of War*, 1995), which will be analysed below, and its companion piece, the television mini-series *Povinnost* (*Confession* 1998), the diary of the commander of a Russian battleship cruising the Barents Sea.

Spiritual Voices: From the Diaries of War is a documentary diary in five 'entries' of variable length, centred on the lives of the 11th brigade of border guards of the Moscow Army along the Tadjik/Afghani frontier.[10] The films, shot for television with Betacam SP cameras over six months in 1995, are a manifestation of Sokurov's idiosyncratic and experimental approach to the documentary format: in between personal essay and testimony, *Spiritual Voices* is a reflective piece with minimal dialogue, stylistically characterised by long takes, prolonged close-ups, a bleached, flat image, and a textured soundtrack that merges natural sounds and music by Tōru Takemitsu. The first instalment, however, is stylistically distinct – it is a pure essay composed of a single, fixed 38-minute-long shot of a frozen Russian landscape, dominated by Sokurov's voice-over, musing on Mozart's music and life.

Aleksandr Sokurov's *Spiritual Voices* (1995): the snowy expanse in Episode One.

The quality of the image, the style and the treatment of the subject matter characterise

Spiritual Voices as a product that exceeds both the video format and the television format; unsurprisingly, it was also screened at several film festivals, and presented at art galleries and museums as an installation, in which the five episodes run simultaneously on different screens. Although the episodic structure clearly owes something to television conventions, the unevenness of the five segments, of 38, 33, 87, 79 and ninety minutes respectively, is unusual for a mini-series; as a documentary film, its fragmentariness is atypical, and its total length of 327 minutes conspicuously excessive. Similarly, the adoption of Beta video – which is normal for television, but anomalous for a film of such quality – is remarkable. *Spiritual Voices*, indeed, tests the limits of the television documentary both in terms of the outstanding care given to the image composition, camerawork and multilayered soundtrack, and in terms of its approach to the subject matter. War and the life of soldiers in a faraway frontier zone are, in fact, depicted in a remarkably pensive, personal, ascetic manner.

From its very title, *Spiritual Voices: From the Diaries of War* claims to be a diary. In my previous analysis of the diaristic form, I privileged two perspectives: the question of authorship, and the question of time. Consonant with the results of my examination of the former issue, authorship in *Spiritual Voices* is perhaps dispersed, but also compelling and unquestioned. The authorial stamp on these films is indeed unambiguous, both in contextual and in textual terms. The circulation of *Spiritual Voices* at film festivals, and as an installation in museums and art galleries, is a clear acknowledgement of Sokurov's authorship – with this film, indeed, he won the first Video Prize at the 1995 Locarno Film Festival. *Spiritual Voices*, which did not receive theatrical distribution, was digitised and distributed by Facets as part of a collection of Sokurov's films, bearing the name and a photograph of the author on the DVD's front cover – thus reinforcing its status as part of the oeuvre of an important auteur.[11]

Textually, the film displays Sokurov's authorship primarily through the adoption of the director's first-person voice-over throughout the five episodes. The voice-over completely dominates the first episode, a personal musing on composers – thus inaugurating the film on a strongly subjective note. Sokurov can only be seen in episode two,[12] while on the vehicle taking him to the military outpost; whereas his images do indeed imply the presence of a different person behind the camera, hence a potential dispersion of authorship, they also strengthen Sokurov's position as the protagonist of the film, and consolidate his stamp on it. The choice of the diary format is an obvious statement of subjectivity, which locates the author at the centre of his work. In addition, the entire film – in spite of the choice of a 'low' format such as Beta or, conversely, because of it, given the control it affords the filmmaker[13] – speaks of a strong authorial vision, through the complexity and continuity characterising a large project in several instalments; through its ostensible unmarketability, and remoteness from commercial cinema; its chromatic austerity; its slow, inquisitive pace; its predilection for both extended close-ups, and for long, fixed or slowly moving shots of a barren, meaningless landscape – which tend to generate not the typical spectatorship of a television documentary, but the mesmerised audience of the highly subjective film of a self-conscious auteur.[14]

The obvious stylistic continuity of *Spiritual Voices* with Sokurov's other films, both documentaries and fictions, further sanctions this work as authorial, as well as suggesting a blurring of boundaries between fiction and nonfiction that, once again, is a marker of Sokurov's distinctive aesthetic project, and systematic and self-conscious approach to the cinema. Sokurov, an artist with a profound interest in classical culture and the fine arts, is, indeed, a true auteur in the tradition of modern cinema, who by his own admission recognises as masters only a few film directors, including Bergman, Eisenstein, Griffith, Fellini, Flaherty, Dreyer and Tarkovsky (see, for instance, Szaniawski 2006: 13). For Fredric Jameson, Sokurov is 'but one of a whole international generation – a word not taken in the biological or chronological sense – of great auteurs, who seem to renew the claims of high modernism in a period in which that aesthetic and its institutional preconditions seem extinct' (2006: 1).

As a diary, *Spiritual Voices* contains the banal and the momentous, the private confession and the recording of public events. Each instalment is an entry devoted to a single day; each is coherent stylistically and thematically, but in many ways distinct from the other entries. The film is, indeed, quite uneven in style, rhythm, content and duration – even though in episodes two to five, the music, the themes explored and, to a lesser extent, the camerawork, lighting and colour convey an overall sense of continuity. Each entry could exist separately, exactly as in a diary: 'Formally, diaries seem to be both collections of fragments and models of continuity; day after day is recorded, but each entry is discrete and self-sufficient' (Hogan 1986: 9). The filmmaker produces an enunciator that directly identifies with the author of the film, and who is embodied into a narrator/diarist who speaks in voice-over, in the first person. The diarist frequently registers the date, the day of the week, or durations ('At the beginning of June...'; 'It was very hot last night'; 'All day long...'; 'It was December. It was coming to December 31st').[15]

The identity of this diarist, as performed in and by the film, oscillates between the soldier among soldiers, and the filmmaker/chronicler of the guards' life at the frontier post. Indeed, Sokurov (who, in the few images of him that we glimpse, wears a uniform), highlights both his closeness to and distance from the Russian soldiers he films. He frequently talks of 'us', ostensibly referring to himself and the guards rather than himself and his crew: 'We sat and rested in silence, looking down at the frontier post' he remarks, for instance, over images of resting soldiers. However, Sokurov is also well aware of the ultimately unbridgeable gap between him and the guards, for example when he sombrely comments: 'I look at these soldiers, and it seems to me they can't have had much in the way of human happiness.' If the feeling of inclusion is induced by the condition of sharing the soldiers' life and destiny ('If they lose, everyone dies'), and by Sokurov's typically extreme human ambition in his approach to his subject matter, the sense of exclusion is due to the realisation that the filmmaker exists under different rules: he can always leave the outpost, and return home. Sokurov's oscillation between these two states of mind and two personae is implied by the following comment from episode three: 'The men seem to treat me as one of them, but perhaps I am wrong to think it.' The same oscillation is encapsulated by the alternation of present and past tense in his speech, as we will see in more detail below – an alternation that tangibly embodies the film diary's double nature, deriving from the interaction between the 'presentness' of the images and the 'pastness' superimposed on them by the editing/commentary.

In order to take up the identity of the diarist, and in line with the characteristics of the diary format, Sokurov frequently notes his own feelings and sensations, those that are potentially ordinary or momentous: 'I'm thirsty'; 'I slept a dreamless sleep'; 'I found the going tough. I often had to ask for a rest'; 'Goodness, it's hot here'; 'When the base was finally attacked, at first it wasn't frightening'; 'War is hideous'. Especially interesting is the fact that Sokurov almost totally succeeds in erasing the presence of his own crew, in order to appear as the solitary diarist in dialogue with himself. Whereas the spectator is directly addressed in the essayistic first episode, the remaining instalments present us with a diarist ostensibly talking in the first person to himself – even though the ultimate address of *Spiritual Voices* to television, film and art gallery audiences demonstrates the deceptiveness of the diaristic 'autocommunicative' structure. The film, in truth, speaks to an 'intimate spectator', while also producing an 'intimist spectacle' of personal and everyday occurrences.

If one wanted to apply James' distinction between 'film diary' and 'diary film', *Spiritual Voices* would certainly be an example of the second, in the sense of a diary that emerged in the editing room from footage filmed some time before. It is, however, also correct to say that Sokurov has the vocation of a diarist, given the considerable number of journals he shot. The post-production is not concealed, and is not irrelevant either, rather the opposite; the choice of altering the colour, for instance, thus creating an austere palette of hues (from red to beige to grey), is a conspicuous intervention, which introduces a strongly subjective perspective on the events and, arguably, a layering of temporal distance.

Furthermore, the refined, multifaceted soundtrack, and the addition of a sparse voice-over, which as mentioned alternately reports and comments on the events from the 'now' of the post-production and from the 'now' of the filming, add a further temporal layer, as well as a subjective reflection on and contemplation of the recorded events. We even learn from the voice-over that, during the shooting, Sokurov kept a written diary (at the beginning of the second episode he states: 'Flicking through my journal, this is what I read'; at the onset of episode three, and again in episode five, we hear him saying: 'This is what I wrote in my diary') – suggesting that *Spiritual Voices* emerges from a combination

This is what I wrote in my diary.

Sokurov's *Spiritual Voices*: the diaristic beginning of episode three

of filmed notes and a written diary; the written entries must have been used in the editing room as a guide to reordering and interpreting the footage. However, the film does not lose any of its immediacy – indeed, the use of video responds to the urgency of witnessing the events 'here and now'. Frequently, we sense that shots are captured instantaneously, especially in episode three, a day of open fighting; the camera is at times in movement with the soldiers, or awaits and observes along with them, creating the effect of the unfolding of events. This effect is amplified by the voice-over, which often highlights the dimension of coping with the present, or of anticipating the unexpected. As Bruno Dietsch writes, the film is 'an experience of immersion from which the spectator does not emerge unscathed' (2005: 25; author's translation).

Time is, I argue, the true subject matter of *Spiritual Voices*, as is thoroughly appropriate for a diary. There are two main dimensions of temporality in the film: the daily time of normal routine and occurrences; and the suspended time of the anticipation of the unforeseen. Isolated in a desolate, no-man's frontier, facing an enemy who is just beyond the border, the soldiers experience both temporal dimensions in their day. As Sokurov explained during a television interview aired before the broadcasting of his film, the war is both daily routine and anguished waiting:

> We began to make our film in summer, then came again in winter. We worked in the places where war is daily routine, where the state of war is not a sudden attack, but normal life itself. Namely – fighting operations on the border between Tadjikistan and Afghanistan. Sometimes it was many days of troubled waiting. Sometimes battle: assault or repulse of it. But always there were victims, and always there was parting from the relatives and friends. And always anguish and abandonment. (n.d.)

Fredric Jameson noted Sokurov's affinity for the depiction of daily time in his films: 'The time of "l'emploi du temps", of routine and schedule, the hours of the day' (2006: 6). The repetitive temporality captured by Sokurov is one that the cinema is well versed to reproduce, as Jameson argues:

> The camera has in any case an 'elective affinity' with the real or the referent that none of the other arts (except photography) can claim, as though what counts as reality is precisely this succession of temporal presents that can do without the great events or the dramatic moments of happening, this never ending sequence of daily cycles and physical preparations, of going about your business, that the camera registers without comment like the passage from morning into noon and from afternoon into evening. (Ibid.)

It is certainly true that Sokurov's representation of historical time in his cinema – for instance in his films on Hitler, Lenin and Hirohito, respectively *Molokh* (*Moloch*, 1999), *Telets* (*Tarus*, 2001) and *Solntse* (*The Sun*, 2005), or in the *tour de force* of *Russkiy kovcheg* (*Russian Ark*, 2002) through three centuries of Russian history – shuns the continuum, the temporal fullness, and does not even try to create a sense of historical truthfulness. Writing about *Russian Ark*, for instance, Yana Hashamova rightly argues that, in this film, 'there is no attempt to transform everyday settings and daily existence into historical time' (2006: 259). *Spiritual Voices* does not transform them either; war along the frontier becomes a Bakhtinian chronotope. We are offered no historical context, no analysis of causes and motivations, no political or ideological commentary, and no assessment of the conflict's progress – in line with the diary's preference for microhistory over macro-history. As Alexandra Tuchinskaya has suggested, writing about the film *Confession*,

> For Sokurov the military theme has long been interpreted as an existential one and so service on the frontiers, be they land or sea, becomes a metaphor for human behaviour. Compulsory military service, an institution that remains in the shattered civic life of Russia, is viewed by the filmmaker as an essential feature of reality, something that touches everyone – males and females, those who have served in the army, those who have avoided it. It is a life of submission, a lack of freedom, a dependence on circumstances, of seclusion and the monotony of the daily routine.[16] (n.d.)

While the existential theme is crucial, *Spiritual Voices* also remains a document of the fighting on the border between Tadjikistan and Afghanistan, and of the life of the Russian guards at frontier post 11.

The registration of daily cycles in *Spiritual Voices* is not only a consequence of the camera's affinity for the representation of reality as a succession of temporal presents, as suggested by Jameson, but also an effect of the adoption of the structure and style of the diary, with its tendency towards immediacy, contingency, micro-history and calendar time. However, through its incremental repetition, the diary also suggests and reproduces the sensation of the flow (and circularity) of time, and evokes the consciousness of both its emptiness and its fullness. In *Spiritual Voices*, Sokurov is attentive simultaneously to the repetition of the daily routine, and to the dimension of the exceptional temporal rarefaction produced by war (especially by war at the frontier, with an enemy always there, just beyond the border) – in which time becomes remarkably dense, thick with anticipation and anguish; or else disappears altogether, as indicated by the following exchange between soldiers, occurring in episode five:

> – The day's over.
> – Tomorrow is another day.
> – We'll go through the day, same as ever.
> – Is it Wednesday or Thursday?
> – Tuesday.
> – Only Tuesday? ... I've lost all account of time.[17]

Spiritual Voices is capable of actually reproducing the feeling of time, in all the acuteness and potency that result from its sheer mobility, from the brute impact of temporality as it emerges from the sensation of time passing, the sense that time can be empty, the act of recording time as it passes, the dimension of waiting, of recurrence and repetition, and the ignorance and expectation of the future.

Partly, this effect is the result of a peculiarly filmic temporal dimension, inscribed in the flow of the very slow-paced, and sometimes fixed, shots, which, for the director, are not contemplative in a self-absorbed, aestheticised manner. Rather, they allow for the spectator's exploration of the image, and participation in the creation of the film's artistic world: 'The most important quality the film image can possess is its capacity to offer the viewer sufficient time to peruse the picture, to participate in the process of attentively looking for something' (Sokurov, in Sedofsky 2001: 2). Temporality is, therefore, literally inscribed in the single shot, thus achieving an acute affective impact on the spectator.

The articulation of the thematic interest of temporality in the five episodes is multilayered. Episode one is a pure essay, on the life, death and music of Mozart and other European composers. Its essayistic structure is indisputable: the single authorial viewpoint manifests itself through an enunciator/narrator who identifies with the real author. In voice-over, Sokurov muses about Mozart, destiny, the frailty of human life, classical music and contemporary music, the inability of the artist to reconcile with his life and his times, the contrast between human imperfection and artistic flawlessness. His speech opens problems, probes ideas and suggests ways of thinking about these topics. In voice-over, Sokurov addresses the spectator directly, as a partner in the communication – he involves him by sharing his opinions and sensations ('what a lightness of touch!'); by pleading with him ('Listen carefully. Listen carefully to the music, and try to feel the sounds'); by creating a close association between the speaking 'I' and listening 'you', based on the essay's implicit humanistic assumption of a sensibility shared by the two partners in the communication ('We are now going to hear the music of Olivier Messiaen'; 'Let us listen to it again, so as to remember it, to keep it in our souls').

Sokurov's argument, however, is not confined to the voice-over; much of it emerges from the interaction between the spoken text, the visuals and the music. The visuals are made up of an angled, fixed long shot of a frozen landscape; a snowy expanse in the foreground is hemmed in by a line of pine trees, behind which we glimpse a lake, bordered by mountains in the background. While the description of this shot suggests fixity, the landscape is, in truth, extraordinarily mobile, thanks to the effects of a highly changeable light, the oncoming of the evening, the arrival of a flock of gulls, the transit of a human figure, the approaching of another figure who stops to light a fire. The landscape contributes two main elements to Sokurov's argument: it introduces the nature/culture divide (culture being obviously represented by the music we hear, which encapsulates the civilisation that Sokurov will leave behind when travelling to the frontier in episode two); and it provides a physical embodiment of one of the main themes of the essay: temporality. Time is inscribed in the frame both through its fixity and stillness, and its changeability and progression – similarly to Andy Warhol's eight-hour-long shot of the Empire State Building in *Empire* (1964), the film comes to resemble a moving painting, which slowly evolves and imperceptibly but profoundly transforms before our eyes. Thirty minutes into the film, when the light has almost disappeared, a fade interrupts the tangible, mesmerising flow of time, and introduces for a few seconds the close-up of a sleeping soldier, and with it the topic of the rest of *Spiritual Voices*. Again, Sokurov fades in on a sleeping soldier about five minutes later – and it is the last image of the episode.

Time is also a major topic of Sokurov's verbal musing, which touches on questions such as the brevity and misery of life (Mozart died at 35 years of age, and the description of his death is heart-rending); the relationship between the limitedness and even ugliness of the human being and the durability and sublimity of artistic creation; the contrast between the past and the present, seen for instance in the different visions and opinions of a man that are held by his contemporaries and by posterity, or in the dissimilarity between classical music (Mozart, Beethoven) and contemporary music (Messiaen, 'a man of our times'). The soundtrack also contributes to the theme, with the particular temporality introduced by the music – by its movements and its tempo.

Travelling, both in space and time, is a key aspect of the diary form. Many diaries are travelogues; and all diaries keep a record of time and of its passing. In the specific experience of the diary film, which is divided between the moment of filming and the moment of editing, travel in time is unavoidable. As Russell remarks: 'The diary film involves a journey between the times of shooting and editing; travelling becomes a form of temporal experience through which the film- or videomaker confronts himself or herself as tourist, ethnographer, exile, or immigrant' (1999: 279). *Spiritual Voices* is, indeed, the diary of a journey; furthermore, the film performs an actual travel in time – bridging the moment of the editing and the moment of the shooting. In *Spiritual Voices*, in fact, Sokurov's voice-over speaks sometimes in the past tense, hence from the 'now' of the post-production, other times in the present, in the 'now' of the filming. In episode two, the passage from one temporal layer to the other is, indeed, performed as a form of travel in time. At the onset of the episode, Sokurov declares that he is reading his own journal; while recollecting the events, he states: 'At the beginning of June, with a light heart, yet also with sadness, I quickly collected my things and left Russia.' The experience of remembering and reconstructing the past imperceptibly mutates and transforms into that of going back in time, and living the events unfolding on the screen, as if they were happening here and now. The film performs this passage via a cross fade, which takes us all the way from the snowy Russian expanse to the scorching landscape of Tadjikistan. The use of tenses in Sokurov's speech abruptly changes: 'In June, Tadjikistan is already very hot. Against all odds, I have arrived here ... Now I know that in a few hours I'll be at the border.' After this point in the episode, Sokurov speaks in the present, hence fulfilling the two rules of the diary, which must say 'I' and 'now'.

Episode two, furthermore, straightforwardly adopts the structure of a travelogue; travelling, thus, truly becomes a form of temporal experience. We witness Sokurov's flight by helicopter to the border with Afghanistan, where a military vehicle then takes him to the frontier post. On the short helicopter flight, the camera frames the faces of the soldiers, insisting on the close-up of a young man who appears particularly tense, and often looks anxiously into the lens, directly at the spectator.[18] It feels as if Sokurov wants to capture on camera even the soldiers' dreams, or their 'spiritual voices', as suggested by the shot of the sleeping soldier in episode one; by the one of soldiers standing in a row with their eyes closed, which is used twice in episode two; and by the soldier's dream of a woman's laughter, gunshots and clouds, visualised towards the end of the third episode.[19] 'God help us all', Sokurov whispers as the helicopter takes off; but it is the following drive which most worries him and the soldiers. Sokurov notes that the road parallels a precipice and the River Panjsher, which marks the border with Afghanistan. This long drive through the mountains is the only route to the frontier post, but is extremely dangerous and the soldiers fear ambushes. The camera seems restrained, possi-

Spiritual Voices: tension and interpellation on the helicopter flight in episode two

bly following orders, and its viewing scope is limited; we glimpse rifles, uniforms, tense gazes; over an image of himself sitting at the back of the car, Sokurov's voice admits: 'I keep a sharp eye all around.' The dimension of travelling that Sokurov highlights is, therefore, decidedly temporal: one made up of duration, anxiety and suspense. When the convoy finally reaches its destination ('We've arrived'), the camera, in a release of tension, looks all around, pauses on soldiers doing nothing, passing the time, chatting and playing. The temporal flow slows down (some slow motion is also used); the rarefaction produced by the anti-climax favours notetaking, the observation of the mundane and inconsequential.

The third episode opens with Sokurov once again marking the temporal distance between the 'now' of the editing and the 'now' of the shooting: 'This is what I wrote in my diary: It was very hot last night. I slept a dreamless sleep.' The voice continues to use the past tense, and describes actions that we actually see unfolding on the screen: 'At that time, we often used to leave the little valley where the company was stationed and climb keeping strictly to the paths, up and up'. After further descriptions of these past treks, the voice ceases and allows the conversations among soldiers to take centre stage. These conversations, and the urgency and presentness of the images (often accompanied by gunshots in the distance), bring the temporal dimension back to the here and now; the gap introduced by the voice fades and disappears. Unsurprisingly, when the voice-over emerges again, it speaks in the present: 'If these soldiers win an engagement, they save their own lives and the lives of those below. If they lose, everyone dies. In this war, it seems, no prisoners are ever taken.' As in the previous episode, from this point onward Sokurov speaks only in the present tense.

The episode covers a day at the outpost – though it is difficult to say whether all the material was shot over a 24-hour period, the strong sensation of the record of a day is conveyed by the opening, diaristic remark about 'last night', and the several references made by the voice-over to 'today' ('Today is a strange, uneasy day'; 'The day is over'); by the changing light, from dawn to daylight, from dusk to night; and by the focus on the succession of daily activities, which include reaching the outpost, chatting, reading, napping under the sun, cooking, eating, smoking, writing, listening to some music on an old tape recorder, coming back to the base, eating, doing night guard, sleeping. Gunshots are often heard in the background; we once see a soldier firing his gun from a fortified hut; later, we hear mortar shots, and are informed of rumours of snipers, wounded soldiers and even a dead Russian guard. Yet, it is a day without open fighting; a day in which, once again, the temporal dimension is one of waiting, of hiatus and suspense, as suggested by the following dialogue between two soldiers:

– I reckon the war is over. They have left us alone today.
– Don't speak too soon.

And again:

– Anyway it's quiet today. What about tomorrow?

This dimension is also emphasised by the sombre extra-diegetic music, which surfaces even at times of apparent relaxation for the soldiers. The episode concludes with the same music, on images of stormy clouds and *The Wounded Angel* (1903), a painting by Hugo Simberg in which two grave-looking boys carry an angel, who has hurt her head and wings. One of the boys stares out of the picture directly at the spectator. The wounded angel on a stretcher anticipates the theme of the next entry.

Episode four, which is solidly linked to the previous one by images of dark clouds and the same musical piece on which episode three ended, starts *in medias res* – both in the sense that Sokurov's speech is in the same tense of the events that unfold on screen, the present; and because the day is advanced: 'All day long, the sun has kept coming out, only to disappear again behind pale clouds. A sultry day, devoid of colour.' While the previous diary entry was devoted mainly to mundane activities, this is a day of preparation for military operations, and then of fighting. A trench is dug alongside the river, orders are given, mines are carefully armed and laid in the ground, strategy is discussed and positions are communicated to the soldiers.

Suddenly, the post is attacked. The camera is kept at short distance from the fighting; either near the senior officers, who communicate over the radio and control the operations from behind the lines, or closer to the action, with shakier shots. We witness explosions and guns being fired, dust lifted; we hear gunshots, occasionally accompanied by the usual, sombre music. Despite the confusion, a sort of narrative of the battle is created through the editing, by alternating images of fighting and those of the officers reacting to the events, exchanging information and making plans. The quality of the image changes significantly; its unsteadiness, errors, lack of focus and sudden shifts are a product of the camera-man's jerky reactions to gunshots, of his running or ducking, or of his attempts to follow the action – the high reactivity of video becomes key to these sequences.

Over a trembling tracking shot along a trench, Sokurov comments: 'War is hideous, from the very first shot to the last. There is nothing but dust, the smell of burning, stones, hot shrapnel, blood, a hint of fear. No room for aesthet-ics.' Whereas the previous episode privileged the daily time of normal routines, which even in a godforsaken place does have its lyrical and aesthetic side, here we experience the concentrated, dense, desperate time of war – which is simul-taneously intense and empty. Fatal wounds are announced over the radio – there are casualties. Probably triggered by such intensity, Sokurov's speech suddenly switches to the past tense, as if to re-establish the emotional safety of a temporal gap between the speaker and the events: 'As if they knew what was going to hap-pen, they decided to lay more mines around the post.' And again, 'When the base was finally attacked, at first it wasn't frightening.' Finally, 'Everything finished as suddenly as it began. The enemy retreated to the mountains to muster reinforce-ments.'

Once the fighting is over, daily routines and the observation of the mundane resume: bread is baked for dinner; the camera focuses on a hazy sun. Unsurpris-ingly, Sokurov's utterance returns to the present tense; what he says, a replica-tion of his earlier words, attracts attention to the circularity and repetitiousness of daily time: 'All day long, the sun has kept coming out, only to disappear again behind pale clouds. A sultry day.' Life resumes. The soldiers eat and relax. There is some talk of everyday occurrences: there was a birthday today; there was one yesterday too. Gunshots, however, are still occasionally heard outside; the faces, explored by long close-ups, betray tiredness and self-absorption. Two soldiers wash and play with water; a wounded guard on a stretcher is attended to. The surreal whistling of a train can be heard on the last images and the ensuing clos-ing titles – probably the signifier of the wounded soldier's dream of returning home.

The last episode is set in winter, after a temporal gap of some months.[20] It opens, once again, with an aural link to the previous episode (the whistling train), with a reference to Sokurov's journal ('This is what I wrote in my diary: a soldier is warming himself in the sun'), and with the use of the past tense. Sokurov's speech is thoroughly focused on time, and the various facets of its experience at the frontier post – the time dense with anxious waiting, the repetitiousness and circularity of both the seasonal year and the daily cycle, time as presentness and time as memory, the end of time.

It is December, and this is December 31st. That winter, there were some sunny days. It hardly ever snowed, but there were some sunny days. Because of this, all the passes were open to traffic in all directions, and none of us could tell what each day would bring. Meanwhile, we had to get through the day. Sooner or later, and God willing, next year it would be all just memories – memories of our dear ones, be they living or dead.

Unlike in the previous episodes, rather than replicating the usual, one-time movement from memory to actuality, here Sokurov's speech keeps drifting back and forth from the past tense to the present; a soldier is writing a letter, for instance, and Sokurov, observing him, comments: 'His trench overlooks the Panjsher and a foreign country. He himself is far from home. This letter will take three months to arrive'. Such temporal *dérive* is designed to draw attention to the circularity of time – a distinctive trait of diaristic incremental repetitiousness. While we listen to a mesmerising Asian chant and are granted the time to visually explore the surroundings, Sokurov's voice emerges again and, in the past tense, repeats verbatim a sentence we already heard in episode three: 'We often used to leave the little valley where the company was stationed and climb keeping strictly to the paths, up and up'. The surroundings, however, have changed, from the bright landscape burnt by the sun to the darker, cold and barren winter – therefore coming full circle, back to the season of the first episode.

The day recorded in this episode appears to be especially empty. The camera lingers on ordinary, trivial things, sometimes even slowing down the pace – like when it focuses for a long time on a bird sitting on a wire, in slow motion. Unhurried, circular panoramic shots abound, and so do long close-ups of faces. Soldiers seem relaxed, write letters, chat, smoke, eat and wait. The winter day is short, the night falls quickly, and the fifth episode, not unlike the first, becomes for a while a visual essay on the effects of changing light on landscape.

The impression of ordinariness is, however, somehow deceptive. Not only are the soldiers' lives always at risk, as Sokurov's voice-over reminds us; but also this is a special day – 31 December. We move indoors, to follow the preparations for the celebratory dinner. At midnight, the officers drink to the new year, eat cake and sing. The mood suddenly shifts: the absence of a dead comrade becomes conspicuous, and a man sheds some tears. Out into the night, two guards receive the visit of a 'Santa Claus'; but Sokurov's voice is there to remind us that these men must find their way in the dark through minefields. The outpost to which some guards come at three am in order to relieve their comrades for the rest of the night looks cold and inhospitable. Gunshots are heard in the distance. A man jokes: 'A NATO soldier would have topped himself long ago'. The harshness of these people's 'normality' becomes tangible again; and, conversely, so does the fact that even the most severe, exceptional conditions, through continuous repetition, ultimately become matters of daily routine. While eating some dinner, the guards talk about the week, the days that have passed and those still to come; one of them admits that he has lost all sense of time. The celebration of the coming of the New Year is utterly absurd: nothing will change, tomorrow will be the same as today, as the day before. The exceptionality of New Year's Eve, then, only serves to underscore the numbing repetitiveness of the daily, weekly and yearly cycles – in which time simultaneously weighs people down, and dissipates in its own recurrence.

At the end of the episode, the camera lingers on a sleeping soldier. A cross-fade introduces a panoramic shot of the river and of misty mountains. Sokurov's voice-over emerges for the last time, to announce the end of his sojourn at the frontier post: 'Yes, it's time to go back to Russia. In Russia it is still cold. Snow and silence. And not a soul.' The circle is now complete: the utterance, half of which is a repetition from episode one, ideally takes us back where the journey began – both spatially (a Russia connoted by silence and solitude) and temporally (a cold, snowy winter). The image fades on black; bells are heard in the distance. While Sokurov is about to go back, the sleeping soldier can only dream of going home, and of breaking the circle of time. A recurrent image in *Spiritual Voices*, the sleeping soldier could, of course, also stand for a dead soldier; and the bells we hear could be tolling the dead.[21] It is here, during the last sequence, that we fully realise how *Spiritual Voices*, a film in which the threat of death is a daily reality, fulfils the requirement that diaries should always ultimately be about the end of time.

chapter seven
THE NOTEBOOK FILM: PIER PAOLO PASOLINI
AND THE FILM THAT CANNOT BE MADE

'To make a film means (at least for me) to tell the truth about oneself and about what one is in reality.' (Pasolini 2001: 2777; author's translation)

If a diary is open and fragmentary, the notebook is much more so. Humble, receptive of the banal, the mundane, the ongoing, like a diary it functions as an aide-mémoire. Indeed, the notebook is very close to the diary not only in terms of function, but also in terms of textual structures: it is a monologue with the self, a private and self-addressed gesture.[1] The diary, however, is already form, imposed by an activity of recollection and reordering that takes place at some temporal and critical distance, even when very modest, from the events. Lighter and more agile, the notepad accompanies us, always at easy reach, and allows us to jot down ideas, impressions and projects as they emerge, while they still are sketchy and magmatic. The intellectual's and the artist's notebook, differently from the personal diary, which is a finished if fragmentary work, has the distinct role as a stage of and an instrument in the process of creative thinking, of which it can be one of the primary tools (see John-Steiner 1997: 5). For these reasons, the notebook has connotations of urgency, of lack of inhibition and control – and the status simultaneously of a tool and a record (of the process of thought), and of programme (in relation to the finished text that will follow).

What is fascinating about the idea of a cinematic notebook is its function as an early version, or a draft for future films. This function implies a freedom, spontaneity and improvisation that are generally not found in a final, polished product. To the critic, it promises to contain revealing details of a film's gestation, traces of the process by which the director has come to make certain choices and has attained the final vision. Because it records the process of thinking, and reflects thought *in fieri*, it is self-reflexive and essayistic. The notebook carries comments made for oneself – as in a diary, the rhetorical structure is that of a dialogue with the inner self.

The metaphor of the notebook is, however, overtly literary/verbal, and thus seems to deny the audiovisual specificity of the notebook film; the most strictly verbal aspect of the analogy is insufficient to an understanding of this filmic form. A comment on his nonfiction short *Le mura di Sana'a* (literal title *Sana'a's Walls*, 1964), by Pier Paolo Pasolini, whose work will be in focus in the ensuing chapter, clarifies the issue (while, simultaneously, evoking Pasolini's conception of realism, his theories of cinematic language and his writer/director in-betweenness):

> Nothing like making a film forces you to observe things. The writer's gaze on a landscape, be it rural or urban, can omit a great quantity of things, and only pick out of the entire scene those elements which communicate an emotion, or which are useful. The director's gaze on that same landscape cannot avoid becoming aware of everything that is in it. In fact, while for a writer things are destined to become words, that is symbols, in the director's expression things remain things: 'the signs' of the verbal system are therefore symbolic and conventional, while the signs of the cinematographic system are indeed the things themselves, in their materiality and in their reality. (Pasolini, in Caminati 2007: 6; author's translation)

If the written notebook tends to be selective and sober, the filmic one indexically records for future use everything that is situated before the camera. In this sense, the notebook film, while being related to the painter's sketchpad as a visual record, supersedes it by its completeness and faithfulness.

There exist a number of different types of filmed notebooks. The most obvious example is the film of auditions and location scouting. However, while most filmmakers take audiovisual notes (of the locations, of the potential actors) with their cameras before making a film, rarely are these then edited and produced as an independent piece of work. An example is Luchino Visconti's *Alla ricerca di Tadzio* (literal title *In Search of Tadzio*, 1970),[2] which documents the director's pursuit for the right actor to play Thomas Mann's striking adolescent, Tadzio, in *Morte a Venezia* (*Death in Venice*, 1971), and includes images of Visconti's journey (with stopovers in Budapest, Helsinki, Warsaw and Venice), the auditions for the role of Tadzio and for minor roles, as well as some location scouting in Venice. The exploration of Visconti's choice of Björn Andrésen for the role sheds some light on his gestation of the film, his reading of the novella and his impression of the characters. *Alla ricerca di Tadzio*, which was shot in 35mm, has the characteristics of a notebook, because it is not a documentary made on the set during the film's making, but ideally and temporally precedes the film. Other notebook films that chronologically and conceptually precede the features they are made in preparation for are, for instance, Jean-Luc Godard's videos *Scénario de 'Sauve qui peut la vie'* (1979) and *Petites notes à propos du film 'Je vous salue, Marie'* (1983), which explore elements of Godard's future films – respectively *Sauve qui peut la vie* (1980) and *Je vous salue, Marie* (1985) – with reference to the films' subject matter, narrative, characters, acting and cinematography. *Scénario du film 'Passion'* (1982), instead, is a commentary that follows *Passion* (1982) – a reflection on the experience of making that film, as well as on the process/work of filmmaking in general.

One must mention the potential paradox inherent in the transformation into a coherent text of a collection of fleeting audiovisual notes, which served a specific purpose and were intended as an aide-mémoire and a trial (as, for instance, was the case of Visconti's film). The point is that, in the conversion into a documentary, the characteristics of the notebook are ostensibly lost – even if the fragmentary and ephemeral style of the notebook is maintained.

A fitting case study for a reflection on this question is provided by Federico Fellini's *Block-notes di un regista* (*Fellini: A Director's Notebook*, 1969), a fifty-minute television film made for NBC. *Fellini: A Director's Notebook* exemplifies the paradoxical encounter between a filmmaker's contradictory desires for, on the one hand, a fragmentary, unfinished and preliminary form such as the audiovisual notebook and, on the other, its transformation into an accomplished, independent work, as well as the tension between the notebook's vocation for the documentary and its drive towards fiction.

Fellini: A Director's Notebook was born, in Fellini's own words, as a television programme 'in the manner of a notebook (the notebook of a director) consisting of sketches and re-proposals not in a journalistic vein but in one of drama and fantasy' (Fellini 1968). In the same letter to the film's producers, Fellini discusses his planned notebook as a series of portraits of people he consulted during the preparatory phase of *Satyricon* (1969), as a homage to the origins of the cinema and to Fellini's own memory of going to a film theatre with his father when he was a child, and as a rendition of the auditions with actors and extras. The process of making a film, as should be captured by the notebook, is described by Fellini in his letter as made up of 'thoughts, abolitions, cancellations, new births of ideas, characters, episodes' (ibid.). It is this open, chaotic and tumultuous creative process that *Fellini: A Director's Notebook* tries (and succeeds) to capture, not only with reference to *Satyricon*, but also to a project that was never to be realised, *The Voyage of G. Mastorna*. Fellini appears in the film as himself, and through voice-over comments and narrates in English for much of the screen time. We see him as a director with his troupe, filming locations, auditioning actors and extras, talking to people who can help with his historical research, and – most importantly – trying to capture in various locations the right atmosphere for his future film. As is to be expected for a director such as Fellini, however, everything is recreated – *Fellini: A Director's Notebook* does not operate at the level of the documentary, or of the recording of actual location scouting and auditions, but of creative re-enactment, repetition and interpretation. Nevertheless, the fragmentation, disorder and unfinished quality typical of the notebook are preserved or, more precisely, are perfectly recreated by Fellini, as a specific style – in a sense, *Fellini: A Director's Notebook* is a true pastiche of the notebook, and a *mise en abyme* of the form. Fellini's film is paradigmatic, as it shows that any notebook film will always be an act of montage and reordering, no matter how minimal, on the actual magma of audiovisual notetaking.

Other declared notebook films were not originally born as notes on location scouting or on actors or on the future films' meaning and form; but, more decidedly, as actual, independent works – I refer to films such as Visconti's *Appunti su un fatto di cronaca* (literal title *Notes on a Local News Item*, 1951), and Wim Wenders' *Aufzeichnungen zu Kleidern und Städten* (*Notebook on Cities and Clothes*, 1989). In both cases, the notetaking is not about a future film, but about a specific topic. The former was made as part of a filmed monthly magazine, directed by Riccardo Ghione, but was screened for the first time in Paris in 1953. Inspired by the rape and murder of a young girl in the Roman suburbs, with a text by novelist Vasco Pratolini read by Giorgio De Lullo, and music by Franco Mannino, the five-minute film was a lyrical examination of the desolate setting of the murder.[3] Wenders' 35mm *Notebook on Cities and Clothes* was commissioned by the Centre Georges Pompidou and filmed in Tokyo and Paris. As Wenders says in voice-over at the start of the film, he called it a notebook because of the progressive, accumulative way in which it came into being, as notes taken by the director on a day-to-day basis, without a clear overall strategy at the onset of the film. Indeed, this structure is typical of the travelogue, in which the openness and unpredictability of the journey dictate the random accumulation of notations.

Similarly to Wenders' *Notebook on Cities and Clothes*, many of the films that could be included in an ideal group of notebooks are, indeed, travelogues – in which the camera is used to record impressions of places and landscapes. One such work is the television series *L'India vista da Rossellini* (literal title *India as Seen by Rossellini*, 1957–58), which contains the images Rossellini shot in 16mm during his trip to India, and which maintains the episodic structure and the freedom of the sketch. Indeed, this film was, literally, the sketchpad for the film *India: Matri Buhmi* (1959), which was instead shot in 35mm. Another interesting example of travelogue/sketchbook is Louis Malle's *Calcutta* (1969), a montage of images of life in the Indian metropolis, which displays next to no narrative intervention and structure. Michelangelo Antonioni's Super8 travelogue on China, *Chung Kuo-China* (1972), is described in the voice-over at the beginning of the film as a set of 'filmed notes'. Furthermore, of course, all of Pasolini's notebook films are travelogues.

My choice of focusing on Pier Paolo Pasolini is dictated by the recurrence of the notebook form in his filmic work (and in his oeuvre in general), as well as by the indisputable interest of his documentaries, which have attracted far less critical attention than his fiction. These films offer one of the most striking examples of audiovisual self-representation by an artist, whose work was profoundly concerned with the 'I', and whose persona was at least as important as his oeuvre.

A director's notebook: Pasolini and the films to be made

Pasolini is one of the modern directors who most consistently made use of the notebook form. The fragmentation and openness that are characteristic of note-taking are to be found not only in his cinema, but also in his essay work and his literary production; it suffices to think of *Petrolio*, on which Pasolini worked from 1972 until his death in 1975. Published posthumously (and unfinished) in 1992, voluntarily marked by disconnectedness and heterogeneity, *Petrolio* was intended by Pasolini as his *magnum opus*, a vast novel in fragments that mixed 'things done and things to be done, polished pages and sketched pages, or just intentional ones' (Pasolini, in Benedetti 1998: 47; author's translation). In its current form, it is organised in 133 'notes', some of which are multiple.

This work is a case in point, an example of the essayistic nature of the literary notebook (and, similarly, of the filmic notebook), not only because reflection is inscribed in it as a process, but also on account of its communicative structure. In a letter to Alberto Moravia, Pasolini writes that *Petrolio* is a novel but, unlike a true novel, it adopts the language 'of the essay, of certain newspaper articles, of reviews, of private letters, or even poetry' (2005: 579; author's translation). Pasolini focuses here on the figure of the enunciator/narrator and his relationship with the reader:

> In the novel, the narrator usually disappears and leaves his place to a conventional figure, the only one that can have a true relationship with the reader. True precisely because conventional. Not by accident ... the real protagonist of the act of reading a novel is, indeed, the reader. In these pages, instead, I addressed the reader directly rather than conventionally. This means that I did not transform my novel into an 'object', a 'form', hence obeying the laws of a language that ensured its necessary distance from me, almost abolishing me, or through which I generously denied myself, humbly disappearing behind a narrator that is the same as any other narrator. Rather, I talked to the reader as myself, in flesh and bone, as I write this letter to you, or as I often wrote my poems in Italian. I made of the novel an object placed between the reader and I, and discussed it together (as one can do with himself, when writing). (2005: 579–80; author's translation)

The relevance of this metacritical passage for an understanding of the notebook form, in terms of essayistic communicative strategy (the direct dialogue), of the coincident enunciator/narrator, and of the performance of the self ('in flesh and bones'), is evident. Here, it is necessary, however, to focus not only on the dialogue enunciator/receiver, and on self-representation, but also on the specificity of the notebook, which coincides with its provisional character and its magmatic openness.

As several critics have noted, the interest for the openness of the work in progress can be traced in Pasolini's theorisation, and especially in the concept of the 'unmade', or 'to be made' (*da farsi*) – a fitting example is the essay on 'The screenplay as a structure which wishes to be another structure', in which Pasolini discusses the screenplay as an autonomous text, alluding to the film 'to be made' (see Pasolini 1988a). The 'unmade' does not simply coincide with an aesthetic of the unfinished art piece, but corresponds to 'the necessity of creating a work with a fluid structure, which on the one hand is capable of reflecting the Marxist socio-political vision of society ... and on the other what Eco, referring to Brecht's theatre, calls "revolutionary pedagogy"' (Caminati 2007: 9; author's translation). The refusal to polish the literary work, as well as the use of an approximate cinematic technique, can be seen as Pasolini's resistance to the process of transformation of the work of art to an object of consumption. It, thus, becomes clear that the adoption of the form of the notebook, which pushes this stylistic research to its limits, not only has an aesthetic but also an ideological motivation in Pasolini.

Four of Pasolini's documentary films are, declaredly, notebooks: *Sopralluoghi in Palestina* (literal title *Location Scouting in Palestine*, 1965),[4] *Appunti per un film sull'India* (literal title *Notes Towards A Film on India*, 1968), *Appunti per un romanzo dell'immondezza* (literal title *Notes Towards a Novel on Rubbish*, 1970)[5] and *Appunti per un'Orestiade africana* (*Notes Towards an African Orestes*, 1970). Pasolini also wrote notebooks on future films; for instance, his *Sopralluoghi* or *La ricerca dei luoghi perduti* (literal titles *Location Scouting* or *The Search For Lost Places*) is a notebook/travelogue written in 1973 during the journey in preparation for *I fiori delle Mille e una notte* (*Flower of the Arabian Nights*, 1974). *Appunti per un poema sul Terzo Mondo* (literal title *Notes for a Poem on the Third World*, 1968) was written instead in view of a filmic project of the same title, in five episodes, one of which was the *Orestiade africana* (*African Orestes*), which only exists in the form of a filmed notebook (these texts are now collected in Mancini & Perrella 1981). *Notes for a Poem on the Third World*, which was meant to include notebook films on India, Africa, Arabia, Latin America and the black ghettos of the United States, shows how serious and still evolving Pasolini's engagement with the notebook form was. *Notes for a Poem on the Third World* was conceived by Pasolini as 'a film to be made on a film to be made': a spurious, complex film where 'The sections in which the story is narrated in a traditional manner will be shot and edited according to normal procedures; the sections of location scouting for the "story to be made" will preserve their casual and immediate quality' (Pasolini 1981b: 37; author's translation).

The rhetoric of the self

In the pages that follow, I will mainly focus on *Sopralluoghi in Palestina*, with a view to discussing the nature of the notebook film in general, and in particular to analysing this film's specific communicative structure, as well as investigating the nature of Pasolini's self-portrait. At the onset of an account of Pasolini's self-representation, it is indispensable to refer, on the one hand, to the importance of the 'I' in Pasolini's work and, on the other, to the process of mythologising what the figure of the artist has undergone since his death in 1975 – when he went from being widely dismissed in Italy as a provocateur, criticised for the thinly-veiled pornographic content of his *Trilogy of Life*, to a figure of moral authority and integrity based on 'a clearly Romantic vision of the artist as an isolated, persecuted figure, who is thereby a privileged source of truth or of an absolute – even mystic – insight into reality and art' (Gordon 1999: 41). Even though my concern here is specifically with the figure of Pasolini as enunciator in the text, and as onscreen persona, and only tangentially with his offscreen personality, it is obvious that the two feed one another; and it is also clear that Pasolini's own strategies of self-representation border and engage with the representations of him that have been made by others.

Pasolini's poetic world is firmly based on the figure of the 'I'. Robert Gordon detected a number of modalities of the expression of the self in Pasolini's poetry, journalistic output and cinema, which go from the presence of autobiographical data to the identification or refiguration of the speaking subject in fictional or mythical figures, from specific stylistic tropes to the writing of the self into ideas of history, ideology and myth. As Gordon clarified, 'Any discussion of the role of self-construction in Pasolini must start from the primary and absolute importance assigned in his value system to selfhood and to the potentially overwhelming expressivity of the self and his desires' (1999: 42). For the author, the value of the private sphere in Pasolini is simultaneously in its innocence and authenticity, and in its projection into a public role. This dynamic is based 'on a paradoxical combination of expression of the self's innermost, guilt-ridden being and an apparent inability to control or dictate the terms of expression' (ibid.) – the self's incapability of deceit, its innocence ultimately attest to the authenticity of its public expression. Of course, Pasolini's construction of his selfhood is a rhetorical process, which can be studied as such. One of the early critics of Pasolini, Franco Fortini, had already suggested in 1959 that Pasolini's work is in the form of a performance and a masquerade, and that 'The idea of an authenticity through the inauthentic ... is the moral formula Pasolini holds dearest' (in Gordon 1999: 44; see also Gordon 1996: 5).

The construction of Pasolini's selfhood took place also outside his work, namely in the public and mediatic spheres. While Pasolini often portrayed himself as a victim of the media, he was of course sophisticated enough to manipulate them and use them to his own advantage. Simona Bondavalli, for instance, has argued that, during the 1960s, Pasolini gradually gave rise to a complex literary and extra-literary operation, willingly blurring the public and the private, the person and the author; an operation that resulted in the affirmation of a 'spectacular authorship': 'Through a manipulation of his own image, he creates a spectacular identity that converses with media culture in order to maintain authority over the critical impact of his works' (2007: 25).

If, on the one hand, Pasolini expertly controlled his image in the media, in order to simultaneously offer the media what they expected of him and to critique them, on the other hand his image was controlled by the society of the spectacle. Not only an outspoken Marxist intellectual, who vehemently opposed Italian bourgeois capitalism, but also an 'out' homosexual at a time when Italy was blatantly and unashamedly homophobic, he made his body the site of a 'scandal', to use one of his most recurrent expressions; he put it constantly at stake. And society did not avert its gaze: indeed, it tried to consume, but also fix, control and discipline the image of Pasolini.

In his analysis of photographs of the artist published by the Italian press from the mid-1960s onwards, John Di Stefano rightly noted that, 'Caught somewhere between revulsion and fascination, Italians developed an obsession with Pasolini's body' (1997: 20). Pasolini was constantly framed in ways that confirmed his 'monstrosity', positioned him against the dominant order, separated him from society, or, as in the final police still of his disfigured body, 'sent a profound and horrific message to anyone who dares challenge the order and assert his or her difference' (1997: 23). Pasolini's body was the site of an ideological battle, which he did not shun but, rather, embraced. He was simultaneously persecuted, and cultivated the myth of his own martyrdom.

Heretical Orientalism

Whilst being ostensibly about location scouting, Pasolini's notebook films, and especially *Sopralluoghi in Palestina*, are deeply concerned with self-representation. This may be explained by the conditions in which they were shot, during journeys in Africa and India, places that constituted for Pasolini the Third World, and radical otherness – an otherness that unavoidably prompted a redefinition of the self. As a consequence, before examining his self-portrait, it is necessary to briefly engage with Pasolini's portrait of the Third World. This is, notoriously, a thorny topic; I have no ambition to exhaust it here, but only to engage with some of its main aspects, and especially those that allow me to introduce my analysis.

According to Keith Richards, *Notes Towards an African Orestes*

> is a puzzling and self-contradictory array of disparate images and oddly in-coherent voice-over commentary. Here, the cinematic medium, allied with Pasolini's cultural preconceptions, results in a palpably alienating mechanism. Africans are filmed not for themselves, but for what resemblance they sug-gest to Aeschylus' characters. Similarly the African situation is forced into the mould of Greek political development. (2006: 57)

Richards is not the first scholar to point out the problematic side of Pasolini's representation of the Third World (as he always called it), not only in the note-book films, but also in written works such as the diary *L'odore dell'India* (literal title *Scent of India*; see, for instance, Bongie 1991; Rinaldi 1981; Riva & Parussa 1997). While Pasolini's 'Oriental' texts are an easy target for postcolonial cultural theorists, Richards' unreserved rejection of *Notes Towards an African Orestes* is almost too unproblematic. Firstly, I dissent from the accusation of incoherence, contradiction and disorder contained in the above quotation; I do not see why films should ascribe to an ideal form – structured, logical and congruous – in or-der to be progressive, and fall into the category of films that (as Richards expect-ed from Pasolini, but was disappointed not to find in his notebook) make 'radical efforts towards a poetics and politics of film' (Richards 2006: 57) – or perhaps, to put it more simply, films that are politically correct. How productive is it to complain about incoherence in a film that is programmatically incoherent? As Pasolini's voice-over recites in *Notes Towards an African Orestes*, when abruptly interrupting the course of his African search in order to return to Europe: 'I am tearing that style without style that is the style of documentary notebooks.' I take this opportunity to begin to signal that, in styleless/open/unfinished forms such as the notebook, the formless is bound to make its appearance (here, in the tear, and in the music, which borders with noise).

At the level of postcolonial critique, I find it problematic that, while we would probably consider it acceptable for a Western/white director to scrutinise una-ware Western/white potential actors in search of character resemblance, Afri-cans should instead be filmed 'for themselves' (a questionable expression in it-self; supposedly without voice-over commentary, and in a *cinéma-vérité* style);

the same goes for Africa, which should never stand for Greece in the eyes of a European director. Pasolini should have simply stayed at home – or should have let the camera roll, refraining from commentary, as well as from paradox and disorder. Pasolini, however, at all levels a true *agent provocateur*, was never politically correct; furthermore, he abhorred naturalism: 'I hate naturalness. I reconstruct everything' (in Stack 1969: 132).

The reason why analyses of this type are ultimately unsatisfactory is that, while pointing out lists of cultural stereotypes and racist tropes, they say more about current cultural perspectives than about the director's, and do not significantly advance our understanding of the examined works. Luca Caminati's recent reassessment of Pasolini's 'heretical Orientalism', to use the critic's own expression, provides us with a more subtle and complete understanding of Pasolini's Third World texts. Rather than expecting from Pasolini, during the second half of the 1960s, an unlikely postcolonial correctness, Caminati knows that his Orient could only be imbued with Western cultural memories and constructs. Reading his *L'odore dell'India*, for instance, Caminati shows how Pasolini was aware of this burden, and employed strategies to counteract it, for instance the notion of originality, used in the attempt to 'guarantee to the reader a unique, exclusive narration, in order to highlight the originality and veracity of the experience' (2007: 20–1; author's translation). Of course, there was nothing unique in Pasolini's dream of innocence, which is imbued in stereotyping, characterised by the normalisation and crystallisation of the Other, and marked by his ahistorical gaze; but his text also bears witness to 'the director's realisation of the inevitability of the residual presence of stereotypical images when one undertakes the representation of otherness' (2007: 22; author's translation). Pasolini struggles against the tradition of Orientalism, which he clearly wishes to reject, but which he can only repress.

The decision to film India after writing about it in *L'odore dell'India* was the result of Pasolini's awareness of the failure to unburden himself of literary traditions. In *Notes Towards A Film on India*, Pasolini – as he explains in voice-over – 'did not come here to make a documentary, a chronicle, an inquest on India, but to make a film on a film on India'. This film on a film on India, presented as a humble, unfinished notebook, does not hide but indeed emphasises and explodes the paradoxical nature of Pasolini's 'metafilms'. It is in this light that Pasolini's study of native peoples through the lens of the camera must be critically assessed. Sam Rohdie pointed out that the faces Pasolini looks for in his location scouting trips are figurative citations, remembered images: 'Reality was in the analogy' (1995: 60). Pasolini did not reject the Western iconographic tradition; rather, he accepted that this tradition shaped his own ideas and expectations of the Orient – as that idealised past that he could no longer find at home. And yet, the faces he filmed also remain real faces, part of the film's indexicality. And it is precisely Pasolini's choice of projecting cultural tropes onto these faces, while simultaneously filming them 'for what they are', that allows them to escape the reduction to a paradigm:

> These Pasolinian faces, so typical of his cinema, are in fact, and at the same time, the real faces of India and the projection of the filmmaker's gaze onto India, the product of his preconstituted, mediated vision of India. Working under the aegis of the 'location scouting' allows Pasolini to portray Indians without reducing them to mere 'types' (in a Lukacsian sense) and stereotypes (in an ethnographic sense) of a culture, where we often see a social actor becoming an example of some ethnographic theory. (Caminati 2007: 62; author's translation)[6]

Third World otherness coincides for Pasolini with premodernity and myth, with the opposite of the Western home. From a political/ideological perspective, it was the place where, after being disappointed by the disappearance of the Western subproletariat at the hands of neocapitalist modernisation, Pasolini hoped to recover/discover the mythical, natural state of a premodern rural culture, not yet tarnished by industrialisation and consumerism. One must remember, however, that Pasolini was well aware of the impossibility of his dream: 'Much of his lament at present reality revolved around the need to recall the ideal, tempered with the knowledge that it was after all only ideal, a myth, a dream, a fiction, a memory, desire, longing' (Rohdie 1995: 52). The Third World, hence, was always already going to simultaneously fulfil and disappoint Pasolini's search for an ideal. But it is also important to recall that his search was linguistic as much as it was ideological.

> The Third World in Pasolini's work figures as part of a problem for a European artist of what to speak and how to narrate ... Pasolini's social regressiveness and reactionary positions were linked to an artistic modernism. He was not simply, or even primarily, in search of a lost innocence, but rather used that search to pose the problem of how to write, that is the relation of writing to reality in the contemporary world. (Rohdie 1995: 55)

Indeed, the simultaneous fulfilment and disappointment of Pasolini's search for his premodern ideal, and for a linguistic form to express it, are both evident in *Sopralluoghi in Palestina*. It is the paradox inherent in this dual movement of fulfilment/disappointment that materialises lack and longing in both the director's lived and cinematographic experience – a lack which informs Pasolini's self-portrait in this film.

None of this material can be used: *Sopralluoghi in Palestina*

Given the direct presence of the author as enunciator 'in flesh and bones', self-representation is important in all Pasolini's notebooks, even those in which he is less present (at least in terms of image; for his voice is ubiquitous). *Notes Towards an African Orestes*, for instance, opens with the image of the director behind the camera, while he comments in voice-over: 'I am reflected with my camera in the shop window of an African town.' The importance of such an opening is self-evident; Caminati rightly points out that this sequence encapsulates Pasolini's participatory, self-reflexive method of approaching the Other. By signalling from the onset his subjective participation, Pasolini simultaneously authenticates his encounter with the Other and undermines the objective/scientific approach traditionally required of a documentary (see Caminati 2007: 69).

I would add that Pasolini here declares more than his participation; by framing himself behind the camera, he unambiguously puts himself forward as the source of the filmic enunciation. Furthermore, via the stratagem of the reflection and self-gazing, he indicates that this film is as much a self-portrait as it is a notebook on a film to be made; and that the film will also be a reflection on cinematic language. Finally, by opening the film with his own image, Pasolini continues his strategy, adopted throughout his oeuvre, to make recourse 'to the essential signifier of an "authentic" body as a public locus of discourse, in response to the exclusion from discourse and from narrative sexual ideologies' (Gordon 1996: 2–3). Perhaps one should also mention here the figure of Narcissus, the 'founding figure in the gallery of figures of identification in Pasolini's poetry ... who embodies a pure self-contemplation which fails to break out of the limits of re-flexivity' (Gordon 1996: 138). Although in this case the narcissistic self-gazing is not unaware, but framed by the self-reflexive presence of the camera, echoes of the eroticism of self-contemplation are perhaps not lost. In this shot, the screen literally becomes a reflective surface, simultaneously implying the author's narcissistic mirroring and offering the spectator the possibility of identifying with him.

Self-representation in Pasolini's fictional cinema, while being active at many levels (for instance, stylistic and thematic), has most directly and overtly taken place via the director's own appearances, for instance in *Edipo re* (*Oedipus Rex*, 1967), *Il Decameron* (*The Decameron*, 1971) and *I racconti di Canterbury* (*The Canterbury Tales*, 1972) or, slightly more covertly, via his (partial) identifications with historical, mythical or fictitious characters, for instance the left-wing intellectual crow in *Uccellacci e uccellini* (*Hawks and Sparrows*, 1966), the director (played by Orson Welles) in *La ricotta* (1963, episode of the omnibus *Ro.Go.Pa.G.*), or Christ in *Il Vangelo secondo Matteo* (*The Gospel According to*

St. Matthew, 1964). The latter association is of obvious importance to *Sopral-luoghi in Palestina*, which was made in preparation of *The Gospel According to St. Matthew*; and it is suggested by the theme of the identification of the poet's self with Christ in Pasolini's poetry and cinema,[7] and confirmed by his desire to have Christ played in his film by a famous poet (Yevtushenko and Kerouac were mentioned), as well as by the 'oblique allusion' (Gordon 1996: 199) of casting his own mother as the older Virgin Mary.[8]

Antonio Masotti's photographs of the projection of the *Gospel* on Pasolini's body during *Intellettuale*, an installation by Fabio Mauri performed at the Modern Art Gallery of Bologna on 31 May 1975 (see Mauri 1994), are suggestive simultaneously of the corporality of Pasolini's cinema and of its inscription in the authorial body, which 'bears' the film like a cross. It must, however, be clarified that the autobiographical/lyrical identification with Christ in *The Gospel According to St. Matthew* is never allowed to become the 'object of static contemplation or inert dreaminess' (Ferrero 1994: 57; author's translation), for it is counterbalanced by the epic/lyrical interpretation of Christ as a symbol of protest, of violent rejection of the norm of iniquity and evilness.

The *Gospel* has often been painted as a surprisingly orthodox reading or almost an illustration of *St Matthew*, an idea probably suggested by the Church's reception of this film, epitomised by the OCIC (Organisation Catholique Internationale du Cinéma et de l'Audiovisuel) Award at the 1964 Venice Film Festival. Critics, however, highlighted elements that diverge from this reading, such as the immanentism infused by the director in all the transcendental elements of the Gospel, the portrayal of Christ as a pre-Marxist, super-human hero, rather than an unearthly God, and the recurrence of Pasolinian topics and obsessions, especially the take on those who are excluded from history, the marginalised, peripheral subproletariat (see Micciché 1999: 46–8). Indeed, many described the period of the 'ideological cinema', from *La rabbia* (1963) to *Uccellacci e uccellini*, and which includes both *The Gospel According to St. Matthew* and *Sopralluoghi in Palestina*, as the years of Pasolini's 'utmost isolation' and 'sociopolitical torment', in which Pasolini confronts and deplores the crisis of a country in deep transformation (see Micciché 1999: 33). This comment is fully relevant to *Sopral-luoghi in Palestina*, a film in which the 'torment' of the director is explicit.

Sopralluoghi in Palestina was the result of a journey of location scouting.[9] Having been granted the requested assistance of the institute for the promotion of Catholic culture, Pro Civitate Cristiana, in the preparation of his film based on the Gospel, Pasolini went to Palestine with Don Andrea Carraro and Dr Lucio Settimi of the Pro Civitate, Walter Cantatore of the production company Arco Film, and cameraman Aldo Pennelli. The tour of Israel and Jordan took place between 27 June and 11 July 1963; visited places included the Sea of Galilee, Mount

Tabor, Nazareth, Capernaum, Bar'am, Jerusalem, the River Jordan, Bethlehem and Damascus.

While one can find some sparse references to Pasolini's presence in *Notes for a Film on India* and *Notes Towards an African Orestes* (see Rohdie 1995; Caminati 2007), almost no critical attention has been paid to his self-portrait in *Sopralluoghi in Palestina*. This comes as no surprise, given the scarcity of published critical readings of this text; such lack may to some extent be due to Pasolini's partial disowning of his film: 'It came about very casually, and in fact I never took any part in the camera set-ups or the shooting or anything else' (in Stack 1969: 73; see also Betti & Gulinucci 1991). However, Pasolini's declaration is unconvincing, and was probably prompted by his disappointment at having been called in suddenly by producer Alfredo Bini to show the material 'to a few distributors and Christian Democrat bosses to help the producers' (Pasolini, in Stack 1969: 73).

Even if Pasolini did not shoot the material himself, it is unlikely that he would have granted a young cameraman full freedom, while being a passive presence on set – a possibility that utterly contradicts Pasolini's notorious practice of fully appropriating every artistic product he came in contact with (both his own or of others), as well as his desire to be in control of his own image and to use all media to fashion his public persona. Indeed, Pasolini's hypothetical disinterest and passivity are disproved by the film itself, in which we see him posing for the camera, talking to it, carrying the microphone and prodding his co-traveller Don Andrea in order to make him turn and face the lens. It is believed that Pasolini did not edit the six reels of film.[10] As he suggests in the same interview: 'I had it put together by someone and then just looked over it, but I left everything, including some very ugly cuts which this person had made – who anyway wasn't even a qualified editor. I had it put on in a dubbing-room and improvised a commentary, so altogether the whole film is rather improvised' (ibid.).

It must be noted, first of all, that the minimal and unrehearsed post-production intervention on the 54-minute *Sopralluoghi in Palestina* only reinforces the status of the film as notebook, as ephemeral, open and unstable text. Secondly, the film completely belongs to Pasolini, who is credited as director, and who dominates every image, from the first to the last (his onscreen presence indissolubly links the film with his vision and will). In addition, he made the film his own by superimposing his authorial voice on it as well as a musical commentary (*The St Matthew Passion*, BWV

Pasolini with microphone and notebook in *Sopralluoghi in Palestina* (1965)

244, by Johann Sebastian Bach, which he had already used in *Accattone*). Besides, the 'ugly cuts' are not at all at odds with his customary editing practice – one only needs to recall *The Gospel According to St. Matthew*, with its incredible mismatches and jump-cuts. Finally, *Sopralluoghi in Palestina* must not have been as insignificant to Pasolini as he would like us to believe in this interview, given that he repeated the experience less than three years later, with *Notes Towards a Film on India*, and seeing that the notebook – the 'film to be made on a film to be made' – became such an important practice for him.

Utterly and unquestionably subjective, characterised by the onscreen presence of a strong director/enunciator through the image of his body and the sound of his voice, *Sopralluoghi in Palestina* is more than a documentary, or even a collection of images resulting from location scouting and the search for actors. It is, also and distinctly, an essayistic work. Even though it ostensibly does not present a strong philosophical argument as the films I have explored in the first section of this book, it does indeed offer the director's musings on various topics, including the work of the filmmaker, the relationship between representation and imagination, between spirituality and aesthetics, Christianity and the Arab world, archaism and modernity, capitalism and the subproletariat.

In line with the essay tradition, Pasolini presents his work in this film as a 'research' and a 'quest' ('the eternal problem of my search',[11] he exclaims for instance towards the end of the film), hinting at the aspect of trial and investigation typical of the essay. Reinforced by the many shots filmed from behind the windscreen of the travelling car, the travelogue structure of this text, which for Anita Trivelli (2008) is a road movie journal, perfectly exemplifies and indeed performs the searching ethos of the intellectual quest. Its performative character is self-evident; as Stella Bruzzi suggests, 'the end point of a journey is unknown, defining the journey embarked upon as a fluid performative act' (2006: 118). The journey of course, with its open-ended, casual structure and lack of narrative cohesion, also parallels the rhetorical configuration of the notebook. Not by accident, we often see Pasolini with a notepad in his hand, taking notes, or even using it to protect his head from the sun. The film, furthermore, adopts interpellation throughout, and establishes an intimate dialogue with the spectator, which, I argue, is one of the most distinctive sites of the emotion produced by this text. It is interpellation that I will now pay attention to.

Pasolini taking notes in *Sopralluoghi in Palestina*

Sopralluoghi in Palestina employs, in truth, not only direct verbal interpellation, but a range of communicative registers. Its rhetorical structure is complex – Pasolini's voice-over, imposed in post-production, at a modest temporal distance from the shooting, alternates with moments of dialogue, in the 'now' of the film, in which the sound was recorded live, or even instances of formal interviews. Indeed, at the onset of the film, we see the microphone being carried around alternately by a member of the troupe or by Pasolini himself. In an early scene, a dialogue between Pasolini and his interlocutor Don Andrea is hardly audible, drowned out by the sound of the wind hissing in the microphone. When the two are not speaking, Pasolini, in post-production, cancelled the sound altogether, in order to eliminate the noise. The carelessness in the quality of the shooting testifies to the occasional, ephemeral nature of the notebook style.

On a number of other occasions, the dialogue between Pasolini and Don Andrea is, instead, clearly audible. Interestingly, these are not so much spontaneous conversations, but are set up as interviews, in which Pasolini either asks a question to the priest, or alternatively the priest acts as the interviewer. These exchanges, which strengthen the documentary nature of the film, are, of course, temporally simultaneous with the travel. They function as moments in which Pasolini records his and his partner's impressions, as they are experienced. The intellectual and emotional distance from the events is near zero; in these instances, the film gives account of the fullness of the experience, and preserves it for future use.

Not in all of the scenes, however, was sound recorded simultaneously with the shooting; the majority of the footage is hence accompanied by Pasolini's voice-over, with a background of classical, 'sacred' music – Bach. The music and, especially, the voice-over evidently problematise the visual status of the notebook – by adding a later commentary, they transform the relationship of the images to the immediacy of their recording, and add a filtered, although improvised, critical dimension that is usually (but not necessarily) missing in the act of jotting down one's thoughts. In this sense, *Sopralluoghi in Palestina* is also diary, as much as it is a travelogue.

Pasolini's voice in the film constantly addresses a 'you', whose identity is never revealed. Instinctively, one is tempted to place Don Andrea in the position of the receiver, because he is Pasolini's interlocutor throughout the film – not only the person with whom he travels and to whom he talks, but also in relation to whom he identifies himself, as we will see below. And yet, this association is to be excluded. In the film, in fact, the two address each other in Italian using the formal you ('Lei'), whereas Pasolini's voice-over speaks to an informal, familial you ('tu'). Another possibility is to see this 'you' as Pasolini, who talks to himself, as is typical in notes jotted down to be used at a later stage by their author.

And yet, even this possibility, although attractive, is unconvincing. True, at times Pasolini seems to address himself, for instance when he makes comments that he is to use at a later stage, as a private aide-mémoire: 'In the case I should shoot my film there...'; or again when he wonders, over images of himself and Don Andrea absorbed in conversation: 'What did Don Andrea and I talk about here?' However, far more numerous are the moments in the film when it becomes distinctly clear that 'you' is another – for instance, when Pasolini asks, as if in the middle of an intimate address to a friend or a partner: 'As you can see, these mountains are very similar to those surrounding Crotone; I wonder if you know them'; or when he recites some verses he wrote during the journey, for the benefit of his addressee: 'Wait, maybe I can remember some verses that I wrote during that memorable journey.'

The interpellation is continuous: 'Look here ... as you can see ... you can easily see ... as you saw ... as I will tell you shortly in person, from the screen'. The tone is, at times, that of the epistle, one is tempted to say of the love letter, which warmly includes the addressee in the filmmaker's project: 'No further comment is needed to explain to you why Nazareth is totally unusable for our film.' It is at this time that it becomes clear the addressee is the film's producer and Pasolini's friend, Alfredo Bini.[12] And yet, Bini is never named, his presence never overtly acknowledged, his voice never heard – hence allowing for the ambiguity of the address, and for the position of the addressee to be filled by the spectator, who feels directly summoned.[13]

The relentless appeal to another person reaches moments of intimate exchange: 'I anxiously strive to remember the names of the places, to communicate the emotion of this moment to you'. I argue that the film establishes a personal, amorous dialogue between Pasolini/enunciator and his spectator, who is summoned as a close, intimate friend, almost as a lover, who is asked to watch the images together with the director, share his search, his personal experience – an experience of which the enunciator wants to communicate and share the emotion. My reading is perfectly in tune with Pasolini's description of the spectator in his 1970 essay, 'Il cinema impopolare' ('The Unpopular Cinema'):

> For the author, the spectator is merely another author. And here he is unquestionably correct, and not the sociologists, the politicians, the pedagogues, etc. If in fact the spectator were in a subordinate position with respect to the author – if he were, that is, the unit of a mass (sociologists), or a citizen to be lectured (politicians), or a child to be educated (pedagogues), then one couldn't even speak of an author, who is neither a social worker, nor a propagandist, nor a school teacher. If then we speak of works by an author, we must consequently speak of the relationship between author and intended recipient as a dramatic relationship between democratically equal individuals. (1988b: 269)

The sound of Pasolini's soft, gentle voice, reaching from the past for his equal, for the individual, for his lover-spectator, as co-author of the film, is an experience for the contemporary audience that has little to do with the imposition of a repressive meaning on the film, as suggested by many theorists of voice-over.[14]

If through his voice he reaches for the spectator, and sites him/her in the position of a loved one, an intimate partner in the communication, with whom to share his experiences, in *Sopralluoghi in Palestina* Pasolini also sketches a self-portrait, which is based on his own performance in the film, as well as his verbal self-description. It is to this performance and to this self-description that I now wish to turn my attention. The first aspect one needs to consider is, of course, the body, for 'the self-portrait bases itself above all on the experience of the body, of the author's own body as the site and theatre of experience' (Bellour 1989: 10). And Pasolini's body is at the centre of his experiences in all his location scouting: 'The search for characters for the fiction interrogates living bodies, which give themselves to the director as *metteur en scène* (and to the director's body) through the language of physical presence' (Mancini & Perrella 1981: xii; author's translation).[15]

Fully-clad in either white or beige trousers and a long-sleeved shirt, most frequently also white, sometimes wearing his by then-customary dark glasses, and often holding a notepad in his hands, Pasolini at less-than-forty looks smart, slender, focused, but also edgy and uneasy, on his Palestinian journey. All the sequences show him to us as a traveller, one with a clear purpose: that of scouting locations and faces, as well as of reaching a clearer understanding not only of the land he is visiting, but of his planned film. Rare are the moments of conviviality or rest; the only parentheses that Pasolini allows are those dedicated to playing with children, met by chance along the road, or sitting pensively (showing his slender body in his underwear) by the Dead Sea. The title of the film is its ethos – the persona that Pasolini lets us see here is that of the scouting director; a searching director/thinker, whose curiosity, intellectual tension and focus on his work are total.

The figure of Pasolini as filmmaker is also highlighted by the visual presence of the camera and microphone in many scenes. His preoccupation with his future film is constant – he is concerned by the unsuitability of the locations, especially the urban ones, which either present too many signs of modernity, or are too miserable; and by the inappropriateness of the faces, which he describes as 'pre-Christian, indifferent, cheerful, animal-like'. Pasolini often

Sopralluoghi in Palestina: Pasolini as purposeful traveller

describes his feelings. Few locations or situations offer 'moments, vague sugges-tions', as he comments, visual annotations for the future *The Gospel According to St. Matthew* – a group of people resting along the road, a man entering Jerusalem on a donkey's back, a woman at a market. The only landscape that truly im-presses Pasolini is the desert of the Dead Sea, which, the director comments, will be impossible to replace with Italian scenery. Costumes, extras and the Catholic audience of the future film are also part of Pasolini's preoccupations.

While being deeply disappointed at one level, Pasolini is also surprised and admiring at another level. As Noa Steimatsky noted:

> The modern, industrial aspect of Israel was, as Pasolini states in the *So-praluoghi*, 'a practical disappointment'. This became the ostensible rationale for filming the Gospel elsewhere. But the plain concreteness of the holy places in Palestine, the modesty of their dimension and placement, bearing neither the epic nor dramatic impact that Pasolini had expected, ultimately consti-tuted 'an aesthetic revelation', one that left its traces in the ultimate choices of location and shooting style of *Il Vangelo secondo Matteo*. (2002: 247)

In particular, the source of intellectual and aesthetic pleasure comes from the discovery of the spirituality (which for Pasolini means aesthetic dimension) of the smaller and the more humble. Much of this pleasure is to be found in the distance allowed by the superimposed commentary. This is not surprising, as Pasolini more than once described the contrast between, on the one hand, his dissatisfaction with the present experience and, on the other, his nostalgia for the experience itself.[16]

Pasolini allows us insight into his state of mind not only by describing his emotions but, in a more subtle manner, by way of comparing himself with Don Andrea. The comparison and disparity between the two is immediately played out visually at the onset of the film, with Don Andrea wearing his long, black

priestly vestment, and Pasolini in all-white lay clothes. It is interesting that no attention what-soever is ever paid in the film, either visually or verbally, to any of the other members of the small crew. Pasolini talks exclusively of and to Don Andrea, and treats him as an equal partner in his quest. Indeed, he presents the priest to us in two main ways: as the ideal spectator of his future film on the Gospel, and as a co-director. He does the first by commenting that Don And-rea's reactions to the visited places were 'perfect',

Pasolini and Don Andrea: complementary dichoto-mies in *Sopralluoghi in Palestina* and gave him a clear idea of the way in which the Catholic audiences would watch his film on the Gospel. The second is achieved by constantly asking for Don Andrea's opinions.[17]

Don Andrea himself is perfectly clued in – he is, indeed, the first to explicitly observe that the locations are unsuitable for Pasolini's film, and who suggests how to use them: 'The purpose should be this: to condense, absorb the spirit of the situation. Then, possibly, relive it, rebuild it, invent it perhaps in another setting, another place.' Don Andrea, hence, is presented almost as a double of the director, as can also be evinced by Pasolini's comment: 'Don Andrea's reactions were clear to me, because, as you will hear from his accent, he is from Veneto, and so we had very similar childhoods. My childhood experience with Venetian liturgical Catholicism is similar to his, so I found in him certain reactions from my childhood.' Furthermore, the documentary is punctuated by their conversations and mutual interviews – I have already noted how their roles as interviewer/interviewee are often interchanged during the film. It is interesting to note that the two take opposing attitudes towards the camera: Pasolini always faces it; Don Andrea always turns away from it.

The idea of the couple (of opposites or of complementary dichotomies) is recurrent in Pasolini's poetic universe; it can even be traced in the autobiographical sphere, in the relationship of young Pier Paolo with his brother Guido.[18] Gordon has suggested that in Pasolini's cinema 'bound' couples (for instance, Jason and Medea, or Totò and Ninetto) are archetypes of the representation of split consciousness, a theme that recurs in Pasolini's oeuvre: 'the figuration of duality is, for Pasolini, an expression of the deepest shape of selfhood, precariously on the cusp between overdetermined excess and dissolute, permanent, violent loss' (1996: 202). It is indeed in the sign of excess and lack that I wish to read the self-representation of Pasolini in *Sopralluoghi in Palestina*. This reading is in tune with Gordon's argument that Pasolini's representation of the self in his cinema is one of crisis and split: 'the power of *La ricotta* lies in its depiction of the *collapse* of the self; and the crow of *Uccellacci e uccellini* is similarly already a self-in-crisis' (1996: 199; emphasis in original).

Excess appears in *Sopralluoghi in Palestina* as restlessness, anxiety and disorder. Pasolini often describes his feelings and reactions by comparing them to Don Andrea's:

What did Don Andrea and I talk about here? We probably had one of our usual discussions in which I tended to see the world in Christ's times a little like what was before my eyes here. A rather wretched world – pastoral, archaic, shattered. While Don Andrea always tended to see, even in the settings that surrounded Christ, a certain dignity.

While Pasolini tends to see disorder and fragmentation in the surrounding land-scape, Don Andrea sees dignity; it becomes progressively clear that their different perceptions reflect their diverse personalities. Pasolini's description of himself as disorderly becomes evident, in fact, through the comparison with the order that characterises Don Andrea. Unlike the director, for instance, the priest was not deeply affected by the 'terrible lunar landscape' of the Dead Sea: 'The only one who was not traumatised by this atrocious panorama was Don Andrea, with his absolute, extreme mental order.'[19]

Through his intense dialogue with Don Andrea – intended both literally (the verbal exchanges and interviews) and metaphorically (the subtle comparison I have just described) – Pasolini is able to offer a self-portrait that exceeds the lim-its of the potentially banal representation of a filmmaker scouting locations. He presents himself instead as a curious intellectual on a journey and a search, which becomes obsessive, as he remarks. As a man and an artist, Pasolini is framed by his intensity, his turmoil, his disorder, his dissatisfaction and discontent. Lack – of order, of contentment, of certainty – is the marker of this self-portrait. This is, of course, not uncommon; indeed, lack is at the very basis of self-portraits, for 'the self-portraitist's inaugural experience is one of emptiness, of absence onto himself' (Beaujour 1991: 4).

It is not surprising, then, that one of the central points in Pasolini's construc-tion of subjectivity in his entire oeuvre is the concept of lack. Discussing the centrality of death in Pasolini's poetry, Gordon has suggested how through it 'poetry acquires part of its negativity, becoming a trace of an absent self, who narrates his life in writing because of a lack of presence to himself and in real-ity' (1996: 93). Again Gordon, discussing the figure of the father in Pasolini's poetry, claimed that, for the poet, 'the lack is a terrifying weak point, where all the imperfections of the self are concentrated ... Lack is written across the body of the subject, who can only compensate with already compromised secondary plenitudes' (1999: 53–4).

Lack in *Sopralluoghi in Palestina* is all-pervasive, the true subtext of all of the film's themes. Lack is, first and foremost, the terrifying weak point of the self, which emerges as an absence of order and assurance. It is, furthermore, the lack of homeliness, of familiarity with the traversed landscapes, which is evident in Pasolini's constant attempt to refer and compare his perception and experience to Italian landscapes and situations, with which he is familiar. This lack is, indeed, a threat: 'The destabilising factor of the journey out of the Western home and into the postcolonial world places the traveller/narrator before the necessity to redefine himself' (Caminati 2007: 18; author's translation), and to acknowledge his own substantial homelessness. Rootlessness is indeed an important theme in Pasolini's poetic world, which has, once again, autobiographical connotations (the many relocations of the youth, the uprooting to Rome). As Sam Rohdie proposed, the lack of a home is at the core of Pasolini's idea of travel itself: 'Home is never anywhere for him. It is the impossible ideal and his voyages to find it inevitably dissatisfied him' (1995: 188).

Another manifestation of lack is, in fact, precisely the absence of the ideal sought by Pasolini in his trip – the ideal locations, the ideal faces. As Rohdie pointed out, 'This was the entire sense in Pasolini's *Sopralluoghi* where nothing at all in the film was of use for the film-to-be-made that was made, *Il Vangelo secondo Matteo*, made in Calabria, an analogous biblical Palestine. Reality points to the absent ideal within it' (1995: 60). The ultimate absence, though, in this sense, is that of the ideal film: *Sopralluoghi in Palestina* is the signifier of such lack, a void which *The Gospel According to St. Matthew* can only partially and unsatisfactorily fill.[20]

All the above-described manifestations of lack, however, are modelled on and epitomised by the key absence in this film: that of Christ. Maurizio Viano rightly noted how Pasolini often muses about places in the light of the past presence of Christ in them: 'Here Christ must have preached'; 'This is the door through which Christ entered': 'In *Sopraluoghi*, Pasolini is recording an absence (He is no longer here) and postulating a presence (He must have been here), an absence and a presence of nothing less than the transcendental signifier of Catholic culture, the sign which keeps all the others in place' (1993: 130). Once again, we are reminded of Pasolini's identification with the figure of Christ in his poetry, in which the 'narcissistic self-contemplation, predicated on absence, evolves into contemplation of the body of Christ as a token of presence' (Gordon 1996: 145). If the body of Christ on the cross, with its connotations of 'display, nudity, scandal, humiliation and martyrdom', becomes a visible and narcissistic figuration of the self, here Christ – the true goal of the search of Pasolini's journey – is only present as absence. Such absence becomes a *mise en abyme* of the absent self, opening to the experience of the sublime.

Pasolini invokes the sublime several times during the film. That he makes recourse to the term in order to define his experience of the visited places is unsurprising; as Rhodes remarked, the rhetoric of the sublime may well be endemic to Pasolini's artistic production: 'Pasolini will often conceive of representation as an agonistic exercise of its impossibility because the world to be represented is essentially beyond being represented' (2007: 81). In *Sopralluoghi in Palestina*, the experience of the sublime is provoked either by the very small, or by the grandiose, and is profoundly connected to the experience of lack. The first time it is mentioned is in Capernaum. Pasolini talks to Don Andrea: 'Capernaum is a sublime place, in its smallness, extreme poverty and absolute lack of scenography.' This theme appeared even before, although without being explicitly named, in the many references to the 'great smallness, great humility' of the places. The opposite type of vista also produces the sublime: before the Dead Sea, Pasolini comments that it was the only landscape that 'counts among its characteristics, as you can see, the impression of grandeur. All the rest is sublime and solemn in its humbleness and smallness, but never grandiose, never cyclopean, if not terrifying'. Finally, it is Jerusalem that displays 'something historically sublime in her appearance'.

While the sense of the sublime was evoked all along by Pasolini's reaction to the visited landscapes, both its causes and effects emerge more powerfully towards the end of the film. Approaching the conclusion of his search, the place in which the story ended (and began) – Bethlehem – Pasolini becomes progressively confused; he no longer remembers places and names; his memory vacillates. 'I don't remember the name of this Church, nor its function'; 'I don't even remember the name of this Church, or what it commemorates'; 'I anxiously strive to remember the names of the places'. Once again, it is the absolute order of Don Andrea's intellect against which Pasolini's disorder is measured:

> I could use the help of Don Andrea in remembering the details of what we are seeing in this moment of the film. Don Andrea's mind: so orderly, so precise, where everything comes together with utmost simplicity. While I was continuously ruffled by historical perspectives and breakdowns, in Don Andrea's mind everything was straightforward, as on the façade of eternity.

This disorder is caused precisely by the ultimate lack, the lack of Christ. The travellers are about to reach the last stage in their search, the Church of the Holy Sepulchre. Pasolini comments: 'This is the place of the supreme act. A stupendous little Romanesque church commemorates the Ascension. The most sublime moment of the entire evangelical story. The moment in which Christ leaves us alone to search for him.' Immediately after, the film comes abruptly to its end.

It is this, hence, the sense of *Sopralluoghi*: the sublime search for an always already lost plenitude; a search that, therefore, is both boundless and formless. Such lack is not only of the self – it is also of the cinema. The key to an understanding of the confusion of all notebook films is that they testify to the director's search for a film not to be made, but that cannot be made.

In Pasolini especially, this search is always doomed: Pasolini's realism is defeated from the start, because it wants to testify to a reality that has already disappeared; and because the film's realism replaces reality itself, thus erasing it. As Rohdie put it, for Pasolini,

> Film provided a knowledge of reality, but at the cost of reality's disappearance. The knowledge of reality included, and even primarily included, the knowledge of the loss of reality engendered by the fact of it being rewritten in film.

Film represented, then, or rather Pasolini's films represented, a consciousness of a lost reality, lost to the effort of making reality known, that is of retaining it. (1995: 52)

In their seminal analysis of the formless in the aesthetic field, *Formless: A User's Guide*, Yves-Alain Bois and Rosalind Krauss claim that the formless is 'nothing in and of itself' and 'has only an operational existence: it is a performative' (1997: 18) – a process at work, both in art and in criticism. The 'style without style that is the style of documentary notebooks' opens up to the operations of the formless. In *Notes Towards an African Orestes*, for instance, the formless makes its appearance in the dissonance that disintegrates the musical soundtrack, often bordering on pure noise. In *Sopralluoghi in Palestina*, the work of the formless is in the editing.

Sopralluoghi in Palestina, as we saw, was spliced together almost haphazardly. This random and unrefined editing process resulted in a curious effect. The vast majority of the cuts are preceded by a swift, barely noticeable downward camera movement, which briefly fades to white. As totally appropriate to the hasty, unfinished style of notetaking, the camera is, simply, carelessly lowered by the operator at the end of each shot while still reeling. All these sudden shifts were not eliminated, but simply left there; they progressively add up, and deeply haunt the spectator. One is tempted to believe that Pasolini did not dislike the result; after all, his style of montage was famously and deliberately rough; many of his films 'are marked by abrupt beginnings and endings and unexplained shifts of scene and setting' (Gordon 1996: 211). *The Gospel According to St. Matthew* is indeed paradigmatic of this unpolished approach, and is striking for the visual discontinuity, jump cuts, the hasty and brusque 'mistakes', which become a marker of Pasolini's cinema: 'The use of both micro- and macro-editing as a rhythmic, temporal dimension to the work of subjectivity represents one of the most alienating and anti-naturalistic effects in Pasolini's cinema' (1996: 212).

Through this repeated slippage or obsessive *glissement*, the formless performs its work in *Sopralluoghi in Palestina*, revealing the gap (between artistic imagination and 'brute reality', the reality searched for and its substitution by the film's reality), and exposing the lack – in the man, and in the text.

chapter eight
THE SELF-PORTRAIT FILM: MICHELANGELO'S LAST GAZE

'A director does nothing but look for himself in his films. They are documentaries, not of an already-made thought, but of a thought in the making.'
(Antonioni 1996b: 57; author's translation)

Though it can be traced far back, the self-portrait as an artistic genre coalesces in the sixteenth century – even if the term itself is more recent, and reflects the notion of the self that prevailed in Western societies in the late-eighteenth century, with Romanticism and its 'invention' of the self as a self-contained object of awareness.[1] The sixteenth century, however, is the period that sees a clear rise in both literary autobiography and the painted self-portrait, probably as a result of increased social mobility and ensuing changes in people's awareness of their individuality (see Trilling 1972) – and as a consequence and a reflection of the new position held by the artist in society (see West 2004: 163–4).

The term has also been borrowed to describe literary texts. Written self-portraits can be seen as a form of autobiography, but one that does not depend on narrative construction. For this characteristic, they have much in common with the essay. Indeed, Philippe Lejeune has thus defined Montaigne's *Essays*: 'One sees that the text of the *Essays* has no connection with, as we define it, autobiography; there is no continuous narrative nor any systematic history of the personality. [It is] self-portrait rather than autobiography' (in Beaujour 1991: 2).

For Michel Beaujour, author of a seminal text on the genre, the lack of continuous narrative is, indeed, a defining characteristic of the literary self-portrait:

This genre attempts to create coherence through a system of cross-references, anaphoras, superimpositions or correspondences among homologous and substitutable elements, in such a way as to give the appearance of discontinuity, of anachronistic juxtaposition, or montage, as opposed to the syntagmat-

ics of a narration, no matter how scrambled, since the scrambling of a narrative always tempts the reader to 'reconstruct' its chronology. The totalisation
of the self-portrait is not *given* beforehand: new homologous elements can
be added to the paradigm, whereas the temporal closure of autobiography already is implicit in the initial choice of a curriculum vitae. (Beaujour 1991: 3)

The above quotation introduces a description of the self-portrait that closely
evokes filmic language. The temptation to borrow such description and use it to
illustrate the features of audiovisual self-portraiture is too much to resist. Indeed,
Raymond Bellour was prompted to write that the self-portrait is perhaps the only
form of autobiography truly achievable in film; defying the shortcomings of the
cinematic apparatus and language in terms of respecting the autobiographical
pact,[2] the self-portrait 'is distinguished from autobiography by the absence of a
story one is obliged to follow' (1989: 8):

> The self-portrait clings to the analogical, the metaphorical, the poetic, far
> more than to the narrative. Its coherence lies in a system of remembrances,
> afterthoughts, superimpositions, correspondences. It thus takes on the ap-
> pearance of discontinuity, of anachronistic juxtaposition, of montage. Where
> autobiography closes in on the life it recounts, the self-portrait opens itself up
> to a limitless totality. (1989: 8–9)

One is struck by the similarity that the above descriptions of the self-portrait
bears with the language of dreams, as defined within a Freudian model, as well
as with the language of cinematic oneirism (see Rascaroli 2002a). Substitution,
juxtaposition and superimposition are operations that the cinematic apparatus
is well able to perform, through framing, camera movement and montage. This
appears to corroborate the hypothesis that the cinema is better suited to the self-
portrait than to autobiography.

If the pact of the self-portrait is 'I won't tell you what I've done, but I shall tell
you *who I am*' (Beaujour 1991: 3; emphasis in original), its rhetorical structure,
as in the diary and related forms (travelogue, notebook) is that of an 'I' talking to
him- or herself, and addressing 'the putative reader only insofar as he is placed in
the position of an overhearing third person' (1991: 9). For Beaujour this is why, in
his *Roland Barthes par Roland Barthes* (1975), for instance, Barthes sometimes
refers to himself as 'he', in order to preserve the I-You relationship, 'despite the
resistance of the discourse adopted, and to reserve in his text a fictional place
for the reader'. Other self-portraits are more solipsistic, as Augustine's soliloquy
destined to God, or Montaigne's dismissal of readership in the foreword to his
Essays. For Beaujour, the reader thus positions himself as *addresser*, which is why

'each reader *knows* himself' in the self-portrait, and 'can become, in turn, the one who writes them' (1991: 9; emphasis in original).

Filmmaking, needless to say, is not literature – while a comparison with the written self-portrait may (partly) elucidate its narrative and verbal components, the film's visual and aural constituents must also be accounted for. It is interesting how, for instance, in her *Les Glaneurs et la glaneuse*, when she clarifies that her film is also an act of self-portraiture,[3] Agnès Varda films one of her hands with the other hand, which holds her DV camera, and is driven to compare the activity of filming herself to a self-portrait by Rembrandt, a postcard of which she brought back from a trip to Japan. A filmic self-portrait will unavoidably be indebted to painting – while being yet another, different form. And the self-portrait has also, of course, a long and (for the cinema) relevant tradition in photography and, more recently, in video art. Artistic visual practices have started, since the 1960s at least, to challenge long-established conventions, so much so that today one no longer needs to think of the self-portrait as a traditional artistic genre:

> Contemporary technologies have broadened the definition of what self-portraiture can be. In the 1960s, the American artist Robert Morris ... was working on ideas based on conceptual portraiture, using bottled body fluids and medical scans. Mona Hatoum produced *Corps Etranger* in 1994, a video installation of an endoscopic journey through the landscape of her own body, and Marc Quinn's cryogenic sculpture *Self* (1997) contains nine pints of his own blood. (Rideal 2005: 10)

Raymond Bellour believes that the medium of video is particularly suitable for audiovisual self-portraiture. He recognises that the tradition can be traced 'in certain obscure corners of the modern cinema' (1989: 9), but then focuses on video art, first (from the early 1970s) American, and then European. His examples range from Vito Acconci's *The Red Tapes* (1976) to *Scénario du film 'Passion'* (1982) by Jean-Luc Godard, from Peter Campus's *Three Transitions* (1973) to Bill Viola's *The Space Between the Teeth* (1976). For Bellour, there are four reasons why 'video seems to lend itself more particularly, and certainly more exclusively than cinema, to the pursuit of the self-portrait' (ibid.): the instant feedback provided by video; the possibility for the author to more naturally include his or her body; the ease of post-production intervention in the image; and the role of mass communication (the television screen to which video is bound) to perform the role fulfilled by rhetoric. Video is indeed, as Rosalind Krauss proposed, an inherently narcissistic medium, in which the body is sited in between two machines: 'The first of these is the camera; the second is the monitor, which re-projects the performer's image with the immediacy of a mirror' (1976: 52). It is certainly true that video, thanks to its inexpensiveness, immediacy, wide availability and versatility, facilitates experimentation more easily than the cinema; this is the reason why pure cinematographic self-portraiture is rare, and there are few 35mm self-portrait films.

While the literary self-portrait is a monologue, with the reader in the paradoxical position of addresser, the visual self-portrait's tradition is one of direct interpellation, thanks to the gaze that the image of the artist/author in the portrait very frequently exchanges with the spectator standing before it. We find a confirmation that this form of 'I-You' relationship continues in video self-portraits in Vito Acconci's description of his own *One Minute Memories* (filmed between 1971 and 1974): 'I was thinking in terms of video as close-up, video as place where my face onscreen faces a viewer's face offscreen – a place for talk, me talking to you, the viewer' (in Bellour 1989: 23). It is interesting that, in Acconci's description, the gaze of the face in close-up is first posed as pure interpellation, but quickly transforms into dialogue.[4]

And yet, similarly to the literary self-portrait, the audiovisual one also has much to do with the monologue, in which the spectator is in the position of an overseeing/overhearing third person. First of all, the self-portrait's gaze is a *mise en abyme* – the spectator looks, through the eyes of the author, at the author: 'The viewer of a self-portrait also occupies a strange position of looking at a metaphorical mirror that reflects back not themselves but the artist who produced the portrait' (West 2004: 165). The identification of the spectator is, therefore, with the author; the spectator becomes the addresser.

Unsurprisingly, the self-portrait is often described as a diary: 'Because self-portraits merge the artist and the sitter into one, they have the allure of a private diary, in that they seem to give us an artist's insight into his or her own personality' (West 2004: 163). As a private,[5] diaristic gesture, self-portraiture implies a paradoxical spectatorship: 'The self-portrait can be compared to a diary: a personal and exclusive viewpoint rarely produced with publication in mind, within which relationships and emotions may be explained and analysed' (Rideal 2005: 43). Hence, while the essay proper is always and explicitly addressed to another – a reader/spectator, with whom the essayist establishes a dialogue – the self-portrait (similarly to the diary, the notebook and the travelogue) is addressed primarily to the self as other. The reader or spectator is let into the privacy of the addresser's dialogue with his or her self; he/she is invited to set up a paradoxical identification with the author as addresser. At the same time, it is easy to argue that the self-portrait, with its aim of self-presentation and its ambition to be a bid for eternity, is also always meant for a public; or, more specifically, for that special audience that is posterity.

Celluloid and beyond: audiovisual self-portraits

A broad and flexible approach to the genre would suggest considering all first-person, autobiographical films which involve self-representation (diaries, travelogues, notebooks, letters, poems and autobiographical documentaries) as instances of self-portraiture.[6] Indeed, critics have, with various degrees of persuasiveness, called films self-portraits, ranging from the radically experimental to fiction to documentary. Examples include the avant-garde piece *Emak Bakia* by Man Ray (1926), on the basis that 'It represents a constellation of Man Ray's formal and iconographic interests and achievements' (Aiken 1983: 240; see also Gambill 1980: 34); *Intervista* (*Federico Fellini's Intervista*, 1988) by Federico Fellini, which was described as a 'self-portrait of the artist as a mature man' (Degli-Esposti 1996: 167); *Manhatta* (1921) by Paul Strand and Charles Sheeler, which was seen by one critic as a 'national self-portrait', because it 'draws together a set of cinematic images to project the American artist's embodied experience' (Gerstner 2006: 158); and Dominique Cabrera's *Demain et encore demain*, on the basis that Cabrera exposes herself onscreen under her various identities of woman, daughter, sister, mother, lover, citizen and filmmaker (see Calatayud 2001).

Within his study of the autobiographical documentary in America, Jim Lane studied a specific form of US nonfiction cinema as 'autobiographical portraiture' (see Lane 2002). These films use 'voice-over narration, formal interviews, home movie footage, and still photographs as well as interactive modes of shooting to establish a less plot-driven and more synchronically organised representation', in this differing from the journal entry style of the autobiographical documentary (Lane 2002: 94).[7] This set of films, which developed since the early 1970s, can be divided for Lane into family portraits (with such early examples as Martin Scorsese's *Italianamerican* (1974) and Alfred Guzzetti's *Family Portrait Sittings* (1975)) and self-portraits. The latter category 'replaces the family with a number of external forces that have connections to the way the portraitists see themselves. Thus the self is constructed in relation to art, film, politics, unemployment, hometown, infertility, and many other places, traditions, and ideas' (2002: 120). Among Lane's examples of self-portraits are Jon Jost's *Speaking Directly: Some American Notes* (1972), Jerome Hill's *Film Portrait* (1972) and Michael Moore's *Roger and Me* (1989).

While it is easy, and indeed unavoidable, to find elements of the representation of the self in all subjective, first-person films, be they experimental or mainstream, fiction or documentary (some examples of which have been explored in the previous chapters of the present book), one has to wonder when this approach ceases to be sound and viable. It is very difficult, indeed, to determine where self-portraiture ends and autobiography begins, or vice-versa. The above-described critical practice poses the question of generic boundaries – how elastic is the self-portrait as a genre? When should we stop talking of self-portrait, given that most art is, to a certain extent, autobiographical?

Take the case of Manoel de Oliveira's *Porto Da Minha Infância* (*Porto of My Childhood*, 2001), an overtly autobiographical account of the director's time in Porto as a child and then as a young man. The film, part documentary, part fiction, mixes reconstructed sequences, with an actor playing de Oliveira, and archival images of the times and events which the director himself describes in voice-over. This autobiographical account of de Oliveira's youth is an account whose authenticity is endorsed by the director's own voice-over. However, the indexicality of the cinematic apparatus means that the artist as a young man is present in absence (he is either evoked/described by the voice-over, or replaced by a stand-in). The film could, however, also be read as a self-portrait of the artist as an old man, of the contemporary de Oliveira, while he reminisces about the past and evokes autobiographical data. The film is also, of course, a documentary on the city of Porto.

I suggest that specific films can be grouped together as more explicit and accomplished representatives of the genre. Thus, I here advocate a selective approach, based on an evaluation of the self-consciousness of the director's gesture – as testified, for instance, by the film's title, by its textual commitments and characteristics, or by the author's comments in interviews and other paratexts.

Three examples of declared self-portraits by well-known film directors are Jonas Mekas' *Self-Portrait* (1990, video printed in 35mm); *JLG/JLG: Self-Portrait in December* (35mm);[8] and *Cinéma, de notre temps: Chantal Akerman par Chantal Akerman* (1997, television), by Chantal Akerman.[9] Two films that their authors have described extra-textually in terms of self-portrait are Jean Cocteau's *Le Testament d'Orphée* (*The Testament of Orpheus*, 1960) and Agnès Varda's *The Gleaners and I*. About the first, Cocteau remarked: 'My film is nothing other than a strip-tease show, consisting of removing my body bit by bit and revealing my soul quite naked' (in Williams 2006: 98); and again: '*Le Testament* is nothing other than an attempt at a self-portrait, a self-portrait concerned with profound likeness' (ibid.). As for the second, Varda frequently described it in interviews as a self-portrait (see for instance Meyer 2001).

An incomplete list of declared self-portrait films includes: Jerome Hill's *Film Portrait* (1972, 35mm), Chuck Hudina's *Self Portrait* (1972, 16mm), Andris Grinbergs' *Pashportrets* (*Self-Portrait*, 1972, 35mm) and his *Pashportrets. Testaments* (*Self-Portrait. Testament*, 2003, 35mm), Maria Lassnig's *Self Portrait* (1973, 16mm), Daniel Singelenberg's *Another Shot* (1973, 16mm), James Broughton's *Testament* (1974, 16mm), Diana Barrie's *Night Movie #1: Self-Portrait* (1974, Super8), Gail Camhi's *Coffee Break* (1976, 16mm), Unglee's *Forget Me Not* (1979, 16 mm), Marcel Hanoun's *Un film, autoportrait* (1985, 16mm), Vilgot Sjöman's *Self Portrait '92* (1992, television), Robert Kramer's *Berlin 10/90* (1993, Beta SP), Anja Czioska's *Roof - Shower - Underwater 3 BandW Hand Developed Film Prints* (1994, 16mm), Olivier Fouchard's *Autoportrait* (1997, Super8) and *Autoportrait Refilmé* (1998, Super8), Brian Frye's *Self-Portrait as Kaspar Hauser* (2000, 16mm), Louise Bourque's *Self Portrait Post Mortem* (2002, 35mm) and Lin Qiu's *Self Portrait 2* (2006, miniDV). Even this incomplete list demonstrates that the audiovisual self-portrait is not confined to video but uses all formats, from Super8 to 35mm, while at the same time being a decidedly experimental form, due to the high level of personal content and the affinity for research that self-portraiture has always displayed. Indeed, these films are extremely diverse in style, format, length and technical specifications, and interpret self-portraiture in totally dissimilar and idiosyncratic ways. This is, somehow, unsurprising. Self-portraiture, in fact, for obvious reasons is necessarily original – hence unique, avant-garde and modern. As Beaujour noted of the written form, 'Self-portraitists make self-portraits without knowing what they are doing. This "genre" proffers no "horizon of expectation". Each self-portrait is written as though it were the only text of its kind' (1991: 3).

And yet, while being necessarily unique, many self-portraits feed on analogous themes, ideas and obsessions. All art historians who have studied self-portraiture in painting, for instance, point to the fact that it is an eminently narcissistic genre, as well as the epitome of self-analysis and intimate dissection. At the same time, the self-portrait was traditionally used as a tool to present and demonstrate one's skills to potential patrons; to ensure one's artistic survival and recognition; and to indicate one's perception of his or her position in society. Hence, the self-portrait is a contradictory genre, which merges the most intimate artistic gesture with the most public display of image-management: 'The self-portrait is the artist's most personal form of expression. It is the ultimate means of self-analysis, presenting an opportunity for self-reflection, self-expression and self-promotion; a bid for eternity' (Rideal 2005: 7). Self-portraits are usually simultaneously statements about the artist's personality and her status in society. Frequently, they include the tools of their author's art, as well as objects situating her in space and time. While being a narcissistic mirror of the self, and a locus for the expression of the artist's most intimate self-concerns and personal legacy, in fact, the self-portrait is never isolated from other discourses, and also always engages with the external world, even just by including the markers of one's time and society: 'Self-portraiture records not only what the artist looks like but also how they interpret themselves and the world around them' (Rideal 2005: 8).

All-important themes of the genre are death and *vanitas*. Each self-portrait freezes a moment in time, hence capturing the work of death; and each is, potentially, the last one; and, therefore, a *memento mori* – the reminder of the transient nature of vanity, and the meaninglessness of earthly life. Furthermore, despite its promise 'to deliver the artist in some capacity to the viewer' (Jones 2002: 951), the self-portrait also poses the problem of whether we can ever 'know' the subject behind the image. This is evidently because 'The subject is neither identical with itself nor with the portrait each one of us paints of ourselves, that consoling fiction of an autonomous ego invested with "attributes of permanence, identity, and substantiality"' (Lomas 2000: 187). Indeed, irrespective of the medium through which they are accomplished, all self-portraits are deeply concerned with the relationship and negotiation between the portrayed self and the original self; so much so that the self-portrait can be seen as a 'transaction', a 'dialectic of self and other' (ibid.). This question entails a corollary of issues and discourses, many of which will be of clear interest for my case study, and which I list here: the contrast between the ideal body and the natural body; the double and the divided self; the mirror image and the processes of recognition and misrecognition; the name and the signature; the act of revealing and the act of concealing.

It is opportune to begin to note here that some of these themes (at least those of the split self and the double, of misrecognition and concealment) are not only relevant to Antonioni's final filmic self-portrait, but in many ways to his entire oeuvre.

Antonioni's final self-portrait: *The Gaze of Michelangelo*

'Which body? We have several.' (Barthes 1977a: 60)

Produced by the Istituto LUCE, first screened at the 2004 Cannes Film Festival,[10] *Lo sguardo di Michelangelo* (*The Gaze of Michelangelo*, 2004, 35mm) was made in the wake of the completion of the 'Progetto Mosè' (Project Moses), the four-year meticulous restoration of Michelangelo Buonarroti's monumental complex of the tomb of Julius II, in the Roman Church of San Pietro in Vincoli. The project had a large audience, and an informational halo: it could be followed live on the Internet thanks to a number of well-placed webcams.[11] Subsequent to the completion of the restoration, Antonioni filmed the 17 minutes of *The Gaze of Michelangelo*, a deceptively simple nonfiction, in which the director goes to San Pietro in Vincoli to admire *Moses* and the other statues.

The short can be read in many ways: as the documentation and exploration of the results of the restoration; as a tribute to Michelangelo; as a study of *Moses*; as a reflection on the relationship between film and the fine arts; as an exploration of digital technologies and their marriage with traditional filmmaking; as a meditation on the relationship between art and life, permanence and transience; and as a contemplation of death. It can additionally be seen as a retracing and repetition of the many visits Sigmund Freud is known to have paid to the statue which fascinated him so much. After seeing it for the first time in 1901, Freud went to study *Moses* daily, and for many hours at a time, during his summer vacation in Rome in 1912; he then wrote the controversial essay *Der Moses des Michelangelo* in 1914 (see Freud 1955: 211–36).

While being all of these things, *The Gaze of Michelangelo* is, I argue, primarily a self-portrait of Michelangelo Antonioni; it has, indeed, all the tenets and functions of the self-portrait. Placed at the very end of his career and his life,[12] containing Antonioni's last self-fashioned images, and being undoubtedly his best post-1985 film, it acquires the function and value of a legacy. When Antonioni leaves the church, seemingly on his own legs, at the end of the film, he leaves simultaneously art, the cinema, his audience and life.

As is well-known, since 1985 Antonioni was confined to a wheelchair as a consequence of an ictus, which deprived him of most bodily movement and almost completely of speech. Yet, in this film we see him standing and walking without aid (although not talking),[13] thanks to a digital alteration of the image. Antonioni's experimentation with image modification was certainly not new – an example is his testing of colour in the video (then reprinted in 35mm) *Il mistero di Oberwald* (*The Oberwald Mystery*, 1981). As the director has suggested, talking of this film: 'Electronic equipment allows you to add, take away, modify colour, from the whole image or a section of it, while you are shooting. In practice, you "paint" your film there and then, while making it' (in Biarese & Tassone 1985: 60; author's translation).

Digital intervention in the self-portrait is far from being surprising or unheard of. Self-portraiture was, indeed, used as a promotional tool even by Renaissance artists, who began to think of identity in new ways, so much so that 'in the sixteenth century there appears to be an increased self-consciousness about the fashioning of human identity as a manipulable, artful process' (Greenblatt 1984: 2). While it is possible to identify paintings that appear to be the product of dispassionate self-awareness, and that offer unforgiving analyses of one's image, self-portraits are frequently a means of narcissistically communicating the idea of the self that an artist is most comfortable with and proud of, and wants us to embrace and remember.

It is, thus, unsurprising that digital technology is today an alluring tool for the refashioning of one's identity: in recent times, for instance, 'Artists eagerly adopted computer-based technology in order to "put themselves in the picture" in the form of digitally manipulated photographs' (Avgitidou 2003: 134). They often did this not in order to 'distort reality but to help redefine the narrow dictates of normality' (Adams 1994: 216). When looking at the possibilities offered by the Internet, then, artists 'have engaged in digital culture beyond manipulated photography, in invented (non-existing) personalities, identities shared by a group of people or subjectivities "constructed" by various others' (Avgitidou 2003: 135). The oncoming of digital technology, in other words, has introduced a whole series of new possibilities in terms of self-fashioning – even though the novelty factor is only relative. As Maureen Turim has convincingly argued,

> the principles of image construction are only in part determined by a technology, since all the techniques associated with that new technology existed before, in a form of prefiguration ... With digital video, the artisanal approximation that performed similar processes include the ways art, photography, film, and video prefigure the work of digital imagery through compositional devices, *mise-en-scène*, constructivism, and collage/superimposition techniques. (1999: 52)

For Antonioni, the use of technology (at that time, video) for the purpose of image alteration appeared to realise the director's old wish of 'painting a film as one paints a picture' (in Tinazzi 1996: xxv).[14] It is also important to recall that self-portraits, because of the freedom they afforded the artist, on account of the lack of a commission and of the constant availability of the model, often originated as opportunities for technical experimentation: 'Artists could use the self-portrait as a means of drawing attention to the medium and the process of production of the work, to show off their skill, or to experiment with technique or style' (West 2004: 165). And yet, if image construction has always been available to artists (even before the advancement introduced by digital technology),[15] fashioning and self-fashioning, especially when a photographic image is involved, do not necessarily sever the link between such an image and its object, or disrupt our ability/tendency to look at it as an indexical trace of reality. As Timothy Dow Adams has correctly noted, 'The recent emergence of computer manipulated photography seems to have done little to shake the belief in a direct, physical link between photographs and their subjects' (1994: 476).

The significance of the digital refashioning of his body by Antonioni in *The Gaze of Michelangelo*, a restoration that echoes the restoration of *Moses*, will become clearer after an exploration of the features of this ostensibly plain and minimalist, but in truth extraordinarily rich and complex self-portrait.

Antonioni appeared as himself in footage by other filmmakers, and especially in various television documentaries, for instance Gianfranco Minghozzi's *Michelangelo Antonioni storia di un autore* (1966); Wim Wenders' *Chambre 666* (1982); and Enrica Antonioni's *Fare un film per me è vivere* (1996), a 'behind the scenes' of *Al di là delle nuvole* (*Beyond the Clouds*, 1995). With regard to self-fashioned images, however, Antonioni's body is almost completely absent from his cinema,[16] as well as from his painting: 'I used to paint even as a child; then, it was faces: my mother's, my father's, Greta Garbo's. Mine, never: because I'm unable to see myself' (1993; author's translation). Despite an almost complete absence of self-produced images, it is possible to argue that Antonioni is immanent in all his films, embedded through his directorial gaze, which is constantly felt by the spectator as a structuring presence; as Sam Rohdie has argued, precisely like his characters, 'Antonioni gazes, equally estranged, on that multiplication and problematisation of looking which extends itself, uncomfortably, to the audience' (1990: 72). It is not coincidental that the title of Antonioni's self-portrait film should be *The Gaze of Michelangelo*.

Such a title immediately evokes a number of themes that are emblematic of self-portraiture: the name, the signature and the double. While 'Michelangelo's gaze' alludes, in the first instance, to Buonarroti and his 'vision', to his style and his signature, a secondary but obvious reference is to Antonioni himself. The film's title, therefore, attracts our attention to the destiny in a name, which Antonioni shares with another Italian artist, who lived between 1475 and 1564 – a fortuitous, but significant and symbolic coincidence. Antonioni, in fact, fashions his self-presentation in the shape of a mirror image of another Michelangelo. The implications are bold, given Buonarroti's widely recognised status as one of the greatest Western artists – or, more precisely, a multitalented genius (sculptor, painter, architect and poet) who, as the archetypal Renaissance man, embodies a (the?) peak of Western civilisation.[17]

Is Antonioni drawing parallels with Buonarroti, hence positioning himself as one of the greatest artists of his century – and promoting his own work as a pinnacle of cinematic achievement, during the period of most radical experimentation and also of maturity of this art, before its decline in the second half of the twentieth century? Is he looking at himself as an utterly original artist – precisely as Buonarroti, who, taking as his point of reference the styles of Florentine and Roman classical Renaissance, produced an utterly novel, revolutionary artistic vision?

It is no coincidence that Antonioni's work is widely regarded by critics to be very conversant with, and bordering on, the fine arts. His first artistic production was as a painter;[18] his cinema is noticeably painterly, characterised by a use of framing, lighting and, when relevant, colour that is clearly inspired by an observation of the work of painters. Frequent in his work are the 'places which are openly non-narrativised, of a pictorial and visual interest which suddenly takes hold, causes the narrative to err, to wander, momentarily to dissolve' (Rohdie 1990: 51). As evidence of this interest and focus, one can note that 'Antonioni's cinema has always thematised the world of image creation – the cinema, photography and painting' (Casetti 2002a: 5; author's translation). Furthermore, Antonioni was, of course, especially sensitive to architecture – his films always frame the built environment in aesthetically striking ways. His interest in technique and experimentation with style and filmic language is close to those traditionally associated with the fine arts. As Antonioni himself recognised:

> I have a great love for painting. For me, it is the one art, along with architecture, that comes immediately after filmmaking. I'm very fond of reading books on art and architecture, of leafing through pages and pages of art volumes, and I like to go to art shows and keep in touch with the latest work being done in art – not just to be *au courant* but because painting is something that moves me passionately. Therefore I believe all these perceptions and this interest have been somewhat assimilated. And, naturally, having followed modern art, my taste and my predilection for a certain style would be reflected in my work. (1996a: 44)

If the suggested comparison with Buonarroti may seem immodest, or even tactless, a number of attenuating circumstances should be considered. The principal one is that Antonioni frames himself as visually towered over by *Moses*. This is also a philological approach – *Moses*, in fact, now at floor level, was initially conceived for a different position in the monumental complex, and was made to be viewed from below; calculations suggest that its head was supposed to be at 6.6m from ground level (see for instance de Tolnay 1963: 284; Macmillan & Swales 2003: 69). Antonioni's choice is also suggestive of his true viewing position 'from below', caused by his being in a wheelchair (on which more below).

Furthermore, Antonioni positions himself as an admired spectator rather than as a fellow artist (no overt reference is made to his role as a filmmaker); and he clearly pays homage to Buonarroti as a superior genius, an unmatchable source of inspiration. It is also highly significant that Antonioni's statement about his own status and achievements as an artist is made by means of an utterly small, modest, understated film, which was not destined to be widely seen – in many ways, the opposite of Buonarroti's *Moses*, which is not only imposing, sublime, titanic and superhuman, but which in Michelangelo's original plans should have been part of a colossal structure for the tomb of Pope Julius II, previously intended for the impressive setting of St Peter's Basilica. Nonetheless, the comparison with Buonarroti is undeniably introduced by the film; Antonioni here makes his claim to fame for posterity – not for nothing is the self-portrait, as I have already suggested, a highly narcissistic genre, deeply linked to self-promotion and the presentation of the way in which the artist positions himself or herself in society.

Part of this positioning is conveyed by the artist's own name, which becomes a true signature – and the self-portrait is always, of course, a form of signature; also because, historically, 'When artists began producing portraits of themselves in the fifteenth century, it was initially as a footnote or signature to another commission' (West 2004: 163). Michelagnolo Buonarroti (as he himself spelled his name) is universally known as 'Michelangelo' – a highly recognisable 'brand name', which stands for a rigorous, commanding, grandiose and austere vision of art and of life, and for a titanic spirit of rebellion against the human condition. The name also becomes Antonioni's signature, which stands for a similarly outstanding and unique, instantly recognisable style, and sober engagement with the subject of the human condition.

It must be noted that the homonymy and the system of correspondences, suggested by the title and implied by the film, also gesture at the uncanny experience of doubling, which is a persistent theme in self-portraiture. The double is also one of the key figures in Antonioni's cinema – examples are films like *L'avventura* (*The Adventure*, 1960), with Anna (Lea Massari) who is first mirrored and then replaced by Claudia (Monica Vitti); and *Professione: Reporter* (*The Passenger*, 1975), with Jack Nicholson's David Locke taking the place of his doppelgänger, the dead David Robinson. For Rohdie, in Antonioni's cinema 'the process of doubling has no starting point: it is not first the reality, then the image of it, first the substance, then the silhouette, but rather the tenuousness of both, their intermingling, the fragility of the line marking them, the constant threat of obliteration and dissolution … Subject and object waver, their very existences at stake' (1990: 111–12).[19] In self-portraiture, the subject/object relation is also a threat to identity: the artist looks at herself from the outside as an *other* body, as a reflection, as a split self or, indeed, as a double.

Buonarroti produced several self-portraits; he appears in a number of his paintings and statues, as a young man, as an adult and, finally, as an old man. Many scholars consider his art to be deeply autobiographical – *Moses* included: 'Michelangelo's oeuvre contains autobiographical allusions, though always indirect, generalised, sublimated. Even though idealised, his works are more personalised than those of any other Tuscan master. The faces of Procolus, David, Moses, Brutus reflect his own fierceness and his stern morals' (de Tolnay 1963: 263; author's translation).

One of the most uncanny of Buonarroti's self-portraits is included in the fresco of the Sistine Chapel: here, Michelangelo's face appears, distorted and deformed but still recognisable, in the skin that St Bartholomew carries with him. This rather disturbing self-representation points at another important facet of self-portraiture: the visual representation of oneself, one's double, becomes a mask, more specifically a mortuary mask, implying the ideas of both death and *vanitas*. This aspect is fundamental for an understanding of Antonioni's self-portrait in *The Gaze of Michelangelo*. Antonioni's image is here a mask, a digitally-modified double, which hints at questions of demise as well as of the instability of the self. Before I come to these all-important issues, one more element of the film's title must be explored: the gaze.

I have suggested above that Antonioni presents himself in his film as a 'consumer', as a spectator rather than as a producer of art, and as a director. This may seem unusual, given the long-standing tradition in visual self-portraiture of representing the author in the act of painting or of photographing, and of including in the representation images of the artist's tools – brushes, easels, canvas and cameras. Even when these objects are not present, an emphasis is usually placed on the artist's 'natural' work-tools: eyes and hands. Indeed, while Antonioni does not carry a camera, the insistent framing of his eyes and hands is ample evidence of his role as an artist, and specifically as a film director. Even though it may seem logical that the director should privilege his eyes only as instruments of his art, there is plenty of evidence that filmmakers consider their hands to be at least as important as their gaze; probably not only on account of the idea of holding the camera, but of the prominent role of montage in filmmaking, and its persistent association, despite the evolution and computerisation of the technique, with basic manual operations of cutting and glueing. Furthermore, the hands aid the gaze, they assist it in organising and 'framing' the viewed object, as Antonioni's hands clearly do here.[20] It is significant that in filmic self-portraits directors often frame their hands – two examples are the already quoted scene in *The Gleaners and I*, and *JLG/JLG: Self-Portrait in December*, in which a long sequence is dominated by a reflection uttered by Godard over images of his hands.

The gaze in the film's title is, obviously, as polyvalent a term as the name 'Michelangelo'. It refers to Buonarroti's artistic vision, as well as to the stern gaze of *Moses*, which is studied and almost brought to life by Antonioni's camera. It is known that Michelangelo considered *Moses* to be his most accomplished, life-like creation; upon completion of the statue, he is thought to have struck its right knee and commanded: 'Now speak!'[21] Through a series of close-ups and detail shots, articulated through a montage that constantly varies the angle of vision, Antonioni seems to ask *Moses* to 'now look'. Antonioni's framing and montage, however, do more than this; as I have already suggested, they philologically recreate the view of the statue from below. By moving the camera around the sculpture and by varying and multiplying the point of view, Antonioni annuls its 'alleged disproportionate, monstrous, and satyr-like characteristics' (Macmillan & Swales 2003: 73), which are perceived by a spectator in the current frontal view, and achieves the effect, intended by the artist, of a 'vital, complex, and lively figure' (ibid.).

The gaze is, of course, also the gaze of the cinema, and especially of Antonioni – both the man's gaze (which, now quite opaque but still searching and intense, is often scrutinised by the camera) and the director's 'vision'. By exchanging glances with *Moses*, and to an extent with Michelangelo (if we take *Moses* to be, at least in some measure, a self-portrait), Antonioni represents himself as the director of a cinema eminently engaged, at an aesthetic, philosophical and linguistic level with the question of the gaze.

The geography of this visual exchange, reproduced by shot/reverse-shot, is a compelling *mise en abyme*; the gazes put in circulation by Antonioni's camera are multiple – including, of course, the spectator's. By this process, Antonioni recreates and simultaneously complicates the typical situation of the visual self-portrait, in which the artist stares out of the painting/photograph/sculpture at the spectator; and the spectator, looking into the eyes of the artist's image, is placed in the position of the artist herself, and doubles her gaze. The paradox of an addressee who becomes the addresser is masterly reproduced. We both look *at* Antonioni (there are at least as many shots of him as of the statues) and *with* Antonioni: several semi-subjective shots, in which the camera is placed just behind Antonioni's head and frames the side of his face (with his glasses in clear evidence), as well as the field of his vision, invite us to look *through* his eyes (indeed, quite literally through his spectacles). In these shots, the spectatorial identification with the director is also suggested by the photography: while his image is sharp, his field of vision is out of focus. Simultaneously, we exchange glances with *Moses*, and thus look into the mirror of Michelangelo's eyes.[22]

The emphasis on matter, form, body and on the activities of fashioning and self-fashioning is overwhelming. One cannot stress enough the importance of

Looking through Antonioni's glasses in *The Gaze of Michelangelo* (2004)

the body in the self-portrait, which 'bases itself above all on the experience of the body, of the author's own body as the site and theatre of experience' (Bellour 1989: 10). Framed at some distance, Antonioni, about to turn 92, enters the church with his right hand casually resting in his pocket, and walks slowly but resolutely towards the tomb. The frailty, thinness and quasi-transparency of his body are highlighted and intensified by his apparition: he enters from an open door, through which a blade of light cuts through the darkness of the church. The importance of this door (which literally opens and closes the film, and frames it) is consonant with the prominent role that 'not only archways, but doorways, entrances, exits, thresholds, often windows' (Rohdie 1990: 66) play in Antonioni's cinema, as boundaries between different spaces. The open, lit door of *The Gaze of Michelangelo* recalls not only the eschatological/supernatural dimension (which will acquire importance at the end of the film) but also, of course, the (im) materiality itself of the cinema – the ray of light tearing the darkness of the auditorium. Antonioni's body is, therefore, an ethereal, fashioned filmic body, a play of shadows and light projected on a screen – as well as an iconic image of a real body, preserved and embalmed by the cinema in its function of death-at-work.

In the film, Antonioni's is a still-flexible and handsome though aged body; stylishly dressed in Armani, he looks confident, smart and blasé, a refined bourgeois intellectual at total ease with himself – an image that fits in with prevalent forms of self-portrayal by male artists in the late-twentieth century, which included 'the tropes of the artist as gentleman, Christ, Bohemian, or technician' (West 2004: 169). The distance of the camera enhances the seamless effect of the digital intervention, which allowed Antonioni to show us his body as he saw it, and as he wanted us to remember it; to express his understanding of his posi-

Walking through the film's threshold: the opening sequence of *The Gaze of Michelangelo*

Contrasting masculinities: the titanic Renaissance hero and the Western bourgeois artist in *The Gaze of Michelangelo*

tion in society, through choice of clothes, bodily shape and posture; as well as his comprehension/fashioning of his masculinity.

This self-portrait is not, however, that of a false, FX body; neither does it become a sublimated or sanitised version of an old man's body. The camera does get near to inspect Antonioni's face in close-up, to frame it from different viewpoints, to linger on the opaque gaze and the wrinkly skin. Furthermore, Antonioni does not attempt to trick the audience as to the reality of his situation – although in the medium-long or full shots he is seen standing, thanks to the digital refashioning of the image, in the close-ups that include the top of his shoulders he is evidently in a sitting position. Hence, his viewing position fully corresponds to his embodied experience (as seen in the view 'from below' of *Moses*). In Antonioni's cinema, bodies are always historicised (see Rascaroli & Rhodes 2008); and the director's body in this film is no exception. This point becomes unmistakably clear through the comparison he mercilessly sets up between his aged, fragile body, connoting a certain type of modern Western masculinity, and the timeless body of the statue, immortalising the Renaissance vision of a heroic, wilful and titanic manliness.

Antonioni's film, hence, brings the body to the fore in multiple ways: as the theatre of experience (an experience that, via the emphasis on sight and touch, is marked as fundamentally sensual); as the site of the specific and embodied experience of an artist, and therefore instrument of abstraction, intelligence, craft, sublimation and of creation; and as the product of an act of self-fashioning, which attests to the man's vision of himself, within his society and within the history of the arts and of the cinema in particular. And again, as the historicised body of a bourgeois, Western, male intellectual; as a filmic body – a flickering,

The ultimate disappearance: Antonioni leaves the church, the cinema and life at the end of *The Gaze of Michelangelo*

insubstantial, but intensely iconic and desirable image, which actualises the myth of bodily intimacy between the film's spectator and a more-than-real, magnified and beautified human figure; and, finally, as embodiment of the frailty and imperfection of human matter, compared to the durability of marble and of artistic creation.

The film evokes death in many ways, and not only because of Antonioni's considerable age at the time of shooting; this is perhaps unsurprising, given that 'There is hardly an Antonioni film in which death is not a central concern' (Rohdie 1990: 106) – and also given that death is the necessary subtext of all self-portraits.[23] The director comes to the church of San Pietro in Vincoli in order to admire Pope Julius II's grave; the church itself inspires thoughts of mortality and transience. The durability of *Moses*, which long outlived its creator, and which will also outlive Antonioni, its admirer, is in contrast with the fragility of this very minor, occasional nonfiction, to which Antonioni entrusted his last (and almost only) self-fashioned images, and which risks being overlooked by the mechanisms of film distribution, and rapidly forgotten.

Aware of being in the process of crafting his final self-portrait, Antonioni does not shun the thought of death; rather, he faces it straight on, and portrays himself in the act of leaving life. When he enters the church through the open door, the chirping of birds invades the silent, dim space of the chapel together with the light – thus giving the impression that the director had arrived from the reality of a bright Roman morning. When he exits through the same door some time later, however, the birds are no longer to be heard; from the offscreen space comes instead the sound of a distant choir singing the 'Magnificat' by Giovanni Pierluigi da Palestrina.[24] Prompted and almost summoned by the incipit of the sacred, otherworldly singing, Antonioni leaves *Moses* and heads towards the brightness, which now looks like a metaphor for the transfiguration of death. In long shot and without cuts, we observe his slender, beautiful figure turn and give a last look at Michelangelo's statues, then walk slowly towards the door. The camera pans to follow him, then stops and lets him go, continuing to observe him at some distance; hand in his pocket, Antonioni nonchalantly walks away from the lens, and steps into the unknown. The filmmaker of the disconcerting uncertainty of subjectivity, the director of so many uncanny disappearances, performs the final, ultimate disappearance – and walking through the door/limen/ frame of the film, transforms himself into the matter of the cinema.

afterword

Essayistic cinema is irreducibly plural. The division of this book into two sections, the first devoted to the essay film, the second to its cognate forms of the diary, the travelogue, the notebook and the self-portrait, has allowed me to argue that different forms of first-person cinema should not be fully equated, because they derive from and are given shape by their relationship with different literary and artistic genres. Each embraces specific textual commitments and communicative structures, and produces distinct spectatorial experiences. In the essay film, the spectator is an explicit partner in the communicative negotiation; indeed, he is overtly asked to enter into dialogue with the filmmaker/essayist, and to contribute to the creation of a constitutively open and unstable textual meaning. Conversely, in the first-person forms that have been explored in the second section of this volume, the audience witnesses a private discourse that is primarily self-addressed. The spectator, then, is asked to identify with the author. But the analysis has revealed an intrinsic paradox in the supposed auto-communication produced by these forms: ultimately, as soon as a camera is switched on, a spectator is implied, and an audience addressed – even in the case of ostensibly narcissistic and self-centred forms such as private diaries, personal notebooks and self-portraits.

So, at the end of this study, it may be timely to overcome such a division and to heal the fracture, for the purpose of highlighting that all these filmic forms belong together, if not to a single genre, at least to a domain, which can be described as the domain of the essayistic. It is to this domain that a cinema in the first person, a cinema of thought, of investigation, of intellectual searching and of self-reflection belongs. This is a cinema in which the filmmaker does not withdraw behind the camera, does not attempt to disguise her presence, thus letting either reality or spectacle speak for themselves; but one in which she comes out in the open, to say 'I' and to take responsibility for her discourse. In these films, then, the enunciator takes up his place in the text, and embodies into visible or audible narrators, often played by the director himself; the *énoncé* directly points to the enunciating subject. And yet, because essayistic cinema is a cinema of doubt and self-scrutiny, these films never postulate subjectivity in an unproblematic manner. Indeed, by analysing specific films, I have argued that authorship in the essay film is interstitial, and is played in the liminal spaces between the empirical author and his or her textual figures.

Given these characteristics, essayistic cinema may appear to be anachronistic – still authorial, still experimental, still radical, at a time when the industrial side of cinema seems to have totally prevailed over the militant and, one is tempted to write, romantic dreams of both second and third cinema, of art film and of the avant-gardes. In fact, essayistic cinema is responsive and germane to concerns that are fully relevant today. This is, indeed, a time in which the waning of objectivity and truth as convincing social narratives invites different forms of expression, and different dimensions and ways of engagement with the real – ways that are more contingent, marginal, autobiographical, even private. It is also a time in which documentary is being reinvented all over the world, and becomes simultaneously more personal and more popular, perhaps more so than ever.

Essayistic cinema is a cinema of today also because it is the expression of a transnational imagination, one which is more germane to our current interest for filmic phenomena that go beyond the national borders, and that more faithfully describe new and widespread intercultural forms of identification. It is transnational, I claim, because it is the cinema of international filmmakers who programmatically experiment and explore new territories, not only spatial, but existential, affective, aesthetic, communicative, political. The absence of rules in this field means that essayistic directors are in conversation with one another, rather than with established national and generic practices.

Though arguably still emergent, essayistic cinema holds an important place in the history of film, because it is an expression and an embodiment of a fundamental desire – specifically, of the filmmakers' wish to use the camera as a highly flexible, personal and responsive means of expression. Such a desire emerged immediately, in the early 1900s, when artists coming from literature, painting and photography approached the new medium with curiosity and experimental enthusiasm, and attempted to use it in the way in which they were accustomed to using pens, paintbrushes and still cameras. Precisely this same desire powerfully surfaced again in the 1940s and following decades, in instances of theoretical writing (those of Zavattini, Richter, Astruc, Truffaut, Pasolini), in the practice of the almost private cinema of the European new waves, in the diaristic cinema of the New York avant-garde, in the experiments of *cinéma vérité*. Since the early 1970s, it continued to be at the core of the North American autobiographical documentary, of accented cinema and of oppositional first-person nonfiction filmmaking produced by postcolonial, migrant, exiled, feminist and gay subjects.

And now personal cinema is currently one of the liveliest expressions of international documentary filmmaking, and is constantly evolving and expanding thanks to the wide availability of new technologies, which are affording easy access to audiovisual production and consumption, as well as new channels for the distribution and the fruition of alternative products.

Essayistic cinema, furthermore, brings to light and encapsulates another historical desire of the cinema. I refer to that sublimely paradoxical wish to communicate directly with the spectator, to bypass the obvious constraints of an apparatus that involves unbridgeable gaps between the three phases of filming, editing and projection. In striving to fulfil such a wish, essayistic cinema recognises that the body of the film exists, and is capable not only of being perceived, but also of perceiving the spectator (see Sobchack 1992). By using all available means, and indeed by constantly inventing new ones, essayistic cinema addresses and interpellates the embodied spectator, asks her to engage with the film and, through the filmic body, with the filmmaker.

Harun Farocki has asked the question: 'What kind of "I" is speaking to me through a film and how does a film in addressing me perceive me?' (in Halle 2001: 61). It is this central issue that is the focus of essayistic cinema. The essay film constructs a speaking 'I' who is inquisitive, pensive, searching and self-searching, engaged and self-reflexive. It is an 'I' who wishes to address and to engage with the spectator within a shared space of embodied subjectivity. The addressed spectator becomes, then, within this filmic space an equal to the director, a partner in the dialogue and in the creation of meaning; as Pasolini has phrased it plainly, 'For the author, the spectator is merely another author' (1988b: 269). Essayistic filmmaking recognises and valorises the spectator not as an empty, abstract position, as a general audience to be persuaded or entertained, but as an embodied subject who goes to the cinema or buys a DVD in order to establish a relationship with a text, and to enter into communication and negotiation with another embodied subject.

Ultimately, essayistic cinema is multiform, unfathomable and exciting because it is an open field of experimentation, in which there are indeed no rules, save for the adoption (and also the constant testing, subversion and reinvention) of the communicative structures and textual commitments described and analysed in this study. It is a field in which there is no truth, only truth making.

notes

introduction

1   I borrow the term 'interpellation' from Francesco Casetti, who defines it as 'the recognition of someone, who in turn is expected to recognise himself as the immediate interlocutor' (1998: 16). While suggesting that interpellation can be achieved in the cinema through either a voice or a look addressed to the camera, or via 'an intertitle or other metanarrative announcement to address the individual following the narrative rather than a character who lives in it' (ibid.), Casetti also recognises various degrees of intensity to the different devices: 'For instance, a direct gaze into the camera carries a greater demand for attention than either an intertitle or an offscreen voice, both of which also aim to inform, solicit or exhort' (1998: 17). Other expressions encountered in the relevant literature include 'direct address' and 'aside'; Paul Willemen uses 'fourth look', which he describes as the 'look at the viewer' – the other three being those identified by Laura Mulvey in her seminal article, 'Visual Pleasure and Narrative Cinema' (1975): 'firstly, the camera's look as it records the pro-filmic event; secondly, the audience's look at the image; and thirdly, the look the characters exchange within the diegesis' (Willemen 1994: 101). In spite of the Althusserian connotation of the construction of a subject/spectator, I favour Casetti's notion of 'interpellation', which not only accounts for the gaze, but also for all forms of enunciational address to the audience; it presupposes the idea of asking a question of the spectator – and interrogation, I will claim, is the core strategy of essayistic cinema.

2   Throughout the book, I will use the term enunciation generally to refer to the 'manner of utterance' (*énunciation*); occasionally, to the utterance itself, which in cinematic terms may mean the entire film, or a sequence or a shot; when necessary to avoid ambiguity, in this second sense I will use the French term, *énoncé*.

3   Examples include Winston (1995), Corner (1996), Plantinga (1996), Bruzzi (2000 and 2006) and Renov (2004).

4   See, for instance, Giddens (1990), Hall (1992) and Bauman (2000).

5   Richter's and Astruc's contributions are widely recognised as foundational for the

establishment of the form; Pasolini's less so, even if the filmmaker is frequently listed among the essayists. The role of Zavattini in the emergence of first-person cinema, on the other hand, was largely overlooked. Zavattini's name is linked to Italian neo-realism, and therefore to the theory of realism; in his many writings on the cinema, however, Zavattini introduced his reflections on a personal and autobiographical approach to filmmaking as early as 1940, and continued to develop them over the following decades.

6   By conflating European and North-American approaches to first-person cinema I am advocating a transnational perspective that is, perhaps, only reliable to a degree; as Maureen Turim reminded us, for instance, Jonas Mekas (foremost representative of US personal filmmaking) saw the popularity of new European cinema as a threat. On the other hand, this is 'not without irony, for the auteur theory and the stylistic freedom of new wave camera work and editing were close to some aspects of personal cinema' (Turim 1992: 199). It is because of this closeness and affinity that, I believe, it is possible to talk of essayistic cinema as a transnational phenomenon.

7   This can obviously only be achieved through devices such as mirrors.

8   For instance, according to Bruss, Kenneth Anger's *Fireworks* (1947) is not autobiographical because, although the story 'is set in his own home and concerned with his own confessed homosexuality ... the particular events the film depicts are entirely fictitious' (1980: 312). This view clearly equates autobiography with factuality. Yet, it seems obvious that, as is customary in literature, distinctions should be made between the different degrees of autobiography that different films set out to achieve – for instance, from fully factual autobiographical accounts to autofiction.

9   For Hamid Naficy, accented cinema, although including very diverse films, is characterised overall by 'what the filmmakers have in common: liminal subjectivity and interstitial location in society and the film industry' (2001: 10).

10   Of course, in all cinematic forms the subject of the enunciation is always referred to by at least one aspect of the film as *énoncé*; and this aspect 'is the point of view from which things are observed, a point which provides the pivot around which to organise the images (and sounds), and which determines their coordinates and form' (Casetti 1998: 19). However, in the case of essayistic cinema, the subject of the enunciation literally inhabits the film, and embodies in a narrator who identifies with the extra-textual author. This is what I refer to as a 'strong enunciator'.

11   As I will discuss in the following chapter, a key characteristic of the essay is that of weaving the process of thought into the text.

12   Indeed, as David Bordwell has suggested, while debating Tom Gunning's theory of the cinema of attractions, 'performers in early films commonly address the camera, turning to the viewer to register a reaction or mimic another actor. This technique suited the "exhibitionist" side of early film' (1997: 127).

13   Errol Morris had to invent new camera technology, Interrotron, in order to create

direct eye contact between the social actor and the director during interviews and, as a result, between social actor and spectator. He employed this system in his television series, meaningfully entitled *First Person* (2000). The effect is that of a strong inter-pellation – most of the time, the spectator feels directly addressed by the social actor, who appears to be talking to and with the audience. The effect is at times amended by the surfacing of the mediating presence of the director who, for instance, may be heard asking the odd question to the interviewee.

14   Other forms that could have been included in the second part of this study, but were not (solely for questions of space), are the travelogue (which is, however, addressed both in the chapter on the diary film and in the following one, on the notebook film), the epistle and the filmed poem, as well as the personal documentary, intended as a documentary in which the director explores his own life or that of his family.

15   While examples in all chapters will be equally drawn from European and North-American cinema, all the in-depth case studies are European, solely as a result of the author's individual preferences and affinities.

chapter one

1   The idea of the flexibility and availability of the pen and of the act of writing, and the dream of attaining a similar agility with the camera, through lighter and cheaper equipment, are of course at the base of the linguistic developments first introduced by Italian neorealism, and subsequently taken up by the new waves, by *cinéma vérité* and by direct cinema. Cesare Zavattini had suggested the metaphor of the pen ear-lier than Astruc; for instance, in a piece first published in *Cinema* on 25 April 1940, Zavattini argues: 'What was crucial was to *take control of the medium* by providing it at a cost so modest as to make it widely accessible; to allow individuals to have ac-cess to it in exactly the same way as paper, ink, plasticine, or paints; to introduce film stock and lenses into homes just as if they were sewing machines' (1979: 38; author's translation; emphasis in original.). Zavattini's contribution to the establishment of a first-person cinema will be discussed in more detail in chapter five. His writings on the diary film will be scrutinised in chapter six.

2   With these observations on the short film I do not wish to suggest that essays are, by nature, sub-feature length in duration; rather, that the artistic freedom and experi-mentalism guaranteed by the short, and its combination with the documentary mode in the above-described French productive context, favoured the emergence of the essay.

3   Among later examples Burch lists Francesco Rosi's *Salvatore Giuliano* (1962) and some of Godard's films, including *Vivre sa vie* (1962).

4   For instance, in some of the essays included in Liandrat-Guigues & Gagnebin (eds) (2004), and in Weinrichter (ed.) (2007).

5   Corrigan had already written of the essay film in a 1995 article, in which he charted the evolution of the essay and its relationship to experience, 'in its multiple discursive senses: experience represented in the essay, the experience of representing a subject writing the essay, and the experience of a public receiving that essay' (1995: 87).

6   Arthur gives the examples of Agnès Varda, Yvonne Rainer, Jill Godmilow, Ngozi Onwurah, Marlon Riggs, Patricio Guzmán, John Akomfrah and Raoul Peck.

7   Here, and in the following pages, I use the term 'voice' in the sense of the author's subjectivity and not of 'voice-over' (although voice-over can be one of the means through which a subjective stance is expressed).

8   Catherine Lupton (2007) is close to this idea when she calls the voice-over of the essay film 'heteroglossic', on the basis that the essay undermines the authority of the singular, omniscient, voice-of-God documentary narrator 'by multiplying the speaking selves or personae who provide the commentary, by deferring or displacing what they have to say into assorted forms of reported speech – such as the letter, the quotation, the recollected saying or conversation – by asserting their fictional or, at least, ontologically ambiguous status with respect to actual people (including and especially the filmmaker), and by fomenting indeterminacies, tensions and disagreements among them'.

9   For a more thorough discussion of these points, see the introduction .

10   I will explore this different communicative structure in the second section of the book.

11   For a detailed engagement with the question of voice-over in documentary in general, and in the essay film in particular, see chapter two.

12   For a discussion of these concepts see the introduction .

13   All these films will be discussed and analysed in the following chapters.

chapter two

1   The key reference here is, of course, Louis Althusser (1971).

2   As a revealing example that proves the necessity of this type of critical engagement one can think of the film-poems of Scottish director and writer Margaret Tait, with their multi-layered, expressive, poetic voice-over. On Tait, see Todd & Cook (eds) (2004).

3   'Acousmatic' is a sound that is heard without its cause or source being visible.

4   A feature that is apparent, for instance, in the work produced in those same years by Godard, Marker and Marguerite Duras.

5   Silverman, admittedly, cannot, in fact, think of any example of female voice-over, with the exception of Joseph L. Mankiewicz's *A Letter to Three Wives* (1949).

6   The process employed to create this musical collage is the following: Farocki recorded sections of the *English Suites* (c. 1715) by Bach and the *Razumovsky Quartets*

(1805–06) by Beethoven on a 16mm tape, then placed the tape into an erasure box, covering the reel with a pair of open scissors, thus protecting some parts of the tape from erasure. The musical score thus created was then paired to the visual track; therefore, the coupling of images and sounds is haphazard (personal communication, Harun Farocki Filmproduktion).

7   To say that this female narrator is simply ventriloquising the director's voice is untenable. Nothing in the film, in fact, unambiguously suggests that Farocki fully embraces and shares the commentary. His positioning in the text as a separate (and silent) narrator denies this interpretation, because it strengthens the voice-over's relative autonomy.

8   The text is transcribed from the English version of the film.

chapter three

1   Among the many examples of collage films which metacritically investigate the image as historical document and the cinema as audiovisual archive and museum are a number of key works of the essay film genre, such as Alain Resnais' *Night and Fog*, Mikhail Romm's *Obyknovennyy fashizm* (*Ordinary Fascism*, 1965) and Jean-Luc Godard *Historie(s) du cinéma*.

2   See chapter one.

3   For a discussion of Freudian versus Proustian elements of Marker's conception of memory, see ffrench (2005).

4   References to relevant writings by Zavattini and Astruc may be found in the introduction , in chapter one and in chapter five.

5   *The Old Place* is an essay film on the New York Museum of Modern Art.

6   This is, however, an idea that some scholars problematise – see, for instance, Charles Saumarez Smith (1989).

7   For a discussion of Resnais' *Last Year in Marienbad* and *Providence* as mental topographies, see Rascaroli (2002b; 2006).

8   Interestingly, the voice-over notices that this book, once it has found its place in the Bibliothèque, no longer is the same book; somehow, similarly to the African artefacts of *Statues Also Die*, it loses its original meaning and becomes part, in this case, of the universal memory that is safeguarded by the library.

9   Catherine Belkhodja, as Sarah Cooper notes, provided voice-overs for several of Marker's films: *L'Héritage de la chouette* (1989), *Berliner Ballade* (1990), *The Last Bolshevik* and *Le 20 heures dans les camps* (1993) as well as featuring as a mute image in the latter. 'Additionally, she figured in *Owl Gets in Your Eyes* (grouped with *Tchaika* and *Petite Ceinture* to constitute the very brief *Three Video Haikus* of 1994) and in stills and imaginary silent film footage within the installation *Silent Movie* (1995)' (2008: 156–7). Her role as a muse in recent years for Marker, and the frequent use of

her voice-over, establishes her as one of the embodiments of Marker's subjectivity in *Level Five*, as I will claim below.

10 Obviously, this is a reference to Marker's widely-known love of this bird, and to his production company Argos Films, of which the owl is the logo.

11 The significance of the Battle of Okinawa for Marker is suggested by the fact that *Sans soleil* already included a sequence devoted to it.

12 Such a divergence and dispute is dramatised by the two films that Clint Eastwood directed about the Japanese/US front of World War Two: *Flags of Our Fathers* (2006), which portrays the Battle of Iwo Jima from the perspective of the American soldiers, and its companion piece, *Letters from Iwo Jima* (2006), which restages the same events from the point of view of the Japanese defenders.

13 Similarly, he claims that in order to reach some museal understanding of Okinawa's tragedy, one would have to go alone into the caves of the horror, where young nurses and wounded civilians and soldiers were crammed, abandoned by Japan, and try to imagine what it might have felt like being a teenage girl awaiting, in the midst of the terrible smell and sound of rotting flesh, her death by flamethrower.

14 Textual multiplicity is also created through 'a fondness for later digressions into humorous anecdote and parable, the insistent working of images through the screens of digital manipulation and mediation … and the elaborate fictional conceits of Laura, her dead lover and her editor friend Chris' (Lupton 2003: 61).

15 There is, however, also a pleasurable side to the repetition afforded by the game. As Marker has argued in an article first published in *Positif* and then reproduced in the CD-ROM *Immemory*, 'What do video games offer us, which say so much more about our unconscious than the complete works of Lacan? Neither money nor glory: a new game. The possibility of playing again. "A second chance." A *free replay*' (quoted in Cooper 2008: 157; emphasis in original).

16 Marker, in other words, argues for the difference between camera/gaze and look also postulated by Farocki in *Images of the World and the Inscription of War* (see chapter two; see also Silverman 1996).

17 Her address is, indeed, both love epistle and confessional/private diary; Cooper writes that 'Level 5 is essentially Laura's video diary, punctuated by log-ins dated from September 7 to November 29 in an unspecified year, with separate entries marked out by a white date on a black screen' (2008: 157). We could venture to call her diary a blog, given that it is composed at the computer, although we do not have evidence of it being posted online.

18 Laura's status as avatar, in the sense of both a site of Marker's subjectivity and an embodied figure with a distinct personality, is reflected by the extra-textual role she took up after the release of *Level Five*, when she became 'spokesperson for and promoter of the film. She appeared in an episode of *Le Cercle de Minuit* television series, devoted to war and cinema on 4 February 1997, and was also interviewed by the French Press' (Cooper 2008: 157).

19 For Lupton, Laura's mediating role is instead ensured by the fact that she was already dead before the beginning of the film, that what we are watching is her diary, and that she has therefore acquired 'the condition that allows her to place herself alongside the survivors and the memory of Okinawa' (2003: 69).

chapter four

1   For Goffman, the 'front' is the general and fixed part of an individual's performance, which may include 'clothing, sex, age, and racial characteristics; size and looks; posture; speech patterns; facial expressions; bodily gestures and the like' (1959: 34).

2   On re-enactment, see Bangma, Rushton and Wüst (eds) (2005); Lutticken (2005).

3   As represented by such photographers as August Sander, Diane Arbus, Wilhelm von Gloeden and Robert Mapplethorpe.

4   Waugh, who mainly writes about American cinema, also attracts our attention to the fact that, since the early 1970s, the presentational mode has become very relevant, with the revival of the interview and, since the 1980s, the 'hybrid experimentation with these presentational modes as well as with stylisations of representational modes, including dramatisation' (1990: 74).

5   See chapter one.

6   For Bordwell, however, the notion of essay used in relation to Godard is only 'an alibi for unusual narrational strategies' (1985: 312).

7   It is, however, more precisely in 1967 that Godard makes his first essay film, the 15-minute short *Caméra-œil* – an episode of the portmanteau *Loin du Viêt-Nam (Far From Vietnam*, 1967).

8   A hybridism that is reinforced by 'the sheer variety of media in which [Godard] is now working and the ease with which he moves between them' (Witt 2004: 74).

9   Indeed, his engagement with performance goes well beyond the cinema. For a commentary on Godard's performances in interviews and in television appearances, see Witt (2004: 83–6).

10 An obvious example is Belmondo's Bogart-like performance in *À bout de souffle*.

11 We should also add *Moi, je*, a key unrealised project of the 1970s, the script of which was published in Brenez, Faroult, Temple, Williams & Witt (eds) (2006).

12 For a detailed discussion of filmic self-portraiture, see chapter eight.

13 Here and elsewhere in this chapter, the translation of the dialogue is taken from the English subtitles of the Cinema Parallel VHS edition of the film.

14 This is a quote, a variation on the closing words of Ovid's *Metamorphoses*.

15 It does, however, present far less audiovisual alteration/reiteration, although it does make use of some of the images we already saw in *Histoire(s) du cinéma*.

16 The Native Americans quote his 1992 poem, 'Les dernières paroles de l'homme rouge' (Darwich 2000: 286–94).

17   There are so many trams in this film that one wonders whether Godard wanted to
     pay homage to F. W. Murnau's *Sunrise* (1927) or to Dziga Vertov's *Chelovek s kino-*
     apparatom (*Man With a Movie Camera*, 1929). Godard makes an explicit connec-
     tion between trams, *Sunrise* and Lotte Eisner in chapter 3B, *Une vague nouvelle*, of
     Histoire(s) du cinéma. Trams were also an important motif in *Voyage(s) en utopie,*
     Jean-Luc Godard, 1946–2006, Godard's exhibition at the Centre Georges Pompidou,
     Paris, 11 May–14 August 2006.

18   'Ainsi, dans le temps des fables, après les inondations et les déluges, il sortit de la terre
     des hommes armés, qui s'exterminèrent' (Montesquieu 1976: 708–9).

19   A visualisation of the spectator's positioning in the film as a partner in the dialogue is
     achieved by a short sequence set in a café towards the end of 'Purgatory'. The camera
     is positioned before a round table, on which three glasses are filled with wine. One
     of the glasses is straight in front of the camera; the impression for the spectator is of
     sitting at the table with two characters, whose hands are visible and whose offscreen
     voices are heard conversing on the subject of democracy.

20   Furthermore, the montage of film excerpts in 'Hell' is interspersed with black frames,
     which suspend the discourse, attract attention to the work of the film, and offer paus-
     es of reflection to the spectator.

21   A visual hint at the film's interrogative structure appears in a scene set at the Sara-
     jevo airport, in which we see a large question mark on the information screen of
     the check-in area. The importance of this image is stressed by the unrealistic, high
     camera angle, which suggests viewing the shot as a comment coming directly from
     the author/enunciator.

22   As he is, for instance, more overtly in *JLG/JLG*; whereas, at least in some of the instal-
     ments of *Histoire(s) du cinéma*, he privileges the thinker, the essayist.

chapter five

1   As we will see, this is especially true of notebook films that were made in preparation
     for subsequent, 'official' films; but also of some diary films (for instance, the work of
     Joseph Morder).

2   Mekas's role in the establishment of the diary film form will be explored in the follow-
     ing chapter.

3   While narrative is obviously relevant to the diary (more so than to the notebook and
     the self-portrait), its openness, occasional nature and vocation to fragmentariness and
     incompleteness differentiate it from other more decidedly narrative forms of writing.

4   See http://www.vidblogs.com/ (accessed 2 July 2008).

5   See http://www.youtube.com/t/about (accessed 2 July 2008).

6   Podcasting is the distribution of multimedia files over the Internet for playback on
     mobile devices and personal computers.

7   Quoted, for instance, in Van Dijck 2006.

8   See chapter one.

9   While in the following chapter I will examine Zavattini's ideas on the diary film, here I will look more generally at his theory of a first-person cinema.

10   As Rhodes notes, 'Pasolini seems to assume that all directors are middle class' (forthcoming).

11   Pasolini's textual examples include films by Antonioni, Bertolucci and Godard.

12   However, it is interesting to note that, while all of his examples are taken from feature fiction filmmaking, his essay was written at the same time as Pasolini was venturing into documentary practice. Furthermore, despite the emphasis on style, there is, in Pasolini's argument, still a belief in indexicality. In other words, Pasolini's approach to subjectivism/formalism is redescribed in terms of realism/indexicality. Hence, Zavattini's and Pasolini's positions are closer than they may seem.

chapter six

1   Arguably due to the rapid expansion of book production and the passage from an oral to a written culture, as well as the spread of revolutionary theologies and the shift induced by the Reformation, which allowed the individual to become a responsible, epistemological subject (see, for instance, Schlaeger 1999).

2   This quotation refers to the 'Lodz diary'. Written in four languages by an unknown person from the Jewish ghetto of Lodz, Poland, eventually deported to Auschwitz in 1944 and killed, the diary documents its author's last four months in Lodz. However, it can be easily argued that a linguistic/rhetorical diversity and a multiplication of the writing self are achieved by most diaries.

3   Here and in the following quotation, 'intimate' and 'intimism' are used in the sense of the French 'intimisme' – with reference to art that concerns itself with the most private, personal thoughts, feelings and ideas, as well as with everyday, domestic, private existence.

4   It must be noted that, for Girard and others, the perceived presence of the diary's potential reader is actually a negative: the other's gaze is experienced by the diarist as a menace, a threat; the potential reader is a judge, and an obstacle to achieving complete sincerity and confession.

5   Of course, some types of diaries do have endings; for instance, travel journals or courtship diaries.

6   See http://www.bbc.co.uk/videonation/ (accessed 22 July 2008)

7   See Zavattini's claim that his aversion to screenplays had already emerged during the war, when he started to plan diaristic films: 'It was the diary already' (Zavattini 1979a: 72; author's translation).

8   See http://www.jonasmekas.com/ (accessed 22 July 2008)

9   Jim Lane is close to this notion when he writes that the filmed events or entries are 'later organised into a narrative where continuities are imposed by identified days, dates, times, and locations. After long periods of editing in which many entries remain in the editing room, the journal entry documentary emerges' (2002: 41).

10   With the collapse of the Soviet Union, Tajikistan gained independence in 1991, but did not have the resources to begin to guard its own frontiers; the existing Russian border troops were therefore kept on site, as it was in Russia's interest to protect itself from Afghani Taliban. The troops we see in *Spiritual Voices* are mostly made up of career soldiers.

11   Underneath Sokurov's photograph on each DVD cover is Susan Sontag's validation of Sokurov's status as auteur: 'Alexander Sokurov is perhaps the most ambitious and original serious filmmaker of his generation working anywhere in the world today.'

12   In episode five, during the night-time sequences, a soldier mentions that 'the cameraman is cold', and asks Alexei (ostensibly, Sokurov) whether he wants a drink; later, we hear Sokurov's voice announcing to the guards that the troupe is leaving: these are the only other direct references to the filmmakers in *Spiritual Voices*.

13   As Sokurov clarified in an interview, 'My coming to video has been perfectly conscious, and it offers me maximum control over the creative process. The unsatisfying distance between the filmmaker and his work is dramatically reduced, while the work's artistic particularities can be developed more extensively and with more variety' (in Sedofsky 2001: 2). After refusing to let his films be shown on television in the 1980s, Sokurov first turned to video in the early 1990s, when Betacam SP equipment became available in Russia, thus expanding the artistic possibilities of working with video.

14   Sokurov's control over his films is considerably high; for instance, 'Sokurov did his own cinematography for *Taurus*, and it is quite likely that he did the job for all his films, even in the presence of a credited director of photography' (Szaniawski 2006: 24).

15   Here and everywhere else in this chapter, dialogue is transcribed from the English subtitles of the Facets DVD edition of the film.

16   Critics have noted not only the existential but also the autobiographical factor of Sokurov's interest in the military, owing to the fact that his father was a Soviet army officer, who was assigned to a number of different places in the USSR and abroad during his career.

17   In *Spiritual Voices* soldiers very frequently talk about time, and especially of what day it is, of when they went home the last time, and of durations – how much is left.

18   Throughout the film the soldiers' expectations and fears are a key subject for Sokurov, whose camera explores faces as if they were emotional landscapes, and whose voiceover often says 'we', thus sharing the fate of the filmed soldiers.

19   This sequence also constitutes Sokurov's eleven-minute short, *Soldatskiy son* (*Soldier's Dream*, 1995).

20   For this last episode, cameraman Alexander Burov was replaced by television camera-man Alexei Fiodorov, who subsequently continued to work with Sokurov until *Moloch*.

21   For Bruno Dietsch, the various elements of the film, among which 'the stifled, drawn-out fragments of the funeral march of the *Twilight of the Gods* and at the end the *Kindertotenlieder* ... converge symphonically on one end, the accomplishment of a work of art on death' (2005: 25; author's translation).

chapter seven

1   Because of this affinity, I will not delve too deeply into an analysis of the notebook's textual structures, and refer the reader to the sections of the previous chapter de-voted to the diary form and its commitments.

2   Produced by Rai-Radiotelevisione italiana for the programme *Cinema 70*, first broad-casted by Rai 2 on 7 June 1970 (see Visconti 1979: 416).

3   An eight-minute version of the film was lost (see Micciché 1996: 24).

4   The title of this film, also in English-language scholarship, is often spelled *Sopraluoghi in Palestina*. I adopt instead the spelling *Sopralluoghi*, as in the film's opening titles.

5   'In 1970, during a city-wide sanitation strike in Rome, Pasolini shot a documentary which he had intended to title *Notes for a Novel on Garbage*. Produced for inclusion in a collective documentary by the Committee of Italian Filmmakers Against Repres-sion, the film was never edited and is seemingly lost' (Gianvito 1999–2000: 41). Reels of this film, although without sound, have recently resurfaced and are at the basis of a documentary on the film made by Mimmo Calopresti, *Come si fa a non amare Pasolini. Appunti per un romanzo sull'immondezza* (2006).

6   In a similar vein, writing of *Notes for an African Orestes* John David Rhodes has argued that 'What saves this political aestheticisation of underdevelopment from becoming merely or only apolitical and condescendingly aesthetic is the fact that these places are being offered to view at all. Sending Greek tragedy into Africa is an allegorical method of meditating on the crisis of modernity and the scandal of third world poverty by not representing these same things' (2007: 148).

7   The Christological theme was already strong in *Accattone* (1961), *Mamma Roma* (1962) and *La ricotta*.

8   However, through the choice of Susanna Pasolini for the role of the *mater dolorosa*, Pasolini also associates Christ with his brother Guido, a partisan killed in the mas-sacre of Porzûs in 1945, thus elevating him to the level of revolutionary martyr.

9   In truth, the journey through Italy for the preceding *Comizi d'amore* (*Love Meetings*, 1965) was also secretly considered by producer Alfredo Bini and by Pasolini as loca-tion scouting for the same film. Pasolini, in his own words, had decided to film in Southern Italy 'even before I went to Palestine, which I only did to set my conscience at ease' (in Stack 1969: 82).

10 However, Alfredo Bini, in a video interview included on the DVD of *Sopralluoghi in Palestina* (Ripley's Home Video, 2005), states that Pasolini himself edited the material.

11 All English translations of dialogue from *Sopralluoghi in Palestina* are adapted from the subtitles of the Ripley's Home Video DVD edition of the film.

12 In the already quoted video interview, Alfredo Bini confirms that he was, indeed, the addressee of Pasolini's commentary.

13 The Ripley's Home Video DVD edition of *Sopralluoghi in Palestina* includes an excerpt that did not make it into the final edit, in which Alfredo Bini addresses Pasolini in voice-over, and comments that it is clear the film should not be shot in Palestine, but in the south of Italy. The dialogue between Pasolini/Bini is only implicit in the final version of the film, in which the absence of Bini's voice allows for the spectator to take up the position of the addressee. This unedited excerpt also raises questions about Pasolini's above-mentioned description of how the film was put together.

14 See chapter two. It is also interesting to note that, in the 15-minute television programme directed by Paolo Brunatto, *Pasolini e la forma della città* (*Pasolini and the Shape of the City*, 1974), Pasolini expresses his opinions on the Italian city of Orte directly to his friend/actor/partner Ninetto Davoli, here truly the ideal spectator/lover, and comments: 'I talk about this problem with you – because I am unable to talk in the abstract, to the void, to a TV audience that I don't even now where to position'.

15 For a discussion of the value and function of Pasolini's body in *Comizi d'amore* see Restivo (2002).

16 Take, for instance, the following passage from a 1940 letter to Franco Farolfi: 'Casarsa disappointed me; on the other hand, everything disappoints me while it is present, but I long for it when it has passed' (in Siciliano 2005: 60; author's translation).

17 Towards the end of the film, while in Jerusalem, Pasolini asks Don Andrea whether the priest considers it acceptable for the film to refer directly to the original image of Christ, and discard the many readings of his figure that have been offered by subsequent generations. Don Andrea's comment is, tellingly: 'Consider yourself authorised.'

18 For instance, see the autobiographical substratum of Pasolini's *I turcs tal Friùl*, in which, according to Andreina Ciceri, 'the two brothers, Pauli and Meni (with continuous, suggestive allusion to the two real-life brothers) are not two dichotomised presences, but interchangeable souls, as by chiasm' (in Siciliano 2005: 83; author's translation).

19 Pasolini thus described Don Andrea in an article written on the occasion of his death: 'As they say in Veneto, he was "on loan" in this life: and this allowed him to have an impartial (and, for what I know, almost angelic) attention to life: an attention that was all the more practical by being contemplative and humbly free' (Pasolini 1981a: 135; author's translation). Note how Pasolini's typical self-description in his oeuvre is

not on the side of contemplation, which here belongs to Don Andrea, but on that of action: his 'desperate vitality'.

20 Indeed, Pasolini's dissatisfaction with his film is well documented; see, for instance, the following comment: 'There are some horrible moments I am ashamed of, which are almost Counter-Reformation Baroque, repellent' (Pasolini, in Stack 1969: 87).

chapter eight

1 Consider, for instance, the Romantic concepts of 'personality' and 'inner life'.

2 See the introduction .

3 As well as being a road-documentary on gleaning, and a travelogue (see Mazierska & Rascaroli 2006: 124–30).

4 This effect is reached in many of his 1970s videos, for instance *Theme Song* (1973).

5 In this sense, it is significant to note that commissioned self-portraits are tradition-ally rare. This fact also contributes to an explanation of the scarcity of 35mm self-portraits.

6 As, for instance, does Muriel Tinel (2006).

7 For a discussion of Lane's category of the journal entry documentary, see chapter six.

8 On this film, see chapter four.

9 In 1998 Akerman also created a video installation entitled *Autobiography – Selfpor-trait in Progress*, which included six monitors showing images from DVDs accom-panied by a narrative written and read by the artist, and which was presented almost simultaneously that year in New York, London and Paris. A section of *Cinéma, de notre temps: Chantal Akerman par Chantal Akerman* is included in the 2007 Car-lotta DVD set *Chantal Akerman: Les Années 70*.

10 The film had limited theatrical distribution, and was released as a bonus in the Warn-er Brothers 2004 DVD edition of the omnibus *Eros*.

11 At the (now unavailable) website www.progettomose.it. Helmut Newton took a se-ries of photographs of the restoration.

12 Only followed by his disappointing instalment in the omnibus *Eros*, *The Gaze of Michelangelo* is, in many ways, Antonioni's true final film. Antonioni died in Rome on 30 July 2007, at 92 years of age.

13 While no word is pronounced, the film is notable for its wonderfully refined sound-track of noises and sounds.

14 Significantly (and also proving Turim's point in the above quotation), Antonioni had already used artisanal means to 'paint' some of his previous films. For instance, when shooting *Il deserto rosso* (*Red Desert*, 1964), his first film in colour, he asked his crew to spray paint on the vegetation on the set, in order to achieve the desired tonal effect.

15 A fitting cinematic example is Woody Allen's *Zelig* (1983), which achieved ample and seamless image manipulation before the advent of digital technology.

16 Antonioni appears in his ten-minute television documentary *Ritorno a Lisca Bianca* (1983, 16mm), a return to the Eolian island of *L'avventura* 24 years after the shooting of the film.

17 It may be useful here to bear in mind that this opinion was already championed by biographer and art historian Giorgio Vasari while Michelangelo was still alive.

18 Michelangelo Antonioni was a painter at least since the 1970s; some of his work is currently displayed at the Michelangelo Antonioni Museum in Ferrara, his birthplace.

19 Although I have here extended them to Antonioni's entire oeuvre, Rohdie's comments were written on a specific film, the documentary *N.U. Nettezza Urbana* (1948).

20 It is also worth recalling here that 'Antonioni's films are often filled with shots of hands moving, groping, reaching out, in search of something which only becomes clear when it is found and sometimes not even then' (Rohdie 1990: 133).

21 According to the legend, a visible scar on the statue's knee is the mark of Michelangelo's hammer.

22 It must also be noted that *Moses'* gaze, together with his posture, and his manner of holding his beard and the tablets, was a crucial point of interest in dissimilar and even conflicting critical readings of the statue (including Freud's).

23 Once again, I would like to recall the example of Varda's *The Gleaners and I* as a 'portrait of the artist as an old lady'; and especially the moment in which she argues: 'No it is not "Oh rage", no it is not despair, it is not "Old age, my enemy", it might even be "Old age, my friend", but still my hair and my hands keep telling me that the end is near' (translation from the English subtitles of the 2002 Zeitgeist DVD edition of the film).

24 It is significant that, as part of the restoration, the large arch window and the four rectangular openings that Michelangelo had inserted in the monument, and that had subsequently been closed, have been reopened. Through these openings both light and sounds originally came – behind the monument, in fact, the choir of the Canonici Regolari Lateranensi used to rehearse, and Michelangelo meant for the voices to enter the church, as a soundtrack.

bibliography

Abbott, H. Porter (1988) 'Autobiography, Autography, Fiction: Groundwork for a Taxonomy of Textual Categories', *New Literary History*, 19, 3, 597–615.

Adams, Timothy Dow (1994) 'Life Writing and Light Writing: Autobiography and Photography', *Modern Fiction Studies*, 40, 3, 459–92.

Adorno, Theodor (1991) *Notes to Literature, vol. 1*, ed. Rolf Tiedemann, trans. Shierry Weber Nicholsen. New York: Columbia University Press.

Agel, Henri (1971) *Esthétique du cinema*. Paris: Presses Universitaires de France.

Agnew, Vanessa (1999) 'Dissecting the Cannibal: Comparing the Function of the Autopsy Principle in the Diaries and Narratives of Cook's Second Voyage', in Rachael Langford and Russell West (eds) *Marginal Voices, Marginal Forms: Diaries in European Literature and History*. Amsterdam: Rodopi, 50–60.

Aiken, Edward A. (1983) '*Emak Bakia* Reconsidered', *Art Journal*, 43, 3, 'Art History and the Study of Film', 240–6.

Aitken, Ian (2001) *European Film Theory and Cinema: A Critical Introduction*. Edinburgh: Edinburgh University Press.

Alter, Nora M. (1996) 'The Political Im/perceptible in the Essay Film: Farocki's *Images of the World and the Inscription of War*', *New German Critique*, 68, 165–92.

_____ (2000) 'Mourning, Sound, and Vision: Jean-Luc Godard's *JLG/JLG*', *Camera Obscura*, 15, 2, 75–103.

_____ (2002) *Projecting History. German Nonfiction Cinema 1967–2000*. Ann Arbor: University of Michigan Press.

_____ (2004) 'The Political Im/perceptible: *Images of the World and the Inscription of War*', in Thomas Elsaesser (ed.) *Harun Farocki: Working on the Sight-Lines*. Amsterdam: Amsterdam University Press, 211–34.

Althusser, Louis (1971) 'Ideology and Ideological State Apparatuses: Notes Towards an Investigation', in *Lenin and Philosophy and Other Essays*, trans. Ben Brewster. London: New Left Books, 127–86.

Anderson, Walter Truett (1997) *The Future of the Self: Inventing the Postmodern Person*. New York: Jeremy P. Tarcher/Putnam.

Antonioni, Michelangelo (1993) 'Le montagne incantate', in *Le montagne incantate e altre opere*, catalogue of exhibition held in Ferrara, 30 July–31 October 1993, ed. Direzione delle Gallerie Civiche di Arte Moderna di Palazzo dei Diamanti, Ferrara Excerpt online. Available at: http://musei.talete.org/musei/antonioni/docdoc.htm (accessed 20 July 2008).

____ (1996a [1961]) 'A Talk with Michelangelo Antonioni on his Work', in *Michaelangelo Antonioni: The Architect of Vision. Writings and Interviews on the Cinema*, ed. Carlo di Carlo and Giorgio Tinazzi. New York: Marsilio, 21–47.

____ (1996b [1964]) 'Preface to Six Films', in *Michaelangelo Antonioni: The Architect of Vision. Writings and Interviews on the Cinema*, ed. Carlo di Carlo and Giorgio Tinazzi. New York: Marsilio, 57–68.

Arthur, Paul (2003) 'Essay Questions: From Alain Resnais to Michael Moore', *Film Comment*, 39, 1, 58–63.

Astruc, Alexandre (1999 [1948]) 'The Birth of a New Avant-Garde: La Caméra-Stylo', in Timothy Corrigan (ed.) *Film and Literature: An Introduction and Reader*. Upper Saddle River, NJ: Prentice-Hall, 158–62.

Avgitidou, Angeliki (2003) 'Performances of the Self', *Digital Creativity*, 14, 3, 131–8.

Bangma, Anka, Steve Rushton and Florian Wüst (eds) (2005) *Experience, Memory, Re-enactment*. Rotterdam: Piet Zwart Institute.

Barthes, Roland (1975) *Roland Barthes par Roland Barthes*. Paris: Seuil.

____ (1977a) *Roland Barthes by Roland Barthes*, trans. Richard Howard. London: Macmillan.

____ (1977b [1964]) 'Rhetoric of the Image', in *Image, Music, Text*, trans. Stephen Heath. Glasgow: Fontana/Collins, 32–51.

____ (1977c [1972]) 'The Grain of the Voice', in *Image, Music, Text*, trans. Stephen Heath. Glasgow: Fontana/Collins, 182–5.

Battistini, Andrea (1990) *Lo specchio di Dedalo. Biografia e autobiografia*. Bologna: Il Mulino.

Bauman, Zygmunt (1996) 'From Pilgrim to Tourist – Or a Short History of Identity', in Stuart Hall and Paul du Gay (eds) *Questions of Cultural Identity*. London: Sage, 18–36.

____ (2000) *Liquid Modernity*. Cambridge: Polity Press.

Bazin, André (2003 [1958]) 'Bazin on Marker', trans. Dave Kehr, *Film Comment*, 39, 4, 44–5.

Beaujour, Michel (1991) *Poetics of the Literary Self-Portrait*. New York and London: New York University Press.

Bellour, Raymond (1989) 'Eye for I: Video Self-Portraits', trans. Lynne Kirby, in Raymond Bellour (ed.) *Eye for I: Video Self-Portraits*. New York: Independent Curators Incorporated, 7–20.

____ (1997) 'The Book, Back and Forth', in Laurent Roth and Raymond Bellour *Qu'est-ce qu'une madeleine? A propos du CD-ROM Immemory de Chris Marker*. Paris: Yves Gevaert Éditeur/Centre Georges Pompidou, 108–54.

Benedetti, Carla (1998) *Pasolini contro Calvino*. Turin: Bollati Boringhieri.

Bensmaia, Reda (1987) *The Barthes Effect: The Essay As Reflective Text*. Minneapolis: University of Minnesota Press.

Betti, Laura and Michele Gulinucci (1991) *Le regole di un'illusione*. Rome: Associazione "Fondo Pier Paolo Pasolini".

Biarese, Cesare and Aldo Tassone (1985) *I film di Michelangelo Antonioni*. Rome: Gremese.

Blanchot, Maurice (2003) *The Book to Come*, trans. Charlotte Mandell. Stanford: Stanford University Press.

Blümlinger, Christa (2004a) 'Lire entre les images', in Suzanne Liandrat-Guigues and Murielle Gagnebin (eds) *L'Essai et le cinema*. Seyssel: Champ Vallon, 49–66.

_____ (2004b) 'Slowly Forming a Thought While Working on Images', in Thomas Elsaesser (ed.) *Harun Farocki: Working on the Sight-Lines*. Amsterdam: Amsterdam University Press, 163–75.

Bois, Yve-Alain and Rosalind Krauss (1997) *Formless: A User's Guide*. New York: Zone Books.

Bondavalli, Simona (2007) 'Charming the Cobra with a Ballpoint Pen: Liminality and Spectacular Authorship in Pier Paolo Pasolini's Interviews', *MLN*, 122, 1, 24–45.

Bongie, Chris (1991) *Exotic Memories: Literature, Colonialism, and the Fin de Siècle*. Stanford: Stanford University Press.

Bonitzer, Pascal (1976) *Le regard et la voix*. Paris: Union Générale d'Éditions.

Bordwell, David (1985) *Narration in the Fiction Film*. Madison: University of Wisconsin Press.

_____ (1997) *On the History of Film Style*. Cambridge, MA and London: Harvard University Press.

Bourdieu, Pierre (1993) *The Field of Cultural Production: Essays on Art and Literature*, ed. Randal Johnson. Oxford: Polity.

Branigan, Edward (1984) *Point of View in the Cinema: A Theory of Narration and Subjectivity in Classical Film*. Berlin, New York, Amsterdam: Mouton.

Brenez, Nicole, David Faroult, Michael Temple, James Williams and Michael Witt (eds) (2006) *Jean-Luc Godard: Documents*. Paris: Centre Georges Pompidou.

Bruss, Elizabeth W. (1980) 'Eye for I: Making and Unmaking Autobiography in Film', in James Olney (ed.) *Autobiography: Essays Theoretical and Critical*. Princeton: Princeton University Press, 296–320.

Bruzzi, Stella (2000) *New Documentary: A Critical Introduction*. London: Routledge.

_____ (2006) *New Documentary*, Second Edition. London and New York: Routledge.

Burch, Noël (1981) *Theory of Film Practice*, trans. Helen R. Lane. Princeton: Princeton University Press.

Butler, Judith (1993) *Bodies That Matter: On the Discursive Limits of 'Sex'.* New York: Routledge.

____ (1999) *Gender Trouble: Feminism and the Subversion of Identity*. New York: Routledge.

Calatayud, Agnès (2001) 'An Ordinary Woman But a Film-maker: *Demain et encore demain* (1997) – Dominique Cabrera's Self-portrait', *Studies in French Cinema*, 1, 1, 22–8.

Calvino, Italo (1986 [1966]) 'Cinema and the Novel: Problems of Narrative', in *The Uses of Literature*, trans. Patrick Creagh. London: Harvest, 74–80.

Caminati, Luca (2007) *Orientalismo eretico: Pier Paolo Pasolini e il cinema del Terzo Mondo*. Milan: Bruno Mondadori.

Carlson, Marvin (2004) *Performance: A Critical Introduction*. New York: Routledge.

Carroll, Noël (1996) 'Nonfiction Film and Postmodernist Skepticism', in David Bordwell and Noël Carroll (eds) *Post-Theory: Reconstructing Film Studies*. Madison: University of Wisconsin Press, 283–306.

Casetti, Francesco (1998) *Inside the Gaze: The Fiction Film and Its Spectator*, trans. Nell Andrew with Charles O'Brien. Bloomington: Indiana University Press.

____ (2002a) 'Introduzione', in Saverio Zumbo *Al di là delle immagini: Michelangelo Antonioni*. Alessandria: Falsopiano, 5–6.

____ (2002b) *Communicative Negotiation in Cinema and Television*. Milan: Vita e Pensiero.

Chion, Michel (1999) *The Voice in Cinema*, trans. Claudia Gorbman. New York: Columbia University Press.

Conomos, John (2001) 'Only the Cinema', *Senses of Cinema*. Online. Available at: http://www.sensesofcinema.com/contents/01/14/godard_conomos.html (accessed 20 July 2008).

Cooper, Sarah (2008) *Chris Marker*. Manchester: Manchester University Press.

Corner, John (1996) *The Art of Record: A Critical Introduction to Documentary*. Manchester: Manchester University Press.

____ (2003) 'Television, documentary and the category of the aesthetic', *Screen*, 44, 1, 92–100.

Corrigan, Timothy (1995) 'The Cinematic Essay: Genre on the Margins', *Iris: A Journal of Theory on Image and Sound*, 19, 85–91.

____ (1999) 'The Essay Film', in *Film and Literature: An Introduction and Reader*. Upper Saddle River, NJ: Prentice-Hall, 58.

Culley, Margo (1985) 'Introduction', in Margo Culley (ed.) *A Day at a Time: The Diary Literature of American Women from 1764 to Present*. New York: Feminist Press at the City University of New York.

Darwich, Mahmoud (2000) *La terre nous est étroite, et autres poèmes 1966–1999*, trans. Elias Sanbar. Paris: Gallimard.

de Baecque, Antoine (2004) 'Godard in the Museum', in Michael Temple, James S. Williams and Michael Witt (eds) *Forever Godard*. London: Black Dog Publishing, 118–25.

de Man, Paul (1984) *The Rhetoric of Romanticism*. New York: Columbia University Press.

de Tolnay, Charles (1963) 'Michelangelo Buonarroti', in Massimo Pallottino (ed.) *Enciclopedia Universale dell'Arte*. Florence: Sansoni, 263–306.

Degli-Esposti, Cristina (1996) 'Federico Fellini's *Intervista* or the Neo-Baroque Creativity of the Analysand on Screen', *Italica*, 73, 2, 157–72.

Di Stefano, John (1997) 'Picturing Pasolini: Notes From a Filmmaker's Scrapbook', *Art Journal*, 56, 2, 18–23.

Didier, Béatrice (1976) *Le Journal intime*. Paris: PUF.

____ (1988) 'Le journal intime: écriture de la mort ou vie de l' écriture', in Gilles Ernest (ed.) *La Mort dans le texte*. Lyon: Presses Universitaires de Lyon, 127–47.

Dietsch, Bruno (2005) *Alexandre Sokourov*. Lausanne: Editions L'Age d'Homme.

Doane, Mary Ann (1980) 'The Voice in the Cinema: The Articulation of Body and Space', *Yale French Studies*, 60, 'Cinema/Sound', 33–50.

Douglas, Kate (2001) '"Blurbing" Biographical: Authorship and Autobiography', *Biography*, 24, 4, 806–26.

Elsaesser, Thomas (2004) 'Political Filmmaking After Brecht: Harun Farocki, for Example', in Thomas Elsaesser (ed.) *Harun Farocki: Working on the Sight-Lines*. Amsterdam: Amsterdam University Press, 133–53.

Ernst, Wolfgang and Harun Farocki (2004) 'Towards an Archive for Visual Concepts', in Thomas Elsaesser (ed.) *Harun Farocki: Working on the Sight-Lines*. Amsterdam: Amsterdam University Press, 261–86.

Feifer, George (2001) *The Battle of Okinawa: The Blood and the Bomb*. Guilford, CT: The Lyons Press.

Fellini, Federico (2001 [1968]) 'Letter to Peter Goldfarb', in Federico Fellini, *8½*, DVD, Double Disc Set, Criterion Collection.

Ferrero, Adelio (1994) *Il cinema di Pier Paolo Pasolini*, ed. Lorenzo Pellizzari. Venice: Marsilio.

ffrench, Patrick (2005) 'The immanent ethnography of Chris Marker, reader of Proust', *Film Studies*, 6, 87–96.

Fihman, Guy (2004) 'L'Essai cinématographique et ses transformations expérimentales', in Suzanne Liandrat-Guigues and Murielle Gagnebin (eds) *L'Essai et le cinema*. Seyssel: Champ Vallon, 41–7.

Fitzpatrick, Ellen F. (1994) 'Introduction: Late-Nineteenth-Century America and the Origins of Muckraking', in Ellen F. Fitzpatrick (ed.) *Muckraking. Three Landmark Articles*. Boston: Bedford/St. Martin's, 1–39.

Fortichiari, Valentina (1992) 'Diario', in Guglielmo Moneti (ed.) *Lessico Zavattiniano*. Venice: Marsilio, 65–77.

Freud, Sigmund (1955 [1914]) 'Michelangelo's Moses', *The Standard Edition of the Complete Psychological Works*, ed. James Strachey, vol. 13. London: Hogarth Press and the Institute of Psychoanalysis, 211–36.

Frodon, Jean-Michel (2004a) 'Jean-Luc Godard: Parmi nous', *Cahiers du cinéma*, 590, 16–19.

_____ (2004b) 'Jean-Luc Godard et *Notre Musique*. Juste une conversation', *Cahiers du cinéma*, 590, 20–2.

Gambill, Norman (1980) 'The Movies of Man Ray', in *Man Ray: Photographs and Objects, exhibition catalogue*. Birmingham: Birmingham Museum of Art, 30–42.

Gerstner, David A. (2006) *Manly Arts: Masculinity and Nation in Early American Cinema*. Durham, NC: Duke University Press.

Giannetti, Louis D. (1975) *Godard and Others: Essays On Film Form*. Rutherford: Fairleigh Dickinson University Press.

Gianvito, John (1999–2000) 'Remembrance of Films Lost', *Film Quarterly*, 53, 2, 39–42.

Giddens, Anthony (1990) *The Consequences of Modernity*. Cambridge: Polity Press.

Gilbard, Florence (1984) 'An Interview with Vito Acconci: Video Works 1970–1978', *Afterimage*, 12, 4, 9–15.

Girard, Alain (1963) *Le Journal intime*. Paris: PUF.

Godard, Jean-Luc (1972a [1962]) 'Interview', in Jean Narboni and Tom Milne (eds) *Godard on Godard: Critical Writings by Jean-Luc Godard*. London: Secker and Warburg, 170–96.

_____ (1972b [1967]) 'One Should Put Everything into a Film', in Jean Narboni and Tom Milne (eds) *Godard on Godard: Critical Writings by Jean-Luc Godard*. London: Secker and Warburg, 238–9.

_____ (1985) *Jean-Luc Godard par Jean-Luc Godard*, ed. Alain Bergala. Paris: Cahiers du cinéma – Editions de l'Etoile.

Godard, Jean-Luc and Youssef Ishaghpour (2005) *Cinema: The Archeology of Film and the Memory of a Century*. Oxford and New York: Berg.

Goffman, Erving (1959) *The Presentation of Self in Everyday Life*. London: Penguin.

Good, Graham (1988) *The Observing Self: Rediscovering the Essay*. London: Routledge.

Gordon, Robert (1996) *Pasolini: Forms of Subjectivity*. Oxford: Clarendon Press.

_____ (1999) 'Pasolini's Strategies of Self-construction', in Zygmunt G. Barański (ed.) *Pasolini Old and New: Surveys and Studies*. Dublin: Four Courts Press, 41–76.

Greenblatt, Stephen (1984) *Renaissance Self-fashioning: From More to Shakespeare*. Chicago and London: University of Chicago Press.

Hall, Stuart (1992) 'The Question of Cultural Identity', in Stuart Hall, David Held and Tony McGrew (eds) *Modernity and its Futures*. Cambridge: Polity Press, 274–316.

Halle, Randall (2001) 'History Is Not a Matter of Generations: Interview with Harun Farocki', *Camera Obscura*, 16, 1, 46–75.

Hashamova, Yana (2006) 'Two Visions of a Usable Past in (Op)position to the West: Mikhalkov's *The Barber of Siberia* and Sokurov's *Russian Ark*', *Russian Review*, 65, 2, 250–7.

Hogan, Rebecca (1986) 'Diarists on Diaries', *Auto/Biography Studies*, 11, 2, 9–14.

_____ (1991) 'Engendered Autobiographies: The Diary as a Feminine Form', *Prose Studies*, 14, 95–107.

Hooper-Greenhill, Eilean (1995) *Museum, Media, Message*. London: Routledge.

_____ (2000) *Museums and the Interpretation of Visual Culture*. London and New York: Routledge.

Huxley, Aldous (1960 [1959]) 'Preface', in *Collected Essays*. London: Harper and Brothers, v–ix.

Huyssen, Andreas (1995) *Twilight Memories: Marking Time in a Culture of Amnesia*. London and New York: Routledge.

Ivens, Joris (1940) 'Collaboration in Documentary', *Films*, 1, 2, 30–42.

James, David E. (1992) 'Film Diary/Diary Film: Practice and Product in Walden', in David E. James (ed.) *To Free the Cinema: Jonas Mekas and The New York Underground*. Princeton: Princeton University Press, 145–79.

Jameson, Fredric (2006) 'History and Elegy in Sokurov', *Critical Inquiry*, 33, 1, 1–12.

Japan International Cooperation Agency (2002) 'Chapter 2: Peace Education in Okinawa', *Post-Conflict Reconstruction of Education and Peace Building: Lessons from Okinawa's Experience*. Online. Available at: http://www.jica.go.jp/english/resources/publications/study/topical/post_conflict/pdf/post03.pdf (accessed 24 April 2007).

John-Steiner, Vera (1997) *Notebooks of the Mind: Explorations of Thinking*. New York and Oxford: Oxford University Press.

Jones, Amelia (2002) 'The "Eternal Return": Self-Portrait Photography as a Technology of Embodiment', *Signs: Journal of Women in Culture and Society*, 27, 4, 947–78.

Katz, John Stuart (ed.) (1978) *Autobiography: Film/Video/Photography*. Toronto: Media Programmes Division of the Education Branch, Art Gallery of Ontario.

Kear, Jonathan (2005) 'The Clothing of Clio: Chris Marker's Poetics and the Politics of Representing History', *Film Studies*, 6, 49–63.

_____ (2007) 'A Game That Must Be Lost: Chris Marker Replays Alain Resnais' *Hiroshima mon amour*', in Frances Guerin and Roger Hallas (eds) *The Image and the Witness: Trauma, Memory and Visual Culture*. London: Wallflower Press, 129–42.

Kozloff, Sarah (1984) 'Humanizing "The Voice of God": Narration in *The Naked City*', *Cinema Journal*, 23, 4, 41–53.

Krauss, Rosalind (1976) 'Video: The Aesthetics of Narcissism', *October*, 1, 50–64.

Lacan, Jacques (1977) *The Seminar XI: The Four Fundamental Concepts of Psychoanalysis*, ed. Jacques-Alain Miller, trans. Alan Sheridan. New York: W. W. Norton.

Lack, Roland-François (2004) 'Sa Voix', in Michael Temple, James S. Williams and Michael Witt (eds) *Forever Godard*. London: Black Dog Publishing, 312–29.

Lane, Jim (1996) '*Finding Christa. In Search of Our Fathers*. Black autobiographical documentary', *Jump Cut*, 40, March, 38–46.

_____ (2002) *The Autobiographical Documentary in America*. Madison: University of Wisconsin Press.

Langford, Rachael and Russell West (1999) 'Introduction: Diaries and Margins', in Rachael Langford and Russell West (eds) *Marginal Voices, Marginal Forms: Diaries in European Literature and History*. Amsterdam: Rodopi, 6–21.

Lejeune, Philippe (1977) 'Autobiography in the Third Person', trans. Annette Tomarken and Edward Tomarken, *New Literary History*, 9, 1, 'Self-Confrontation and Social Vision', Autumn, 27–50.

____ (1980) *Je est un autre. L'autobiographie de la litterature aux medias*. Paris: Seuil.

____ (1988) 'Le journal intime: écriture de la mort ou vie de l'écriture', in Gilles Ernest (ed.) *La Mort dans le texte*. Lyon: Presses universitaires de Lyon, 127–47.

____ (1989) 'Cher cahier...', *Témoignages sur le journal personnel*. Paris: Gallimard.

____ (1996) *Le pacte autobiographique*. Paris: Seuil.

____ (1998) *Les brouillons de soi*. Paris: Seuil.

____ (2003) *Un journal à soi*. Paris: Textuel.

____ (2005) *Le journal intime: Genre littéraire ou écriture ordinaire* Paris: Téraèdre.

Lejeune, Philippe and Catherine Bogaert (1997) *Un journal à soi (ou la passion des journaux intimes)*, catalogue of the exhibition at the Bibliothèque municipale de Lyon of 30 September – 27 December 1997. Lyon: Association pour l'Autobiographie et le Patrimoine autobiographique and Amis des Bibliothèques de Lyon.

Leyda, Jay (1964) *Films Beget Films: Compilation Films from Propaganda to Drama*. New York: Hill and Wang.

Liandrat-Guigues, Suzanne (2004) 'Un Art de l'équilibre', in Suzanne Liandrat-Guigues and Murielle Gagnebin (eds) *L'Essai et le cinema*. Seyssel: Champ Vallon, 7–12.

Lomas, David (2000) *The Haunted Self: Surrealism, Psychoanalysis, Subjectivity*. New Haven and London: Yale University Press.

Lopate, Phillip (1998 [1992]) 'In Search of the Centaur: The Essay Film', in *Totally, Tenderly, Tragically*. Amsterdam: Anchor, 280–311.

Lukács, György (1974) 'On the Nature and Form of the Essay', in *Soul and Form*, trans. Anna Bostock. London: Merlin Press, 1–18.

Lupton, Catherine (2002) 'Chris Marker: In Memory of New Technology'. Online. Available at: http://www.vajramedia.com/cm/cm_memtech.htm (accessed 24 April 2007).

____ (2003) 'Terminal replay: Resnais revisited in Chris Marker's *Level Five*', *Screen*, 44, 1, 58–70.

____ (2005) 'Imagine Another: Chris Marker as Portraitist', *Film Studies*, 6, 74–80.

____ (2006) *Chris Marker. Memories of the Future*. Second Edition. London: Reaktion Books.

____ (2007) 'Speaking Parts: Heteroglossic Voice-Over in the Essay Film'. Paper presented at the conference *Der Essayfilm: Aësthetik und Aktualitaët*, Leuphana University, Luëneburg, 29 November – 2 December 2007.

Lutticken, Sven (2005) *Life, Once More: Forms of Re-enactment in Contemporary Art.* Rotterdam: Witte de With.

Lyotard, Jean-François (1984) *The Postmodern Condition: A Report on Knowledge*, trans. Geoff Bennington and Brian Massumi. Minneapolis: University of Minnesota Press.

Macdonald, Sharon (1996) 'Introduction', in Sharon Macdonald and Gordon Fyfe (eds) *Theorizing Museums*. Oxford: Blackwell, 1–18.

Macmillan, Malcolm and Peter J. Swales (2003) 'Observations from the Refuse-Heap: Freud, Michelangelo's *Moses*, and Psychoanalysis', *American Imago*, 60, 1, 41–104.

Maderna, Giovanni (1996) 'Film saggio: Intervista a Edgar Morin', in Silvano Cavatorta and Luca Mosso (eds) *Filmmaker 5 Doc*. Milan: Edizioni A&M, 4–5.

Mallon, Thomas (1984) *A Book of One's Own: People and Their Diaries*. London: Picador.

Mancini, Michele and Giuseppe Perrella (1981) 'Introduzione', in Michele Mancini and Giuseppe Perrella (eds) *Pier Paolo Pasolini: corpi e luoghi*. Rome: Theorema, ix–xiii.

Martin, Carol (2006) 'Bodies of Evidence', *TDR: The Drama Review*, 50, 3, Fall, 8–15.

Mauri, Fabio (1994) *Opere e azioni 1954–1994*, ed. Carolyn Christov-Bakargiev and Marcella Cossu. Milan: Giorgio Mondadori.

Mazierska, Ewa and Laura Rascaroli (2004) *The Cinema of Nanni Moretti: Dreams and Diaries*. London: Wallflower Press.

_____ (2006) *Crossing New Europe: Postmodern Travel and the European Road Movie*. London: Wallflower Press.

Mekas, Jonas (1978) 'The Diary Film (A Lecture on *Reminiscences of a Journey to Lithuania*)', in P. Adams Sitney (ed.) *The Avant-Garde Film: A Reader of Theory and Criticism*. New York: New York University Press, 190–8.

_____ (2003) 'Presentation of *Diaries, Notes and Sketches* (Reels 1 and 2) at Millenium, New York, December 14 1969', in Pip Chodorov and Christian Lebrat (eds) *The Walden Book*. Paris: Èditions Paris Expérimental/Re:Voir Vidéo.

Metz, Christian (1974) *Film Language: A Semiotics of the Cinema*, trans. Michael Taylor. New York: Oxford University Press.

Meyer, Andrea (2001) 'Interview: 'Gleaning' the Passion of Agnès Varda', *IndieWire*. Online. Available at: http://www.indiewire.com/people/int_Varda_Agnes_010308. html (accessed 20 July 2008).

Micciché, Lino (1996) *Luchino Visconti. Un profilo critico*. Venice: Marsilio.

_____ (1999) *Pasolini nella città del cinema*. Venice: Marsilio.

Montaigne, Michel de (1700) *The Essays of Montaigne*, trans. Charles Cotton. Third Edition. London: Printed for M. Gillyflower, *et al.*

Montesquieu, Charles-Louis de Secondat de (1976 [1748]) *De l'esprit des lois*, in *Œuvres complètes*, 2 vols. Paris: Gallimard.

Morrey, Douglas (2005) *Jean-Luc Godard*. Manchester: Manchester University Press.

Moure, José (2004) 'Essai de définition de l'essai au cinéma', in Suzanne Liandrat-Guigues and Murielle Gagnebin (eds) *L'Essai et le cinema*. Seyssel: Champ Vallon, 25–40.

Mulvey, Laura (1975) 'Visual Pleasure and Narrative Cinema', *Screen*, 16, 3, 6–18.

Murray, Timothy (1999) 'By Way of Introduction: Digitality and the Memory of Cinema, or, Bearing the Losses of the Digital Code', *Wide Angle*, 21, 1, 2–27.

____ (2000) 'Wounds of Repetition in the Age of the Digital: Chris Marker's Cinematic Ghosts', *Cultural Critique*, 46, 102–23.

Naficy, Hamid (2001) *An Accented Cinema: Exilic and Diasporic Filmmaking*. Princeton: Princeton University Press.

Nichols, Bill (1981) *Ideology and the Image: Social Representation in the Cinema and Other Media*. Bloomington: Indiana University Press.

____ (1987) 'History, Myth, and Narrative in Documentary', *Film Quarterly*, 41, 1, 9–20.

____ (1991) *Representing Reality: Issues and Concepts of Documentary*. Bloomington and Indianapolis: Indiana University Press.

____ (1994) *Blurred Boundaries: Questions of Meaning in Contemporary Culture*. Bloomington and Indianapolis: Indiana University Press.

Olney, James (1972) *Metaphors of Self: The Meaning of Autobiography*. Princeton: Princeton University Press.

Pasolini, Pier Paolo (1981a) 'Don Andrea: una vita "in prestito"', in *Il caos*. Rome: Editori Riuniti, 134–6.

____ (1981b [1968]) 'Appunti per un poema sul Terzo Mondo', in Michele Mancini and Giuseppe Perrella *Pier Paolo Pasolini: corpi e luoghi*. Rome: Theorema, 35–7.

____ (1988a [1965]) 'The screenplay as a structure which wishes to be another structure', in *Heretical Empiricism*, ed. Louise K. Barnett, trans. Ben Lawton and Louise K. Barnett. Bloomington and Indianapolis: Indiana University Press, 187–96.

____ (1988b [1970]) 'The Unpopular Cinema', in *Heretical Empiricism*, ed. Louise K. Barnett, trans. Ben Lawton and Louise K. Barnett. Bloomington and Indianapolis: Indiana University Press, 267–75.

____ (2001 [1966]) 'Confessioni tecniche', in *Per il cinema*, ed. Walter Siti and Franco Zabagli. Milan: Mondadori, 2768–81.

____ (2005) *Petrolio*. Milan: Mondadori.

Plantinga, Carl (1996) 'Moving pictures and the rhetoric of non-fiction: two approaches', in David Bordwell and Noël Carroll (eds) *Post-Theory: Reconstructing Film Studies*. Madison: University of Wisconsin Press, 307–24.

Rancière, Jacques (2001) *Film Fables*, trans. Emiliano Battista. Oxford and New York: Berg.

Rascaroli, Laura (2002a) 'Like a dream. A Critical History of the Oneiric Metaphor in Film Theory', *Kinema*, 18, 5–22.

____ (2002b) 'The Space of a Return. A Topographic Study of Alain Resnais' *Providence*', *Studies in French Cinema*, II, 1, 50–8.

____ (2006) '*L'année dernière à Marienbad/Last Year in Marienbad*', in Phil Powrie (ed.) *The Cinema of France*. London: Wallflower Press, 101–10.

Rascaroli, Laura and John David Rhodes (2008) 'Antonioni and the Place of Modernity: a Tribute', *Framework*, 49, 1, 42–7.

Renov, Michael (2004a) 'Surveying the Subject: An Introduction', in *The Subject of the Documentary*. Minneapolis and London: University of Minnesota Press, xi–xxiv.

____ (2004b) 'Lost, Lost, Lost: Mekas as Essayist', in *The Subject of the Documentary*. Minneapolis and London: University of Minnesota Press, 69–89.

Repetto, Antonio (1998) *Invito al cinema di Pasolini*. Milan: Mursia.

Restivo, Angelo (2002) *The Cinema of Economic Miracles: Visuality and Modernization in the Italian Art Film*. Durham, NC and London: Duke University Press.

Rhodes, John David (2007) *Stupendous, Miserable City: Pasolini's Rome*. Minneapolis and London: University of Minnesota Press.

____ (forthcoming) 'Pasolini's Exquisite Flowers: "The 'Cinema of Poetry'" as a Theory of Art Cinema', in Rosalind Galt and Karl Schoonover (eds) *Global Art Cinema: New Theories and Practices*. New York: Oxford University Press.

Richards, Keith (2006) 'Export Mythology: Primitivism and Paternalism in Pasolini, Hopper and Herzog', in Stephanie Dennison and Song Hwee Lim (eds) *Remapping World Cinema: Identity, Culture and Politics in Film*. London: Wallflower Press, 55–64.

Richter, Hans (1992 [1940]) 'Der Filmessay. Eine neue Form des Dokumentarfilms', in Christa Blümlinger and Constantin Wulff (eds) *Schreiben Bilder Sprechen: Texte zum essayistischen Film*. Wien: Sonderzahl, 195–8.

Ricoeur, Paul (1992) *Oneself as Another*, trans. Kathleen Blamey. Chicago: University of Chicago Press.

Rideal, Liz (2005) *Self-Portraits*. London: National Portrait Gallery Publications.

Rinaldi, Rinaldo (1981) 'Dell'estraneità: tra il giornalismo e il saggismo dell'ultimo Pasolini', *Sigma*, XIV, 2–3, 95–124.

Riva, Massimo and Sergio Parussa (1997) 'L'autore come antropologo: Pier Paolo Pasolini e la morte dell'etnos', *Annali d'Italianistica*, XV, 237–65.

Rivette, Jacques (1977 [1955]) 'Lettre sur Roberto Rossellini', in Jean Narboni and Jonathan Rosenbaum (eds) *Rivette: Texts and Interviews*, trans. Amy Gateff and Tom Milne. London: British Film Institute, 54–64.

Rohdie, Sam (1990) *Antonioni*. London: British Film Institute.

____ (1995) *The Passion of Pier Paolo Pasolini*. London: British Film Institute.

Rottman, Gordon (2002) *Okinawa 1945: The Last Battle*. Oxford: Osprey Publishing.

Rousset, Jean (1983) 'Le Journal intime, texte sans destinataire?', *Poétique*, 56, 435–43.

____ (1986) *Le Lecteur intime. De Balzac au journal*. Paris: Corti.

Rumble, Patrick (1999) 'Contamination and Excess: *I racconti di Canterbury* as a "struttura da farsi"', in Zygmunt G. Barański (ed.) *Pasolini Old and New: Surveys and Studies*. Dublin: Four Courts Press, 345–62.

Ruoff, Jeffrey (2003) 'Conventions of Sound in Documentary', *Cinema Journal*, 32, 3, 24–40.

Russell, Catherine (1999) *Experimental Ethnography: The Work of Film in the Age of Video*. Durham, NC and London: Duke University Press.

Saumarez Smith, Charles (1989) 'Museums, Artefacts, and Meanings', in Peter Vergo (ed.) *The New Museology*. London: Reaktion Books, 6–21.

Schlaeger, Jürgen (1999) 'Self-Exploration in Early Modern English Diaries', in Rachael Langford and Russell West (eds) *Marginal Voices, Marginal Forms: Diaries in European Literature and History*. Amsterdam: Rodopi, 22–36.

Sedofsky, Lauren (2001) 'Plane Songs: Lauren Sedofsky Talks With Alexander Sokurov', *Artforum International*, XL, 3, November. Online. Available at: http://artforum. com/inprint/id=1837 (accessed 24 April 2008).

Sherman, Stuart (1996) *Telling Time: Clocks, Diaries, and English Diurnal Form, 1660–1785*. Chicago: University of Chicago Press.

Siciliano, Enzo (2005) *Vita di Pasolini*. Milan: Mondadori.

Silverman, Kaja (1988) *The Acoustic Mirror: The Female Voice in Psychoanalysis and Cinema*. Bloomington and Indianapolis: Indiana University Press.

_____ (1996) *The Threshold of the Visible World*. New York and London: Routledge.

_____ (2001) 'The Author as Receiver', *October*, 96, Spring, 17–34.

Sitney, P. Adams (1979) *Visionary Film: The American Avant-Garde 1943–1978*. Second Edition. New York: Oxford University Press.

Snyder, John (1991) *Prospects of Power: Tragedy, Satire, the Essay, and the Theory of Genre*. Lexington: University Press of Kentucky.

Sobchack, Vivian (1992) *The Address of the Eye: A Phenomenology of Film Experience*. Princeton: Princeton University Press.

_____ (2004) *Carnal Thoughts: Embodiment and Moving Image Culture*. Berkeley: University of California Press.

Sokurov, Aleksandr (n.d.) 'Spiritual Voices', *The Island of Sokurov*, filmography section, trans. Tatiana Ussova with Benjamin Halligan. Online. Available at: http://www. sokurov.spb.ru/island_en/mnp.html (accessed 23 March 2008).

Solanas, Fernando and Octavio Getino (1976 [1969]) 'Towards a Third Cinema', in Bill Nichols (ed.) *Movies and Methods, Vol. 1*. Berkeley: University of California Press, 44–64.

Sorapure, Madeleine (2003) 'Screening Moments, Scrolling Lives: Diary Writing on the Web', *Biography*, 26, 1, 1–23.

Sorlin, Pierre (2005) 'France', in Ian Aitken (ed.) *Encyclopedia of the Documentary Film*. London: Routledge/Taylor and Francis, 434–42.

Spielmann, Yvonne (2000) 'Visual Forms of Representation and Simulation: A Study of Chris Marker's *Level 5*', *Convergence*, 6, 2, 18–40.

Stack, Oswald (1969) *Pasolini on Pasolini: Interviews with Oswald Stack*. London: Thames and Hudson/British Film Institute.

Steimatsky, Noa (2002) 'Pasolini on Terra Sancta: Towards a Theology of Film', in Ivone Margulies (ed.) *Rites of Realism: Essays on Corporeal Cinema*. Durham, NC and London: Duke University Press, 245–69.

Szaniawski, Jeremi (2006) 'Interview with Aleksandr Sokurov', *Critical Inquiry*, 33, 1, 13–27.

Taylor, Alan and Irene Taylor (eds) (2003) *The Assassin's Cloak: An Anthology of the World's Greatest Diarists*. Edinburgh: Canongate Books.

Temple, Michael and James S. Williams (2000) 'Introduction to the Mysteries of Cinema 1985–2000', in Michael Temple and James S. Williams (eds) *The Cinema Alone: Essays on the Works of Jean-Luc Godard 1985–2000*. Amsterdam: Amsterdam University Press, 9–32.

Testa, Bart (1990) 'Un Certain Regard: Characterization in the First Years of the French New Wave', in Carole Zucker (ed.) *Making Visible the Invisible: An Anthology of Original Essays on Film Acting*. Metuchen and London: The Scarecrow Press, 92–142.

Tinel, Muriel (2006) 'Cocteau, Wenders, Akerman, Kramer... Le cinéma et l'autoportrait: de l'expression de soi à l'expérience d'un support', *Hors Champ*, April. Online. Available at: http://www.horschamp.qc.ca/article.php3?id_article=220 (accessed 20 July 2008).

Tinazzi, Giorgio (1996) 'The Gaze and the Story', in Michelangelo Antonioni *Michelangelo Antonioni: The Architecture of Vision. Writings and Interviews on the Cinema*, ed. Carlo di Carlo and Giorgio Tinazzzi, New York: Marsilio, xiii–xxvii.

Todd, Peter and Benjamin Cook (eds) (2004) *Subjects And Sequences: A Margaret Tait Reader*. London: Lux.

Trilling, Lionel (1972) *Sincerity and Authenticity*. London: Oxford University Press.

Trivelli, Anita (2008) 'Zwischen Experiment und Nomadentum. Pasolini als Dokumentarfilmer in Indien und Palästina', in Thomas Koebner and Irmbert Schenk (eds) *Das goldene Zeitalter des italienischen Films. Die 1960er Jahre*. München: Edition text + kritik, 279–90.

Truffaut, François (1976 [1954]) 'A Certain Tendency of the French Cinema', in Bill Nichols (ed.) *Movies and Methods, Vol. 1*. Berkeley: University of California Press, 224–37.

____ (1987) *Truffaut by Truffaut*, ed. Dominique Robourdin, trans. Robert Erich Wolf. New York: Abrams.

Tuchinskaya, Alexandra (n.d.) 'Confession', *The Island of Sokurov*, filmography section, trans. Tatiana Ussova with Benjamin Halligan. Online. Available at: http://www.sokurov.spb.ru/island_en/mnp.html (accessed 23 March 2008).

Turim, Maureen (1992) 'Reminiscences, Subjectivities, and Truths', in David E. James (ed.) *Jonas Mekas and The New York Underground*. Princeton: Princeton University Press, 193–212.

____ (1999) 'Artisanal Prefigurations of the Digital: Animating Realities, Collage Effects, and Theories of Image Manipulation', *Wide Angle*, 21, 1, 48–62.

Van Dijck, Peter (2006) 'My Vloggercon Keynote: How Values Get Embedded in Technology', Peter Van Dijck's Weblog, posted June 18th. Online. Available at: http://poorbuthappy.com/ease/ (accessed 2 July 2008).

Vaughan, Dai (1999 [1986]) 'What do we mean by "What?", in *For Documentary: Twelve Essays*. Berkeley and Los Angeles: University of California Press, 84–9.

Vergo, Peter (1989) 'Introduction', in Peter Vergo (ed.) *The New Museology*. London: Reaktion Books, 1–5.

Viano, Maurizio (1993) *A Certain Realism: Making Use of Pasolini's Film Theory and Practice*. Berkeley, Los Angeles, London: University of California Press.

Vincendeau, Ginette (2005) 'Notre musique', *Sight & Sound*, 15, 6, 69–70.

Virilio, Paul (1994) *The Vision Machine*, trans. Julie Rose. London: British Film Institute.

Visconti, Luchino (1979) *Il mio teatro*, ed. Caterina d'Amico de Carvalho and Renzo Renzi, 2 vols. Bologna: Cappelli.

Wahlberg, Malin (2004) 'Inscription and reframing: at the editing table of Harun Farocki', *Konsthistorisk Tidskrift/Journal of Art History*, 73, 1, 15–26.

Waugh, Thomas (1990) '"Acting to Play Oneself": Notes on Performance in Documentaries', in Carole Zucker (ed.) *Making Visible the Invisible: An Anthology of Original Essays on Film Acting*. Metuchen & London: The Scarecrow Press, 64–91.

Wees, William C. (2002) 'The Ambiguous Aura of Hollywood Stars in Avant-Garde Found-Footage Films', *Cinema Journal*, 41, 2, 3–18.

Weinrichter, Antonio (2007) *La forma que piensa. Tentativas en torno al cine-ensayo*. Pamplona: Punto de Vista/Gobierno de Navarra.

West, Shearer (2004) *Portraiture*. Oxford: Oxford University Press.

Willemen, Paul (1994) *Looks and Frictions: Essays in Cultural Studies and Film Theory*. London: British Film Institute.

Williams, James S. (2006) *Jean Cocteau*. Manchester: Manchester University Press.

Winston, Brian (1995) *Claiming the Real: The Documentary Film Revisited*. London: British Film Institute.

Witt, Michael (2004), 'Shapeshifter: Godard as Multimedia Installation Artist', *New Left Review*, 29, 73–89.

____ (2005) 'The Godard Interview: I, a Man of the Image', *Sight & Sound*, 15, 6, 28–30.

Zavattini, Cesare (1979a [1951]) 'Basta con i soggetti', in *Neorealismo ecc*, ed. Mino Argentieri. Milan: Bompiani, 70–3.

____ (1979b [1950]) 'Cinema italiano domani', in *Neorealismo ecc*, ed. Mino Argentieri. Milan: Bompiani, 74–6.

____ (1979c [1951]) 'Il cinema, Zavattini e la realtà', in *Neorealismo ecc*, ed. Mino Argentieri. Milan: Bompiani, 81–5.

Zolberg, Vera L. (1996) 'Museums as Contested Sites of Remembrance: The Enola Gay Affair', in Sharon Macdonald and Gordon Fyfe (eds) *Theorizing Museums*. Oxford: Blackwell, 69–82.

Zryd, Michael (2003) 'Found-footage film as discursive metahistory: Craig Baldwin's *Tribulation 99*', *The Moving Image*, 3, 2, 40–61.

index

365 Films 124

À bout de souffle 14, 91
À propos de Nice 28, 110–11
accented cinema 10–11, 190
Acconci, Vito 172–3
Adler, Sarah 95
Adventure, The, see *Avventura, L'*
Afghanistan 136–8, 140–1
Akerman, Chantal 2, 122, 175
Al di là delle nuvole 180
Aleksandr Nevskiy 95
Alexander Nevsky, see *Aleksandr Nevskiy*
al-Janabi, Abeer Qasim Hamza 127
All the World's Memory, see *Toute la mémoire du monde*
Alla ricerca di Tadzio 147
Allen, Woody 7
Andersen, Thom 2
André Malraux Cultural Centre 96
Andrei Rublev, see *Andrey Rublyov*
Andrésen, Björn 147
Andrey Rublyov 12
Andy Warhol Story, The 107
Angela's Ashes 4
Angelo, Yves 74
Angels of the Streets, see *Anges du peché, Les*

Anges du peché, Les 95
Année dernière à Marienbad, L' 71, 75
Another Shot 175
Anthology Film Archives 124
Antonioni, Enrica 179
Antonioni, Michelangelo 2, 17, 60, 114, 149, 177–88
Apocalypse Now 95
Appunti per un film sull'India 151
Appunti per un'Orestiade Africana 151
Appunti per un poema sul Terzo Mondo 151
Appunti per un romanzo dell'immondezza 151
Appunti su un fatto di cronaca 149
Aprile 126
Arbeiter verlassen die Fabrik 1, 60, 61, 62
Arco Film 158
Argos Films 28
As I Was Moving Ahead, Occasionally I Saw Brief Glimpses of Beauty 124
Astruc, Alexandre 6, 24–6, 65, 190
Aufzeichnungen zu Kleidern und Städten 149
Austin Plant (Birmingham) 61
Autoportrait 176
Autoportrait Refilmé 176

Avant-Garde Home Movie, An 107, 123
Avventura, L' 182

Bach, Johann Sebastian 55, 160, 161
Backyard 107
Bacon, Francis 30
BandB 126
Bar'am 159
Barents Sea 132
Barrie, Diana 175
Barthes, Roland 9, 31, 49, 59, 171, 177
Battista, Gérard de 74
Battleship Potemkin, see *Bronenosets Potyomkin*
BBC 109, 122
Belkhodja, Catherine 73
Belle Étoile, La 126
Belmondo, Jean-Paul 14
Bergman, Ingmar 7, 14, 134
Bergounioux, Pierre 96, 103
Berlin 10/90 176
Bethlehem 159, 168
Bewerbungen, Die 40–1
Beyond the Clouds, see *Al di là delle nuvole*
Bibliothèque Nationale 71
Bilder der Welt und Inschrift des Krieges 39–40, 52–8, 59, 61, 62
Bini, Alfredo 159, 162
Bitomski, Hartmut 60

Blanchot, Maurice 5

Block-notes di un regista
148–9

Blood of the Beasts, see *Le Sang des bêtes*

Blue 125, 130–1

Bourque, Louise 176

Brakhage, Stan 6, 107, 123

Braunberger, Pierre 28

Breathless, see *À bout de souffle*

Brecht, Bertolt 14, 55, 88, 91, 93, 100, 151

Brechtian, see Brecht

Bresson, Robert 25, 26, 128

Bridget Jones' Diary 4

Bright Leaves 107

Bronenosets Potyomkin 95

Broomfield, Nick 86

Broughton, James 175

Budapest 86

Bullot, Erik 126

Buñuel, Luis 1, 28, 128

Buonarroti, Michelangelo 177, 180–3

Cabrera, Dominique 126, 174

Calcul du sujet, Le 126

Calculus of the Subject, see *Le Calcul du sujet*

Calcutta 149

Camhi, Gail 176

Campus, Peter 172

Cantatore, Walter 158

Canterbury Tales, The, see *Racconti di Canterbury, I*

Canudo, Ricciotto 6, 24, 109, 110

Capernaum 159

Capturing the Friedmans 126

Carabiniers, Les 68

Caro diario 126

Carraro, Andrea 158–68

Case of the Grinning Cat, The, see *Chats perchés*

Cavalcanti, Alberto 28, 110

Cavalier, Alain 126

Centre Georges Pompidou 149

Chambre 666 179

Charleen 107

Chatman, Seymour 5

Chats perches 66

Chelovek s kinoapparatom 1

Chinoise, La 89

Chronicle of a Summer, see *Chronique d'une été*

Chronique d'une été 6, 28

Chung Kuo-China 149

Cicero, Marcus Tullio 30

Cinegiornali della pace 112

Cinegiornali liberi 112

cinéma vérité 6, 28, 44, 48, 66, 190

Cinéma de notre temps: Chantal Akerman par Chantal Akerman 175

Citron, Michelle 2

Cocteau, Jean 26, 175

Coffee Break 176

Color of Water, The 4

Confession 107

Confession, see *Povinnost*

Counter-cinema 107, 109–13

Curnier, Jean-Paul 96

Czioska, Anja 176

Damascus 159

Darwich, Mahmoud 95, 96, 100

Dauman, Anatole 28

David Holzman's Diary 128

De Lullo, Giorgio 149

De Palma, Brian 127

Dear Diary, see *Caro diario*

Death and the Singing Telegram 128

Death in Venice, see *Morte a Venezia*

Decameron, Il 157

Decameron, The, see *Decameron, Il*

Delluc, Louis 6, 24, 109, 110

Demain et encore demain 126, 174

Deren, Maya 107

Deux ou trois choses que je sais d'elle 88

Dialogues with Solzhenitsyn, see *Uzel*

Diari della Sacher, I 126

Diaries 128

Diaries, Notes and Sketches 130

Diario di un uomo 123

Diario di una donna 123

Diary for My Children, see *Napló gyermekeimnek*

Diary for My Father and Mother, see *Napló apámnak, anyámnak*

Diary for My Loved Ones, see *Napló szerelmeimnek*

Diary for Timothy, A 123

Diary of a Chambermaid (Renoir; Buñuel) 128

Diary of a Country Priest, see *Journal d'un curé de campagne*

Diary of a Lost Girl, see *Tagebuch einer Verlorenen*

Diary of a Man, see *Diario di un uomo*

Diary of a Woman, see *Diario di una donna*

Diary of St. Petersburg. Kozintsev's Flat, The, see *Peterburgskiy dnevnik. Kvartira Kozintseva*

Diary of St. Petersburg: Inauguration of the Monument to Dostoevsky, The, see *Peterburgskiy dnevnik. Otkritie pamyatnika Dostoeskomu*

Diary of St. Petersburg: Mozart. Requiem, The, see *Peterburgskiy dnevnik: Mozart. Rekviem*

Diary, see *Yoman*

Dieu, Nade 95

Dieutre, Vincent 126

Dirty Pictures 126

Dog Star Man 123

Dukhovnye golosa. Iz dnevnikov voyny. Povestvovanie v pyati chastyakh 39, 132–45

Dullac, Germaine 109, 110

Edipo re 157

Eiffel Tower 79

Ein Bild 40–1

Eine, Simon 95

Elegiya dorogi 132

Elegy of a Voyage, see *Elegiya dorogi*

Emak Bakia 174

Empire 139

Empire State Building 139

Employees Leaving the Lumière Factory, see *Sortie des usines Lumière, La*

Epstein, Jean 6, 24

European Literary Encounters 95, 96

Eye/Machine I–III 50

F For Fake, see *Vérités et mensonges*

Fahrenheit 9/11 1, 22, 41, 42

Family Portrait Sittings 174

Fare un film per me è vivere 179

Farocki, Harun 2, 16, 33, 39–40, 44–5, 49–63, 192

Federico Fellini's Intervista, see *Intervista*

Fellini: A Director's Notebook, see *Block-notes di un regista*

Fellini, Federico 2, 7, 23, 134, 148–9, 174

Femme coquette, Une 90

Fielding, Helen 4

Film Culture 124

Filmeur, Le 126

Filmkritik 50

Film-Makers' Cinematheque 124

Film-Makers' Cooperative 124

Film Portrait 175

Fiori delle Mille e una notte, I 151

Flower of the Arabian Nights, see *Fiori delle Mille e una notte, I*

Forget me not 176

Forster, E. M. 123

Fort Apache 95

Fouchard, Olivier 176

France/tour/detour/deux/ enfants 89

Franju, Georges 28, 29

Fredrich, Sue 122

Free Newsreels, see *Cinegiornali liberi*

Freud, Sigmund 65, 171, 178

Freudian, see Freud

Friedman, Arnold 127

Friedman, Peter 128

Frozen War 126

Frye, Brian 176

Fuses 107

Gaze of Michelangelo, The, see *Sguardo di Michelangelo, Lo*

Genette, Gérard 5

Ghione, Riccardo 149

Gina Kim's Video Diary 126

Glaneurs et la glaneuse, Les 1, 172, 175, 183

Gleaners and I, The, see *Glaneurs et la glaneuse, Les*

Glimpse of the Garden 122

Glitterbug 125

Godard, Jean-Luc 2, 14, 17, 22–3, 28, 29, 33, 39, 68, 72, 84, 88–103, 107, 128

Gospel According to St. Matthew, The, see *Vangelo secondo Matteo, Il*

Goytisolo, Juan 96

Great Train Robbery, The 14

Grierson, John 28, 32

Griffith, D. W. 60, 134

Grinbergs, Andris 175

Groupe Dziga Vertov 2

Guttenplan, Howard 123

Guzzetti, Alfred 174

Hanoun, Marcel 176

Hawks and Sparrows, see *Uccellacci e uccellini*

Helsinki 147

Here and Elsewhere, see *Ici et ailleurs*

Herzog, Werner 2

Hill, Jerome 175

Himeyuri Peace Museum 75

Himeyuri War Memorial 75

Hippocampe, L' 28

Hirohito (Emperor Shōwa) 137

Hirsch, Storm de 122

Histoire(s) du cinema 2, 22, 68, 89, 91, 95

Hitchcock, Alfred 13, 65, 74

Hitler, Adolf 137

Holocaust, see Shoah

Home Movies 123

Hôtel des Invalides 29

Hotel Diaries 126

Hout, Robert 123

Hubert Robert, A Fortunate Life, see *Hubert Robert. Schastlivanya zhizn*

Hubert Robert. Schastlivanya zhizn 2, 132

Hudina, Chuck 175

Huillet, Danièle 2

Hurdes, Las 1, 28

Huston, John 74

I Thought I Was Seeing Convicts, see *Ich Glaubte Gefangene Zu Sehen*

Ich Glaubte Gefangene Zu Sehen 54

Ici et ailleurs 2

Image, An, see *Ein Bild*

Images of the World and the Inscription of War, see *Bilder der Welt und Inschrift des Krieges*

Immemory 34–5, 72–3, 78

India: Matri Buhmi 149

India vista da Rossellini, L' 149

Indoctrination, see *Schulung, Die*

Intellettuale 158

Interview, The, see *Bewerbungen, Die*

Intervista 174

Israel 99, 159, 164

Italianamerican 174

Itoman 76

It's My Life, see *Vivre sa vie*

Ivens, Joris 87

Japan 75–6, 126, 172

Jarecki, Andrew 126

Jarman, Derek 2, 125, 130–1

Jarre, Maurice 71

Je t'aime, je t'aime 75

Je vous salue, Marie 148

Jennings, Humphrey 123

Jerusalem 159

Jetée, La 65, 68, 70, 78

JLG/JLG - autoportrait de décembre 91–2, 94, 98, 175, 183

JLG/JLG: Self-Portrait in December, see *JLG/JLG - autoportrait de décembre*

Jordan 159

Joslin, Tom 128

Journal d'un curé de campagne 128

Julius II 177, 181, 187

Kapital, Das 24

Keep Your Right Up, see *Soigne ta droite*

Keiller, Patrick 2

Keller, Marjorie 122

Kerouac, Jack 158

Killers, The 61

Kim, Gina 126

King Lear 91, 92

Kinjo, Shigeaki 74

Kiss Me Deadly 95

Kisvilma: Az utolsó napló 126

Kitch's Last Meal 107

Kramer, Robert 176

Kramer, Rony 95

Kuchar, George 125

L'esprit de lois, De 96

Land Without Bread, see *Hurdes, Las*

Lang, Fritz 60

Lassnig, Maria 175

Last Bolshevik, The, see *Tombeau d'Alexandre, Le*

Last Year in Marienbad, see *L'Année dernière à Marienbad*

Laura 73, 74

Leçons de ténèbres 126

Lejeune, Philippe 5, 8, 9, 12, 117, 119, 170

Lenin, Vladimir Ilyich 137

Les Films de la Pléiade 28

Letter from Siberia, see *Lettre de Sibérie*

Lettre de Sibérie 2, 26, 64, 66

Level Five 67, 70, 73–83

Lightning Over Water 125

Little Vilna: The Last Diary, see *Kisvilma: Az utolsó napló*

Los Angeles Plays Itself 2

Lost, Lost, Lost 124

Lukács, György 22, 23

LUCE 177

Lumière, Auguste 30

Lumière, Louis 30, 60, 61

Lyotard, Jean-François 5, 38

Mabuni 76

'Magnificat' 188

Malle, Louis 149

Malraux, André 68

Man Ray 123, 174

Man with a Movie Camera, see *Chelovek s kinoapparatom*

Manhatta 174

Mann, Thomas 147

Mannino, Franco 149

Marcel, Gabriel 8

Marker, Chris 1, 2, 17, 22, 26–8, 33, 34–5, 39, 64–82

Marx, Karl 13, 24, 29, 151, 153, 158,

Marxist, see Marx

Masculin féminin: 15 faits précis 29

Masotti, Antonio 158

Massari, Lea 182

Mauri, Fabio 158

McBride, James 4

McBride, Jim 128

McCourt, Frank 4

McElwee, Ross 2, 7, 107, 125, 128

Mekas, Jonas 2, 6, 7, 31, 107, 109, 123, 124–5, 127, 128, 129, 130, 175

Mémoires d'un juif tropical 125

Menken, Maria 122

Mészáros, Márta 126

Michelangelo, see Buonarroti, Michelangelo

Michelangelo Antonioni storia di un autore 179

Miéville, Anne-Marie 95

Minghozzi, Gianfranco 179

Mirror, see *Zerkalo*

Mistero di Oberwald, Il 178

Modern Art Gallery of Bologna 158

Moloch, see *Molokh*

Molokh 137

Montaigne, Michel de 23, 24, 26, 30, 31, 35, 42, 170, 171

Montesquieu, Charles-Louis de Secondat de 96

Moore, Michael 1, 2, 22, 41–2, 86, 174

Moravia, Alberto 150

Morder, Joseph 125

Moretti, Nanni 126

Morin, Edgar 6, 39

Morris, Errol 1, 86

Morte a Venzia 174

Moscow Elegy. Andrei Tarkovsky, see *Moskovskaya elegiya*

Moses 177–9, 181–4, 186–8

Moskovskaya elegiya 132

Mostar Bridge 95, 96

Mount Tabor 159

Mozart, Wolfgang Amadeus 39, 132, 138, 139, 140

Mura di Sana'a, Le 147

Muriel, or the Time of Return, see *Muriel ou Le temps d'un retour*

Muriel ou Le temps d'un retour 175

Museum Piece 126

Mystère Koumiko, Le 1

Naples 126

Napló apámnak, anyámnak 126

Napló gyermekeimnek 126

Napló szerelmeimnek 126

Nazareth 159

NBC 148

Neorealism 108, 111, 112, 124

New American Cinema 6, 124

Nicholson, Jack 182

Night and Fog, see *Nuit et brouillard*

Night Movie #1: Self-Portrait 175

Noren, Andrew 123

Notebook 122

Notebook on Cities and Clothes, see *Aufzeichnungen zu Kleidern und Städten*

Notes for a Poem on the Third World 151

Notes Towards an African Orestes, see *Appunti per un'Orestiade Africana*

Nothing but the Hours, see *Rien que les heures*

Notre musique 39, 94, 95–103

nouvelle vague 6, 24, 27, 28, 90, 113

Nuit et brouillard 2, 30, 95

Number Two, see *Numéro deux*

Numéro deux 91

Oberwald Mystery, The, see *mistero di Oberwald, Il*

objet trouvé 51, 57

OCIC (Organisation Catholique Internationale du Cinéma et de l'Audiovisuel) 158

Odore dell'India, L' 154, 155

Oedipus Rex, see *Edipo re*

Oh oh oh! 126

Okinawa 73–81

Okinawa, Battle of 73

Okinawa Prefectural Peace Memorial Museum 76

Old Place, The 68

Oliveira, Manoel de 175

On Nice, see *À propos de Nice*

One Minute Memories 173

Opération béton 90

Operation Concrete, see *Opération béton*

Oshima, Nagisa 74

Ozu, Yasujiro 126

Pabst, G. W. 128

Painlevé, Jean 28

Palestrina, Giovanni Pierluigi da 188

Paris 123, 149

Pashportrets 175

Pashportrets. Testaments 175

Pasolini, Pier Paolo 2, 6, 9, 17, 29, 60, 109, 112–14, 147, 149, 150–68, 190, 191

Passenger, The, see *Professione: Reporter*

Pathé 61

Peace Newsreels, see *Cinegiornali della pace*

Pecqueux, Gilles 96

Pennelli, Aldo 159

Perlov, David 126

Persona 14

Peterburgskiy dnevnik. Kvartira Kozintseva 132

Peterburgskiy dnevnik. Otkritie pamyatnika Dostoeskomu 132

Peterburgskiy dnevnik: Mozart. Rekviem 132

Petites notes à propos du film 'Je vous salue, Marie' 148

Petrolio 150

Pincus, Ed 2, 7, 46, 123, 125, 127

Plumb Line 107

politique des auteurs, La 26, 27

Porter, Edwin S. 14

Porto Da Minha Infância 175

Porto of My Childhood, see *Porto Da Minha Infância*

Povinnost 132

Power of Speech, The, see *Puissance de la parole*

Pratolini, Vasco 149

Prelinger, Rick 51

Preminger, Otto 73, 74, 80

Pro Civitate Cristiana 158

Professione: Reporter 182

'Progetto Mosè' 177

Proust, Marcel 65

Providence 71

Puissance de la parole 89

Pyramids/Skunk 126

Qiu, Lin 176

Quentin, John 130

Rabbia, La 158

Racconti di Canterbury, I 157

Rainer, Yvonne 2, 123

Rance, Mark 128

Ray, Nicholas 126

Red Tapes, The 172

Redacted 127

Redgrave, Michael 123

Rembrandt van Rijn 172

Reminisces of a Voyage to Lithuania 124

Renaissance 115, 178, 180, 186

Renoir, Jean 25, 26, 128

Resnais, Alain 2, 28, 30, 68–9, 70, 71, 73, 75, 80, 95

Ricerca dei luoghi perduti, La 151

Richter, Hans 6, 24, 27, 28, 190

Ricoeur, Paul 8, 9

Ricotta, La 157, 165

Rien que les heures 28, 110

Riva, Emmanuelle 75

River Jordan 159

River Panjsher 141, 144

Ro.Go.Pa.G. 158

Roger and Me 174

Romanticism 170

Rome 126, 167, 178

Roof - Shower - Underwater 3 BandW Hand Developed Film Prints 176

Rosi, Francesco 29

Rossellini, Roberto 26, 97, 149

Rotschild, Amalie 123

Rouch, Jean 6, 107, 109

Russian Ark, see *Russkiy kovcheg*

Russkiy kovcheg 137

Sacher Diaries, The, see *I diari della Sacher*

Saipan 79

San Pietro in Vincoli 177, 187

Sang des bêtes, Le 29

Sans soleil 22, 52, 56, 66, 73

Sarajevo 95, 96, 97, 99

Satyricon 148

Sauve qui peut la vie 148

Scénario de 'Sauve qui peut la vie' 148

Scénario du film 'Passion' 89

Schneemann, Carolee 107, 123

Schulung, Die 40–1

Scorsese, Martin 174

Sea Horse, The, see *L'Hippocampe*

Sea of Galilee 159

Self Portrait (Hudima; Lassnig) 175

Self Portrait 2 176

Self Portrait '92 176

Self Portrait Post Mortem 176

Self-Portrait 175

Self-Portrait as Kaspar Hauser 176

Self-Portrait, see *Pashportrets*

Self-Portrait. Testament, see *Pashportrets. Testaments*

Seneca, Lucius Annaeus 30

Settimi, Lucio 158

Sguardo di Michelangelo, Lo 177–88

Sheeler, Charles 174

Sherman's March 106, 128

Shoah 58, 76

Silverlake Life: The View From Here 128

Simberg, Hugo 142

Sincerity I 107

Sincerity II 107

Sincerity III 107

Sincerity V 107

Singelenberg, Daniel 175

Siodmak, Robert 61

Sistine Chapel 182

Six fois deux - Sur et sous la communication 89

Six O'Clock News 106

Sjöman, Vilgot 176

Smith, John 126

Soft and Hard 89

Soigne ta droite 91

Sokurov, Aleksandr 2, 17, 39, 114, 115, 132–45

Solntse 137

Sonbert, Warren 123

Sopralluoghi in Palestina 151, 153, 153, 156–69

Sortie des usines Lumière, La 60

Space Between the Teeth, The 172

Speaking Directly: Some American Notes 174

Spiritual Voices: From the Diaries of War, see *Dukhovnye golosa. Iz dnevnikov voyny. Povestvovanie v pyati chastyakh*

Spurlock, Morgan 1

St Bartholomew 182

St Matthew Passion, BWV 244 160

St Peter's Basilica 181

Statues Also Die, see *Statues meurent aussi, les*

Statues meurent aussi, les 68, 69, 70

Straub, Jean-Marie 2

Strand, Paul 174

Sun, The, see *Solntse*

Supersize Me 1

surrealism 25, 28, 109

surrealists, see surrealism

Swinton, Tilda 131

Tagebuch einer Verlorenen 128

Takemitsu, Tōru 132

Tarkovsky, Andrei 13, 14, 134

Tarus, see *Telets*

Tel Aviv 95

Telets 137

Terry, Nigel 130

Testament 175

Testament d'Orphée, Le 175

Testament of Orpheus, The, see
  Testament d'Orphée, Le
Thin Blue Line, The 1
Third Cinema 29
Three Transitions 172
Throwing Stones 126
Tierney, Gene 73
Tokitsu, Kenji 74
Tokyo 149
Tokyo-Ga 125
Tombeau d'Alexandre, Le 66
Tomorrow and Tomorrow, see
  Demain et encore demain
Toute la mémoire du monde
  70, 71, 73
Tribulation 99 51
*Two or Three Things I Know
  About Her*, see *Deux ou
  trois choses que je sais
  d'elle*

Uccellacci e uccellini 157,
  158, 165
Un film, autoportrait 176
Under the stars, see *La belle
  Étoile*
Unglee 176

Ushiyama, Ju'nishi 74
Utrecht 126
Uzel 132

Vangelo secondo Matteo, Il
  158, 160, 164, 167, 169
Varda, Agnès 1, 2, 28, 172,
  175
Venice 147
Venice Film Festival 111, 158
Vérités et mensonges 1
Vertigo 74
Vertov, Dziga 1
Viaggio in Italia 26
Video Diaries 108, 122
Video Nation 108, 122
Vigo, Jean 28, 110
Viola, Bill 172
Visconti, Luchino 147, 148,
  149
Vitti, Monica 182
Vivre sa vie 128
Voix du silence, Les 68
Voyage of G. Mastorna, The
  148
Voyage to Italy, see *Viaggio in
  Italia*

Walden 124
Warhol, Andy 6, 107, 139
Warsaw 147
Weather Diaries 125
Weill, Claudia 123
Welles, Orson 1, 25, 157
Wenders, Wim 2, 125, 126,
  149, 179
Window Water Baby Moving
  123
Workers Leaving the Factory,
  see *Arbeiter verlassen die
  Fabrik*
World War Two 74, 76, 123
Wounded Angel, The 142

Yevtushenko, Yevgeny
  Aleksandrovich 158
Yoman 126

Zavattini, Cesare 6, 65, 109,
  111–13, 124, 190
Zefiro torna 124
Zerkalo 13, 14
Zulu 95